Weird Confucius

Also Available from Bloomsbury:

The Netherworld in Ancient Egypt and China, Mu-chou Poo
Spirits and Animism in Contemporary Japan, Edited by Fabio Rambelli

Weird Confucius

Unorthodox Representations of Confucius in History

Zhao Lu 趙璐

BLOOMSBURY ACADEMIC
LONDON • NEW YORK • OXFORD • NEW DELHI • SYDNEY

BLOOMSBURY ACADEMIC

Bloomsbury Publishing Plc, 50 Bedford Square, London, WC1B 3DP, UK
Bloomsbury Publishing Inc, 1359 Broadway, New York, NY 10018, USA
Bloomsbury Publishing Ireland, 29 Earlsfort Terrace, Dublin 2, D02 AY28, Ireland

BLOOMSBURY, BLOOMSBURY ACADEMIC and the Diana logo are trademarks of
Bloomsbury Publishing Plc

First published in Great Britain 2024
This paperback edition published 2025

Copyright © Zhao Lu 趙璐, 2024

Zhao Lu 趙璐 has asserted his right under the Copyright,
Designs and Patents Act, 1988, to be identified as Author of this work.

For legal purposes the Acknowledgements on pp. x–xii constitute
an extension of this copyright page.

Cover design: Rebecca Heselton
Cover image © Lisa-Blue/ Getty Images

All rights reserved. No part of this publication may be: i) reproduced or transmitted in any form, electronic or mechanical, including photocopying, recording or by means of any information storage or retrieval system without prior permission in writing from the publishers; or ii) used or reproduced in any way for the training, development or operation of artificial intelligence (AI) technologies, including generative AI technologies. The rights holders expressly reserve this publication from the text and data mining exception as per Article 4(3) of the Digital Single Market Directive (EU) 2019/790.

Bloomsbury Publishing Plc does not have any control over, or responsibility for, any third-party websites referred to or in this book. All internet addresses given in this book were correct at the time of going to press. The author and publisher regret any inconvenience caused if addresses have changed or sites have ceased to exist, but can accept no responsibility for any such changes.

A catalogue record for this book is available from the British Library.

Names: Zhao, Lu, 1985- author.
Title: Weird Confucius : unorthodox representations of Confucius in history / Zhao Lu 趙璐.
Description: London ; New York : Bloomsbury Academic, 2024. | Includes bibliographical references and index.
Identifiers: LCCN 2023031227 (print) | LCCN 2023031228 (ebook) |
ISBN 9781350327528 (hardcover) | ISBN 9781350327603 (paperback) |
ISBN 9781350327580 (ebook) | ISBN 9781350327573 (adobe pdf)
Subjects: LCSH: Confucius. | History–Errors, inventions, etc. | Social psychology.
Classification: LCC B128.C8 Z44 2024 (print) | LCC B128.C8 (ebook) |
DDC 181/.112–dc23/eng/20230811
LC record available at https://lccn.loc.gov/2023031227
LC ebook record available at https://lccn.loc.gov/2023031228

ISBN:		
HB:	978-1-3503-2752-8
PB:	978-1-3503-2760-3
ePDF:	978-1-3503-2757-3
eBook:	978-1-3503-2758-0

Typeset by Integra Software Service Pvt. Ltd.

For product safety related questions contact productsafety@bloomsbury.com.

To find out more about our authors and books visit www.bloomsbury.com
and sign up for our newsletters.

To my parents

Contents

Illustrations and Tables ... ix
Acknowledgements ... x

Introduction ... 1

1 Confucius as Prophet ... 13
    Apocrypha and its History ... 14
    The Image of Confucius at the End of the Western Han ... 16
    Confucius as a Prophet ... 19
    Concluding Remarks ... 30

2 Confucius as Ghostbuster ... 33
    Confucius and his Strange Adventures with his Disciples ... 34
    The Power of Chanting ... 43
    Concluding Remarks ... 48

3 Confucius as Diviner ... 51
    Dunhuang and its Textual World in Medieval China ... 52
    Confucius and his Disciples in Dunhuang Divination ... 55
    Perceptions of Sages and Divination in Dunhuang Texts ... 69
    Concluding Remarks ... 73

4 Confucius as Stereotype ... 75
    The Jesuit Depiction of Confucius and its Impacts ... 76
    The Universal Philosopher in Antebellum America ... 80
    The Rise of the Heathen Confucius ... 84
    Concluding Remarks ... 96

5 Confucius as Villain ... 99
    Revolutions toward the Cultural Revolution ... 100
    Confucius Could Be Anyone ... 106
    Villain as the Hero ... 113
    Concluding Remarks ... 122

6	Confucius as Cute	125
	Making Confucius Cute	126
	The Many Meanings of Cute	132
	Managing the Cute Confucius	139

Conclusion 147

Notes 149
Bibliography 191
Index 214

Illustrations and Tables

Figures

1	The Civilization of Blaine. Courtesy of HathiTrust Digital Library	94
2	A Matter of Taste. Courtesy of HathiTrust Digital Library	95
3	Portraits of Kong Lao'er 孔老二 (a. bodily gesture, b. facial details, c. fingernail details, d. facial hair details). Redrawn by Sarah E. Brooker	120

Tables

1	Succession by Generation 相生. Made by Sarah E. Brooker	20
2	The distribution of 1 to 3 through the yearly cycle.	65

Acknowledgements

This book is a pursuit of personal relationships with Confucius, both mine and others. But when I was young, Confucius was just a name to me. Like many people in China, I grew up hearing his name, memorizing what he said for class. He seemed to me to be paper thin, a character in a book. During my time in graduate school, Confucius suddenly became a person. In one of my classes I presented about Confucius' rather harsh criticism toward his disciples in the *Analects*, trying to bust the myth of a kind Confucius and arguing that he was not as moderate as everyone had been led to believe. During the presentation, however, I accidentally called him an "asshole." My classmates and professor burst into laughter, with their laughter peeling back the formal façade and illusion surrounding Confucius. Our focus pivoted from who he was to how we saw him, and the combination of laughter, irony, and a sense of taboo brought us all together. Since then, I have often reflected on these seemingly insignificant, but uniquely personal moments surrounding Confucius. This book is a summary of my reflections, and I am extremely lucky that so many people have lifted me up through the process.

My parents, Wu Shangping 吴尚平 and Zhao Jianfei 趙鑒非 have always indulged me in challenging any common-sense assumptions. At the dinner table, for example, our conversations have ranged from the necessity of going to school to whether parents secretly hate their children, topics that were often on my mind as a teenager. They did what responsible parents do—they either meticulously pointed out the logical inconsistencies in my statements, or giggled at my strangely constructed, but outwardly reasonable argument while saying, "Just don't say this to others!" Without their indulgence, this book would have remained a murmur in my head.

In 2015, Paul R. Goldin invited me to write a chapter for *A Concise Companion to Confucius*, and this chapter, namely, "Representations of Confucius in Apocrypha of the First Century CE," became the first piece of this book. Through the process, Paul always left great freedom for me to pursue the topic, while also being extremely generous in providing me with specific guidance. It was thanks to writing this chapter, that I started to put together this book. In a way, this book would still be no more than a concept without Paul's unfailing guidance. I also thank Wiley for letting me include a revised version of the chapter in this book.

I owe a debt of gratitude to Sophia Katz, especially for Chapter 2 of the book. In 2015, Sophia invited me to the workshop "Divination and the Strange in Pre- and Early Modern Asia and Europe," where I presented my paper, "Demon Hunters and Performers of Miracles: Common Ground between the So-called Confucians, Buddhists, and Daoists in Early Medieval China." With her support, this paper became Chapter 2. Moreover, her workshop also opened the door for me to explore discussions of the strange across different fields.

During the workshop, I benefited greatly from the comments and suggestions from Hon Tze-ki, Joachim Gentz, Esther-Maria Guggenmos, Fabrizio Pregadio, Terry Kleeman, Tiziana Lippiello, and Donatella Rossi. Their insightful comments on my paper and vigorous discussion of the concept of strange transformed my paper into its current form.

Chapter 3 resulted from my tenure at the International Consortium of Research in the Humanities (IKGF), University of Erlangen-Nuremberg. It was a privilege to work with many leading scholars in the field of Chinese divination, which inspired the topic of the chapter. I am especially grateful to the director of IKGF, Michael Lackner. His insightfulness, generosity, and interest in finding meaning in the marginal have given me the lasting momentum to complete this book.

Two anonymous reviewers provided invaluable comments, and I am especially thankful for one of them suggesting an additional chapter on contemporary societies, which has become Chapter 6 of the book. In addition to their meticulous corrections, their comments have given this book a more cohesive and balanced structure.

Since the conception of the project, Sarah Basham and Kate Baldanza have given me priceless advice and suggestions and provided unfailing moral support; after the completion of the first drafts, they meticulously read through each chapter. Their friendship is in the details.

I am also grateful for the work of my research assistants, Sarah Brooker and E'jane Li. Sarah not only copy-edited nearly half of the book, she is also responsible for many images in the book, including the cover image. She has tirelessly looked over the manuscript at different stages and triple checked the most minute details. Her professionalism and work ethic have carried this book to the finish line. E'jane helped meticulously organize the wealth of primary sources in Chapters 4 and 5.

Calling Confucius weird is bound to raise a few eyebrows. For this reason, I am particularly grateful for my two editors, Lucy Carroll and Lily McMahon from Bloomsbury. Lucy was especially encouraging from the moment she heard about this project and laid the foundation for me to work with the press. Lily as her successor has continued to safeguard it until publication. Her periodic check-ins lent structure to an otherwise chaotic and sporadic writing period, as most authors experience. I would also like to thank my copy-editors Kate Greig and Maria Whelan and indexer Avril Ehrlich who brought this book into a much more complete form. Of course, all remaining mistakes are mine.

The publisher and I gratefully acknowledge the permission granted to reproduce the copyright material in this book. Every effort has been made to trace copyright holders and to obtain their permission for the use of copyright material. However, if any have been inadvertently overlooked, the publishers will be pleased, if notified of any omissions, to make the necessary arrangements at the first opportunity. The third party copyrighted material displayed in the pages of this book are done so on the basis of "fair dealing for the purposes of criticism and review" or "fair use for the purposes of teaching, criticism, scholarship or research" only in accordance with international copyright laws, and is not intended to infringe upon the ownership rights of the original owners.

Last but not least, I thank all of my mentors, colleagues, and friends who have shared with me their relationship with Confucius one way or another. Without you, I would think I was alone: Bian He, Chang Chia-Feng, Chen Jian, Connie Cook, Brandon Dotson, Fei Siyen, Anna Greenspan, Melanie Hackney, Martin Kern, Lian Jiani, Victor Mair, Maria Montoya, Michael Nylan, Nathan Harkness, Michael Puett, Dagmar Schäfer, Lena Scheen, Matthias Schumann, Tansen Sen, Nathan Sivin, Nancy Steinhardt, Lillian Tseng, Joanna Waley-Cohen, Brad Weslake, Zhang Jianwei, and Zuo Lala.

Introduction

Would you believe it if I told you that Confucius, or Kongzi (551–479 BCE) 孔子, was a half-human half-divine prophet who fought demons and designed divination manuals? Or that, although he looked like an adorable Yoda, he viciously oppressed the working people of his time? One might object to my depictions, or even ridicule the absurdity of it. They may cite Confucius as a moral philosopher who wore traditional Chinese attire and practiced moderation. Or they might insist that Confucius is famous for his version of the Golden Rule, his failed political career, and his role in developing Confucianism, the underlying ideology of Imperial China. But as we will see in this book, those more unconventional depictions of Confucius are also rooted in history, and some of them were even popularly accepted. Some of us might dismiss them as inferior or erroneous portraits of Confucius by ill-informed or less-educated individuals.[1] However, what if that is not the case? This book attempts to take seriously the seemingly weird images of Confucius in history.

There is no one single perception of Confucius, but there are centers and peripheries. On the one hand, individuals have perceived Confucius differently, and the perceptions also change across time.[2] On the other hand, certain attributes are more well-accepted than others by communities of people when imagining Confucius, ranging from aspects of his physical appearance, like his advanced age, ample forehead, and bearded face; to his inner qualities, such as his devotion to filial piety and benevolence; and even to the evaluation of his life, viewing him as one of the most important philosophers in history.[3] Different individuals might rank these attributes differently, and at a particular historical moment certain communities emphasized certain attributes more than others. Nevertheless, these attributes have formed the center of conceptualizing him, responsible for rendering the most conventional, popular, and thus mainstream images of Confucius. Other attributes, such as his height (reportedly 1.91 m) slip to a more peripheral space.[4] Violations of the central attributes or novel combinations of them have tended to be even more peripheral, if not all together rejected.

These weird attributes of Confucius have received little attention in comparison with their conventional counterparts. Understandably, this is because the mainstream images by definition are more popular, and the violations of these images could be easily perceived as historically inaccurate or even an insult to the ancient sage. For example, the 2007 study of Confucius and his thought, *Homeless Dog: My Interpretations of the Analects* received much criticism in China because of the provocative title. The pejorative connotation of "homeless dog" contradicts the common perception of Confucius as a celebrated sage, even though as we will see in Chapter 1, the term was reportedly acknowledged by Confucius himself based on a well-accepted biography of Confucius from the second century BCE.[5]

Some of the peripheral and rejected attributes of Confucius even challenge our basic assumptions of the world. This is particularly the case for the images introduced in this book. For example, in an increasingly secular world, it is difficult to accept anyone being half-divine. Encounters with demons might make a good TV series or cocktail party story, but would not be taken factually in court or on an insurance application. Similarly, modern readers would dismiss the divination practices of tenth-century Dunhuang as superstitious and irrational. Likewise, modern readers would view the nineteenth-century American representation of Confucius as a symbol of all Chinese as harmful racial stereotyping. Therefore, when viewing Confucius in these ways, we feel compelled to reject it out of hand. As a result, these weird images of Confucius are largely left unexplained—as mistakes worthy of correction, not attention.[6]

Are there other ways to approach these apparently appalling attributes? In the recent decades, scholars have increasingly reflected on how much the perceptions of Confucius are historically made. For example, Lionel Jensen has pointed out the Jesuit missionaries' crucial roles in forging an understanding of Confucius that was impactful to our modern perception, including popularizing the Latinized transliteration of the name "Confucius." Michael Nylan and Thomas Wilson have surveyed the "lives" of Confucius in traditional China and insightfully point out the malleability of his image. More recently, Michael Hunter has made attempts to reevaluate the historical Confucius, especially his association with the text the *Analects*.[7] Despite different approaches and emphases, they all point to Confucius as a construct and seek to historicize it.

This book follows the same path, but does so in a more radical way by focusing on the peripheral and rejected Confucius. It goes beyond the construct of a historical Confucius and examines the outrageously fictitious representations of him. In doing so, it asks the question of why different communities of people would potentially risk contradicting the well-accepted image of Confucius with such representations. It takes the representations as reflections of specific anxieties of certain communities and reveals not only how people across history perceived Confucius in diverse ways, but more importantly, how they used Confucius in daily life, ranging from calming their anxieties about the future and legitimizing a dynasty, to stereotyping Chinese people, and even to forging a new sense of history. In other words, this book explores the instrumentality of these images.

With instrumentality as our guide, we can perceive these weird images of Confucius as innovations. Certainly, the creators of these images might not view them as such, but they are innovative, if we define intellectual innovations as addition, truncation, or recombination of existing knowledge. From this perspective, these images were not simply ignorant mistakes; on the contrary, they were the recombination of their own worldviews with the existing knowledge of Confucius. More importantly, they were created to achieve purposes that the existing or mainstream images of Confucius could not.[8] This view can help us shift our focus from chasing an accurate depiction of the historical Confucius to asking what people needed "Confucius" to be in the first place. That is to say, this book is ultimately about the individuals who imagined Confucius and their agency in so doing.

For our purpose, it is necessary to first clarify what the mainstream images of Confucius look like before diving further into the deviations from the norm. Nowadays, Confucius is most commonly perceived and pictorially depicted as a wise old man who attempted to spread his moral philosophy to both his disciples and the rulers of his time; although he failed his political mission, his thought led to Confucianism, which in turn became the dominant ideology of Imperial China and a foundation of Chinese culture in general. Because of this, he is remembered as a great teacher and one of the most important philosophers in human history.[9] All the above attributes form a mainstream image of Confucius in our time. These attributes, seemingly organic and natural, in fact are a mosaic with pieces from different time periods and sources.

Two textual sources have defined the parameters of the mainstream Confucius: the *Analects* (*Lunyu* 論語) and the biography of Confucius from the *Records of the Grand Historian* (*Shiji* 史記) compiled by Sima Qian 司馬遷 (145–90? BCE). The former is a compilation of sayings by Confucius and his disciples, many of which originated from the Warring States period (476–221 BCE) and became an independent, stable text in the second century BCE. The latter narrates the chronology of Confucius' life and periodizes some of the sayings from the *Analects*. Since the first century BCE, these two texts became the apex of literati culture and have been studied until this very day. They have been accepted as the most reliable sources to study the life and thought of Confucius as a historical figure. Subsequently, this search for the historical, authentic "Kongzi" has become an underlying motivation and justification when imagining Confucius.

According to the two texts, the historical Confucius was a worthy teacher who failed to realize his political vision. Born in Zou (modern day Qufu, Shandong Province), he was the bastard son of a minor noble. His given name was Qiu 丘, literally "mountain." Although he grew up poor, he showed interest in rituals at a young age. Reaching adult life, two missions occupied him: finding an official position and attracting students. He worked for the nobles from the State of Lu and the State of Qi. At the age of fifty-one (501 BCE), he was appointed as the Grand Minister of Crime (Dasikou 大司寇) in the State of Lu, holding a substantial amount of power. During his tenure, he attempted to weaken the Lu aristocratic families' power by dismantling the fortifications of their cities. It was only partially successful and initially enhanced the ruler, Duke of Lu's power. Worried that the Duke of Lu was making his state too powerful, the State of Qi sabotaged the relationship between Confucius and the Duke of Lu by sending the duke good horses and dancing girls. The duke indeed became too distracted to pay attention to his daily work, and disappointed by this, Confucius left the State of Lu.[10]

In the next fourteen years, from 497 to 484 BCE, Confucius travelled with his disciples to more than half a dozen states. He sought to convince the lords of these states to follow his political vision without success. Instead, he only met with predicaments and humiliation: in the State of Song, he was chased after because he looked like the traitor of a Lu aristocratic family, Yang Hu 陽虎; in the same state, he barely escaped an assassination attempt by Xiang Tui 向魋; he was starved for seven days near the border between the States Chen and Cai; and at the State of Zheng, local people described him as a "homeless dog," which Confucius considered an accurate description. According to Sima Qian's narrative, his failure to gain employment was due to the ministers' fear of his worthiness. In 484 BCE, Confucius was welcomed back to the State of Lu at the age of almost seventy. However, he was not appointed to any substantial position, and hence focused on teaching. After experiencing his son's death in 483 BCE and his favorite disciple Yan Yuan's 顏淵 death in 481 BCE, Confucius died on March 9, 479 BCE.[11]

Sima Qian's biography of Confucius crystalizes his image as a sage unrecognized in his own time. In early China, taking the position of Grand Minister of Crime and having devoted followers were already extraordinary achievements in comparison with the majority of people. But the biography still laments that Confucius did not wield as much political power as he should have. More tellingly, the *Records of the Grand Historian* categorizes individuals' biographies according to their social status—the biographies of kings and emperors are called "Annals" (*benji* 本紀); the nobles and aristocrat family members, "Hereditary Houses" (*shijia* 世家); and the more common people, "Listed Biographies" (*liezhuan* 列傳). Given this convention, Confucius should have been put in the category of Listed Biographies, but Sima Qian named his biography the "Hereditary House of Confucius," suggesting that Confucius should have taken a noble position as the right-hand man of his duke. In other words, Sima Qian is responsible for creating a sense of dissatisfaction around Confucius' career.[12]

This sense of dissatisfaction comes from Sima Qian's admiration for Confucius. His biography borrows the words of others to hint that Confucius was comparable to the ancient sage kings. For example, he was considered to be a descendant of the sage (*shengren* 聖人), referring to the sage king and legendary founder of the Shang dynasty, Tang 湯. He was also reported to physically resemble ancient sages like Yao 堯 and Gao Yao 皋陶. To Sima Qian, Confucius' sagehood particularly comes from his preservation and transmission of the teaching of the ancient sage kings. The biography records that Confucius compiled and edited the *Rites, Book of Documents, Book of Poetry, Book of Changes*, and the *Spring and Autumn*, also known as the Five Classics. As Sima Qian exclaims at the end of the biography, Confucius was an ultimate sage (*zhisheng* 至聖) because his teaching had been remembered and valued for generations.[13]

The biography depicts a complex relationship between Confucius and Heaven. Since the eleventh century BCE, Heaven was understood as the ultimate power that decided the fate of individuals and dynasties.[14] According to the biography and the *Analects*, Confucius seemed to believe that Heaven had entrusted him with the mission to transmit culture (*wen* 文), and because of this, he was special. In the texts, he was also symbolically associated with mythological animals whose appearances conveyed the will of Heaven, such as the phoenix (*fenghuang* 鳳凰) and the *qilin* 麒麟. Meanwhile, he also believed that Heaven fated him not to accomplish his mission. When his favorite student Yan Yuan died, he cried: "Heaven is going to forsake me!" Seeing the appearance of a *qilin*, he said "My Way has ended!" The biography of Confucius uses them to craft the narrative that Heaven mysteriously prevented Confucius from advancing in his official career.[15] As we will see in Chapter 1, the relationship between Confucius and Heaven becomes a lasting issue in understanding the sagehood of Confucius.

This ultimate sage Confucius was recognized and sanctioned through imperial sacrifices. This tradition could be traced back to as early as 195 BCE, when the founder of the Han dynasty sacrificed to Confucius in Qufu an ox, a sheep, and a pig, the highest sacrifice. By the third century CE, sacrifice to Confucius became part of the regular imperial rituals. In 472 CE, a Confucius Temple was built in Pingcheng (modern day Datong), the capital of the Northern Wei. This marked one of the first times when the sacrificial place of Confucius was no longer just in Confucius' hometown but also in the imperial center. In 739 CE, Confucius was posthumously entitled King of Transmitting Culture (*Wenxuan wang* 文宣王) by the Tang imperial house, and since then, the sacrifices to him have been comparable to those for an emperor. In this way, Confucius achieved the high position that he should have had. Until the end of Imperial China in 1911, the sacrifices became more elaborate over time, and Confucius temples were built locally beyond the capital and the hometown of Confucius and as far away as Hanoi, Tainan, and Seoul. In this imperial cult, he was the ultimate sage who transmitted the teaching of the ancient sage kings through the Five Classics, and his accomplishments earned him the status comparable to an emperor.[16]

Imperial courts of China promoted this ultimate sage Confucius through education and officialdom. By the second century BCE, learning the Five Classics became part of the imperial curriculum and was increasingly required as part of the credentials for official positions. Since 605 CE, the civil examination was the main way to recruit officials. And the Five Classics together with the *Analects* and *Mencius* were the essential textbooks for the civil examination, and students usually learned them by heart from a young age. The learning process cemented Confucius as the ultimate sage and grand master, and it required young students to regularly pay respect to Confucius and his disciples in addition to honoring the classics. As a result, no matter if one could pass the highly competitive civil examination or not, this imperial image of Confucius spread throughout Chinese society and beyond and became well known, especially among the literati. The ultimate sage Confucius was undoubtedly the mainstream image throughout Imperial China.[17]

Meanwhile, our current mainstream image of Confucius owes more to the Jesuits. As I will elaborate on Chapter 4, the Jesuit missionaries in the seventeenth century encountered the ultimate sage Confucius and transformed him into the "Chinese philosopher," which focused on rather different aspects of his story. By "philosopher," they meant someone who could reason in the Socratic sense. They further specified that morality was the main theme of Confucius' philosophy in the *Analects*. By "Chinese," the Jesuits not only meant that Confucius was from China, but, because his teaching was dominant in Imperial China, he also represented the learning of China. In this way, the Jesuits created a world of philosophers based on the standards of Western philosophy at the time, and Confucius became an eminent part of this world.[18]

This Chinese philosopher Confucius greatly contributes to the modern-day mainstream image of Confucius. It was the Jesuits' intention to de-emphasize Confucius' religiosity, so that the Vatican would not recognize the worship of him as idolatry. On the one hand, they downplayed the practice of sacrificing to Confucius, which could be seen as treating him as a god. On the other hand, they focused on the *Analects* as the source of his thought and portrayed it as moral philosophy which was focused on human relations and decisions. The de-emphasis of religiosity might seem to take him down from the pedestal of the ultimate sage, but the Jesuits compensated it by putting him into the pantheon of philosophers, together with Plato, Aristotle, etc. And like Sima Qian and the imperial court, they lauded his profound impact in establishing an entire school of thought, known as "Confucianism."[19] This moral philosopher and founder of Confucianism image still dominates our modern understanding of Confucius both in academia and by the public.[20]

In twentieth-century China, a more "modified" version of Confucius evolved from the Jesuits' legacy. In the beginning of the twentieth century, scholars like Hu Shi (1891–1962) 胡適 systematically studied early Chinese masters and reintroduced them as philosophers to Chinese readers. After the founding of the People's Republic of China (PRC) in 1949, the official narrative of Confucius followed the philosopher narrative, calling him one of the greatest "thinkers" (*sixiang jia* 思想家) in traditional China. But since the PRC considered traditional China pejoratively as a feudal society, the narrative sidelined Confucius' moral thought. Instead, it praised his pedagogical achievements, rendering him the greatest "educator" (*jiaoyu jia* 教育家) in traditional China. Combined with Marxist materialism, it also moved Confucius further away from religion and the supernatural, rendering him as an increasingly secular figure.[21] As we will see in Chapter 5, this secular thinker-educator Confucius has become the official image in China and has been uniformly taught in elementary and middle schools across the country.

From Sima Qian and the Jesuits to the modern Chinese textbooks, we have accumulated a list of attributes about Confucius and his life. They include: "greatness," "sagehood," "moral philosophy," "education," "representative of Chinese culture," and more. Nowadays, it is common to find this great philosopher-teacher Confucius in social media, textbooks, academia, and government projects. For example, in a 2022 CNN report, the champion tennis player Rafael Nadal was favorably compared to Confucius, in addition to Aristotle and Stoics. Nadal's on-court rituals are justified by "China's greatest philosopher," who "emphasized the importance of developing rituals to lead a good life."[22] Surprising as it is, the comparison decisively acknowledges Confucius as a world philosopher. For a more expected example, in 2004, the Ministry of Education of the PRC initiated a project to create Confucius Institutes, which aimed to establish Chinese language and learning centers at universities and research institutes outside China to facilitate cultural exchange. While these institutes stirred much controversy about cultural imperialism and government interference, people inside and outside China all recognize Confucius as a representative of Chinese culture.[23]

To call this image mainstream is not to deny the diversity of images of Confucius but to stress the contrast between conventional and novel. Although the term "mainstream" often suggests an institutional influence, these images might or might not be established by institutions such as the imperial court. And as the communities and times changed, the "mainstreams" also changed as each chapter will specify. In this book, I also use "classical Confucius," which more specifically refers to the image of Confucius in the *Records of the Grand Historian* and the *Analects*. However, both "mainstream" and "classical" Confucius are not necessarily the "historical" Confucius, indicating the historical figure named as Kong Qiu 孔丘, whose life might or might not be accurately recorded in the sources we have seen.

This book looks at the images of Confucius that deviated from or even violated the mainstream attributes of Confucius. It particularly intends to provoke the sense of novelty, and hence I refer to these images as "weird" in the colloquial sense of the word, where it conveys a feeling of oddity and unexpectedness. In this usage, this feeling could be resolved upon further exploration, contextualization, or explanation. Something weird might not end up being strange, by which I mean phenomena possessing intrinsically alien, anomalous, or unexplainable characteristics.[24] That is to say, the images in this book are not necessarily strange, but have violated certain attributes of the mainstream Confucius, and hence could create a sense of weirdness, either to historical actors or to contemporary people like us. The book intends to resolve this weirdness by making sense of them. It argues that none of these images are intrinsically strange or exotic, for all of them were conscious creations of their time and place.

The six chapters of this book introduce six weird images of Confucius. The first three chapters play with the mainstream image of Confucius being a secular sage who did not engage in strange or supernatural phenomena. Chapter 1 surveys the image of Confucius as a half-human and half-heavenly prophet who predicted the rise of the Han dynasty (205 BCE–8 CE). This first century CE image seems particularly anachronistic because it was rooted in contemporary cosmology that was developed after Confucius' time. In this chapter, we will see how this otherwise peculiar image was in fact a fitting development of Sima Qian's depiction of Confucius. Chapter 2 moves on to early medieval China (220–589 CE) and discusses Confucius' image as a demon hunter in a genre of short stories called "Records of the Strange." In direct contradiction to his secular reputation, Confucius and his disciples in these stories encounter and eventually thrive on strange phenomena that were caused by demons and ghosts. The chapter will contextualize this "ghostbuster" Confucius as part of the expansion of the world of the supernatural. Chapter 3 focuses on the image of Confucius as a diviner in tenth-century Dunhuang in northwest China. It might not be a surprise to see Confucius involved with divination, as the mainstream images of Confucius also portray him as fond of the *Book of Changes*, which was originally a divination manual. Nevertheless, Confucius' interest was still linked to the moral teaching in the text. In contrast, the diviner Confucius did not profess moral lessons but only announced one's fortune in the tenth-century Dunhuang divinatory manuals. This chapter shows what the local people of Dunhuang needed from an ancient sage like Confucius.

Chapters 4 through 6 move to the more modern and global stage, where Confucius encountered transregional trends of ideas both inside and outside China. The images of these chapters challenge the authority of Confucius, as a great philosopher or a teacher. Focused on the nineteenth-century USA, Chapter 4 explores how US newspapers associated Confucius with heathenism and accused him of misleading the Chinese population. This heathen Confucius became the representative of all Chinese people and the totality of Chinese culture, a marked contrast to the great sage worthy of emulation in the previous chapters. If the heathen Confucius in Chapter 4 represents a whole ethnicity, in Chapter 5 he even represents a whole period of the Chinese past. Chapter 5 takes place in the twentieth-century PRC and introduces the treatment of Confucius during the radical, iconoclastic Cultural Revolution (1966–1976). During the movement, Confucius was portrayed as a villain who represented feudal society. Using comic books as a main source, the chapter explores how Confucius was visually and symbolically connected to the Chinese past. In contrast with the iconoclastic attitudes toward Confucius in Chapters 4 and 5, we will see a more playful way to regauge his authority in Chapter 6. This chapter concerns present-day consumerism and examines a merchandized character called Hello Kongzi, a cute version of Confucius. Designed by a Shenzhen based company, Hello Kongzi's cuteness is an attempt to dissolve the authoritativeness of Confucius and make him playful. Turning him into a friend, this image potentially shakes loose his attribute as a teacher.

The choice of these six images is not meant to be comprehensive, but rather, illustrative. The book has no ambition to make a general introduction to non-mainstream images of Confucius through history, as the abundance of images would demand multiple volumes and the expertise of many other scholars. It instead intends to use the six examples to illustrate some of the mechanics behind how individuals and communities appropriated Confucius as a well-accepted character. The six examples sample how far an image of Confucius could deviate from the mainstream ones while still being "Confucius."

This book also does not mean to argue that the mainstream images of Confucius should be dismissed. They have their places in history and societies, ranging from promoting moral ways of living to uniting communities of people. In many ways, they have responded well to people's concerns too. The weird images might have addressed the issues that the mainstream images could not cover, but the weird images are still derivative of and constantly in conversation with the mainstream ones. In this sense, the mainstream and weird images of Confucius are all products of our perceptions, but with one kind at the center of our collective memory and the other at the periphery, at least for the moment.

Using the weird images of Confucius as the topic, the book does want to point out that beneath the seemingly monotonous, centrifugal image of Confucius, there is a wide variety of perceptions. This variety of perceptions is not exclusive to China or outside China, traditional or modern societies, nor are they due to ignorance of the historical Confucius. They are the innovative products of people's anxieties and demands. These innovations did not happen in a lab, but in daily life and emerged from communities of ordinary people. They could substantiate into physical forms like statues and architecture, but also fade away as phantoms of ideas. They are driven by rationality as much as by emotions like anxiety and fear. They could succeed and go on to be remembered in history as *the* Confucius; they could also fail fantastically and slip into oblivion. But either way, behind them is human agency, pushing through the difficulties of life, and this book intends to capture it.

1

Confucius as Prophet

It is weird to refer to Confucius as a prophet. This is not only because the word contains a specific Christian connotation, where the person proclaims the will of God, but the image of Confucius in the *Analects* is also contradictory to the idea of a prophet in a more general sense, as in proclaimer of any supernatural powers.[1] In the first century CE, a story emerged that he was miraculously born in a hollow mulberry tree, physically resembled the constellation Big-Dipper, and prophesized the establishment of a dynasty that would rule almost 300 years after his death. As the spokesman of Heaven, he becomes a prophet. This chapter will make sense of this seemingly weird image of Confucius, which comes from the apocrypha (chenwei 讖緯), a corpus particular to the intellectual and political context of China's first two centuries CE. In the Introduction, we have seen the mainstream image of Confucius as a thinker, a sage, and an unsuccessful politician. We will certainly find all of these attributes in apocrypha. But more visibly, as the product of the literati world in the first century BCE, apocrypha reflect the intellectual and political changes of the time, such as the rising zeal for establishing an ideal society based on the Five Classics (*wujing* 五經) and the restoration of the Han dynasty (202 BCE–9 CE; 25–220 CE), the first mature imperial dynasty in Chinese history. The prophet Confucius emerges in accordance with these changes. In this chapter, we will see Confucius as a prophet and a messenger of Heaven who not only encoded his political teaching in his work, the *Annals of Spring and Autumn* (*Chunqiu* 春秋), but also foretold the ruling house of the Han dynasty, the Liu 劉 family. His seemingly deviant image and extraordinary attributes are rooted in the shared knowledge among the literati of the time.

We will start with a general introduction to apocryphal texts and the political and intellectual world of the first century BCE. Then we will examine Confucius' image in this world. We will specifically focus on a potential tension created by narratives about Confucius: while Confucius was one of the greatest sages in human history, he did not obtain any significant political position. I will argue that apocrypha forged an image of Confucius based on that of ancient sages, which was well-accepted at the time, and by doing so, apocrypha reacted to this tension by portraying him as a heavenly prophet with the special mission of revealing the mandate of Heaven to the world. This image of Confucius was designed to cope with the new political and intellectual environment in first-century CE China.

Apocrypha and its History

Around the first-century CE in China, a corpus of texts appeared under the generic names *chen* 讖, *wei* 緯, or as a binome, *chenwei* 讖緯.[2] *Chen*, a word seldom used before the Han dynasty, indicates prophecies, either in words or images. *Wei* derives its semantic meaning from weaving. In weaving, a warp sets up the frame based on which the woof is woven. Thus "warp," or *jing* 經, is borrowed to designate the classics because of its connotations of "foundation" and "constancy." Following this metaphor, the name "weft," or *wei* 緯, claims to explicate, supplement, or elaborate the classics.[3] In addition, related to prophecies and prognostication, this corpus also includes a large amount of astrological information.[4] Scholars of China have used the word "apocrypha" to refer to this corpus of texts both in the sense that these texts were considered associated with, but not part of the core of, the classics and in the sense that some of the texts claimed to be secretive with a heavenly provenance.[5]

Apocrypha contain several main themes: astrology, explanation and elaboration of the Five Classics, anecdotes of the ancient sages, and prophecies, especially regarding the rise of the ruling Liu family. All of them are deeply rooted in the political and intellectual world in the beginning of the first century CE. After the rule of Emperor Wu 武 (r. 140–87 BCE), the Han empire suffered from overexpansion.[6] The consequential social and economic crises raised doubts about state policies and even the Liu family's rule. People in the court thus became more and more anxious about the destiny of this dynasty: would it last long, or die out soon like the short-lived Qin dynasty (221–207 BCE)? They had good reason to worry, especially because the Han empire adopted a good portion of Qin bureaucratic practices.[7]

In the mid-first century BCE, most intellectuals perceived the fate of a dynasty as dictated by Heaven (*tian* 天). Heaven sent its mandate to the rightful person to establish a new dynasty, and it will send it to someone else if that person, or his descendants, fail to satisfy Heaven's standards for ruling the world.⁸ Based on this assumption, the literati in the imperial court perceived the issue as: the Han empire was on the edge of losing the mandate of Heaven, so it urgently needed to adjust to Heaven's standards.⁹ Where could one find these standards, and how did one know they were the right ones? Through heated debates, most literati at the end of the first century BCE agreed that ancient sage kings' rule (such as under the legendary kings Yao 堯 and Shun 舜) accorded with Heaven, for Heaven sent down auspicious omens as confirmation.¹⁰ Thanks to Confucius' effort in compiling and editing the Five Classics, their rule was at least partially preserved. Emerging from this context, apocrypha inherited this enthusiasm for the Five Classics, the ancient sage kings, and Heaven's will.

The prophecies about the ruling Liu family were particular to the restoration of the Han dynasty. Two hundred and ten years after the establishment of the Han dynasty, a powerful official, Wang Mang 王莽 (45 BCE-23 CE), usurped the throne of the Liu family and established the Xin 新 dynasty (9-23 CE). As an enthusiastic, but unrealistic advocate of the ancient ideal, Wang lost his crown in less than fifteen years due to his frequent but ineffective reforms together with several natural disasters.¹¹ After his death, China fell into civil war for more than a decade. Liu Xiu 劉秀 (6 BCE-57 CE), putatively a remote descendant of the founder of the Han dynasty Liu Bang 劉邦 (256-195 BCE), ended the civil war and restored the Han dynasty.¹² He competed against his rival warlords with more than just military power, but also with legitimacy. His supporters used many strategies to achieve this, especially using prophecies to claim him as the rightful ruler chosen by Heaven. These prophecies, originally short passages, were later expanded into the apocryphal texts. This political message became a trademark of apocrypha.

Because of the sensitive political information in these prophecies and astrological readings, apocryphal texts no longer exist as a full corpus. In 267 CE, Emperor Wu 武 of the Western Jin 西晉 (265-317 CE) banned public access to apocrypha with astrological knowledge because rebels tended to manipulate these texts to claim political authority. From that time on, Southern Dynasties emperors occasionally issued bans against texts in the corpus. The deathblow came from Emperor Yang 煬 of the Sui 隋 dynasty in 593 CE, whose ban, unlike earlier ones, was actually enforced. After this ban, most apocryphal texts were lost.¹³

Fortunately, generations of scholars have made painstaking efforts to reconstruct apocryphal texts with critical textual studies. Based on texts from China, Ma Guohan 馬國翰 (1794-1857 CE) compiled the fragments in his *Jade*

Sack Mountain House's Collection of Lost Books (*Yuhan Shanfang jiyi shu* 玉函山房輯佚書). Yasui Kōzan 安居香山 and Nakamura Shōhachi 中村璋八 gathered fragments found in texts from Japan with previous scholars' compilations to provide us with an even more informative reconstruction. In this chapter, we will rely on their works to explore the image of Confucius. But at the same time, we should bear in mind that no matter how complete their compilations might appear to be, we are still faced with the possibility that several important sections of the original corpus remain lost.

The Image of Confucius at the End of the Western Han

Nowadays when we think of Confucius, we usually recognize him as a teacher and thinker. These attributes also existed in the mind of the literati in early Imperial China. However, they might disagree on what specifically he taught and thought, and they might add more attributes to his image. In this section, we will sketch how Confucius appeared in the eyes of the literati in the Western Han dynasty.

Most people since the Warring States period would agree that Confucius was a great sage. Mencius (372–289 BCE), one of the early advocates of Confucius, compared him to the ancient sage kings, such as Yao 堯, Shun 舜, and King Wen of Zhou 文王.[14] Mencius even considered him as unprecedented in human history.[15] Similarly, in his *Records of the Grand Historian* (*Shiji* 史記), Sima Qian 司馬遷 (145–86 BCE) referred to him as the ultimate sage (*zhisheng* 至聖).[16] Even though Confucius did not achieve any high official position, Sima lifted his biography to the "Hereditary House" (*Shijia* 世家) category, which was for people with noble titles.

Confucius' sagehood created a potential tension between his greatness and his failure to have a successful political career.[17] Confucius, like many of his contemporaries, traveled to various states seeking official positions. Unfortunately, he barely landed an influential position during his life. This might not be an issue if we only considered him to be an ordinary person. But it would create a problem if one compares him to the ancient sage kings. One might ask, if Confucius was a great sage, why was his political career a failure?

One more factor also comes into play: the authorship of the *Annals of Spring and Autumn* (*Chunqiu* 春秋), a chronicle of the state of Lu 魯, recording its state affairs from 722 to 481 BCE. Most people in early Imperial China believed that Confucius wrote the text. While there is little historical ground for this assumption, it was considered one of Confucius' great achievements through Chinese history. *Mencius* contains the earliest extant discussion on Confucius' authorship of the *Annals*:

> [孟子曰]世衰道微，邪說暴行有作，臣弒其君者有之，子弒其父者有之。孔子懼，作《春秋》。《春秋》，天子之事也。是故孔子曰："知我者其惟《春秋》乎！罪我者其惟《春秋》乎！"[18]
>
> [Mencius said:] Again the world fell into decay, and principles faded away. Perverse claims and oppressive deeds waxed rife again. There were instances of ministers who murdered their sovereigns, and of sons who murdered their fathers. Confucius was afraid, and wrote the *Annals of Spring and Autumn*. What the *Spring and Autumn* contains are matters proper to the son of Heaven. On this account Confucius said, 'Yes! It is the *Spring and Autumn* which will make men know me, and it is the *Spring and Autumn* which will make men condemn me.'[19]

For Mencius, the declining social order stimulated Confucius to compose the *Annals* as a critique and rectification of his contemporary world. It is not entirely clear in the citation why Confucius would think people would condemn him for that. However, as Mencius implies, Confucius thought so because writing the *Annals* was a work that belonged to the son of Heaven, and as a person without substantial political power, it was not his position to make such judgments.

Among Western Han scholars, Confucius' authorship of the *Annals* was at the heart of this tension between his sagehood and failed political career. In *Huainanzi* 淮南子 (ca. 139 BCE), the author describes Confucius' many talents:

> 孔子之通，智過於萇弘，勇服於孟賁，足躡效菟，力招城關，能亦多矣。然而勇力不聞，伎巧不知，專行教道，以成素王，事亦鮮矣。《春秋》二百四十二年，亡國五十二，弒君三十六，采善鉏醜，以成王道，論亦博矣。[20]
>
> The capacity of Confucius was such that his intelligence surpassed that of Chang Hong; his courage exceeded that of Meng Ben; his feet were faster than a nimble rabbit; his strength was such that he could hold up a portcullis. His abilities were indeed numerous. But he is not known to the world for his courage or his dexterity. Solely through practicing the way of teaching, he became an uncrowned king. This would indicate that his affairs were indeed few. The 242 years of the Spring and Autumn period saw fifty-two states destroyed and thirty-six cases of regicide. By singling out the good and condemning the bad, he established the Kingly Way. This would indicate that his discussion was indeed broad.[21]

For *Huainanzi*, it is not that Confucius was not talented enough to accomplish his political goals, but that he chose a specific mission: teaching. As part of this mission, his composition of the *Annals* completed the Kingly Way. Aware of Confucius' lack of political status, *Huainanzi* designates the title "uncrowned king" to Confucius. The term came from *Zhuangzi* 莊子, where it was used to describe people who were virtuous enough to become a king without holding a real position as a king.[22] Borrowing this term, *Huainanzi* thus resolves the tension by claiming him as a sage king in a different sense.

In his *The Garden of Persuasion* (*Shuiyuan* 說苑), Liu Xiang 劉向 (ca. 77–6 BCE), one of the great erudites in the first-century BCE China, explains Confucius' authorship of the *Annals* more explicitly in the context of his failure in officialdom:

[孔子]卒不遇, 故睹麟而泣, 哀道不行, 德澤不洽, 於是退作《春秋》, 明素王之道, 以示後人。[23]

[Confucius] was not being appreciated at his end, so he wept when he saw the *qilin*. He lamented the Way not being practiced and that virtue was not harmonized. Therefore, he retreated to compose the *Annals* and illuminate the way of the uncrowned king in order to show it to later generations.

Both Liu Xiang and *Huainanzi* recognize Confucius' sagely nature. But unlike *Huainanzi*, Liu does not consider Confucius' composition as his priority, but a second choice after his political career fell through. For him, Confucius could not practice the Kingly Way, so he instead recorded it in the *Annals* so later generations could practice it. The *qilin*, a mystical animal as well as an omen from Heaven, informs Confucius of his fruitless destiny.[24] In this scenario, even Heaven ensured his failure.

During the last years of the Western Han dynasty, scholars' zeal for pursuing the Kingly Way made Confucius an even better sage.[25] This made the tension between his sagehood and his political setback so obvious to the extent that a great scholar of the time, Yang Xiong 揚雄 (53 BCE–18 CE), felt the need to address it:

或問: "孔子之時, 諸侯有知其聖者與?"
曰: "知之。"
"知之則曷為不用?"
曰: "不能。"
曰: "知聖而不能用也, 可得聞乎?"
曰: "用之則宜從之, 從之則棄其所習, 逆其所順, 強其所劣, 捐其所能, 衝衝如也。非天下之至, 孰能用之!"[26]

Someone asked: "During the time of Confucius, did any of the rulers of the states know that he was a sage?"

I answered: "they did."
"If so, then why did not they use him?"
"Because they could not."
"Can I know about this recognizing his sagehood without employing him?"
"If one employed him, it is likely that they will follow him. If so, then they would discard what they were used to doing, go against what they followed, improve what they were bad at, and give up what they were capable of doing. And they would be uneasy. If they are not the best among All-Under-Heaven, who else could employ him?"

Unsurprisingly, Yang Xiong recognizes Confucius' sage nature, and he believes that it was universally recognized even during Confucius' time. Unlike Liu Xiang, Yang does not mention anything about Heaven regarding Confucius' failure, but instead focuses on the vicious and mediocre rulers and officials. Yang states that Confucius was not employed solely because he was too good to be employed.

Explicitly or implicitly Western Han scholars gave several solutions to the tension. But there are still questions remaining. If Heaven is responsible for the birth of a sage as Mencius and others believed,[27] then was it also responsible for his failure? If Heaven just brought him to the world to fail him, then what was the point of bringing him to the world to begin with? If there is no point, then was Heaven an arbitrary or amoral agent? If so, then does Heaven also arbitrarily choose a new ruler?[28] The image of Confucius in apocrypha emerged from this series of "what if" questions and the anxiety behind them. In the next section, we will see how apocryphal texts engage with this series of questions and create their own answers that not only accord with the political atmosphere but also the intellectual context.

Confucius as a Prophet

In the first century CE, it would have been hard to argue that Heaven is an arbitrary agent. Such a stance not only disagrees with the imperial agenda that Liu Xiu received the mandate of Heaven to restore the Han dynasty, but it also goes against most literati's understanding of Heaven's will based on the Five Classics. Similarly, given what we have seen about Confucius, diminishing his sagehood would also be outlandish. With these specific assumptions of Heaven and Confucius, apocryphal texts take another strategy to tackle this tension:

聖人不空生，必有所制，以顯天心。丘為木鐸，制法天下。²⁹

The sage was not born in vain. He had to institute something to show the heart of Heaven. Confucius was the wooden mallet. He made standards for All-Under-Heaven.

Confucius was born for a specific reason: to set up a standard for the world. The wooden mallet (*mu duo* 木鐸) alludes to Confucius' contemporary's comment on him in the *Analects*: "All-Under-Heaven has been chaotic a long time, so Heaven will use Confucius as the wooden mallet" (天下之無道也久矣，天將以夫子為木鐸。).³⁰ The *Analects* passage suggests a sense of mission for Confucius, and the metaphor "wooden mallet" suggests admonition and warning. Piling up on this passage, apocryphal texts more specifically point out that Heaven does have a special mission for Confucius.

This part alone does not resolve the tension; one can still ask why Confucius did not bring order to the world by being a ruler or a high official, which seems to be a more direct path. In responding to this potential doubt, apocrypha engage in a wide-spread cosmological framework of the time: the theory of the Five Phases. In this theory, Wood, Fire, Earth, Metal, and Water are part of a sequence in which each generates the one after it. Each dynasty, or more specifically the founder of a dynasty, represents one of these phases and follows the previous phase in the sequence (Table 1). This theory highlights continuity in terms of virtues. If a ruler of a dynasty no longer rules virtuously, Heaven will send its mandate to a virtuous person who represents the sequential phase.³¹ Even though people occasionally establish dynasties outside this

Table 1 Succession by Generation 相生. Made by Sarah E. Brooker.

Wood	Fu Xi 伏羲	Di Ku 帝嚳		King Wen of Zhou 周文王
Water	Gong Gong 共工	Qin 秦		
Fire	Shen Nong 神農	Yao 堯		Liu Bang 劉邦
Earth	Yellow Emperor 黃帝	Shun 舜		
Metal	Shao Hao 少昊	Yu 禹		
Water	Zhuan Xu 顓頊	Tang 湯		

sequence, these dynasties are bound to fail (like Gong Gong or the Qin dynasty in Table 1).

According to apocrypha, Confucius is not in the right phase to become a ruler:

孔子母徵在, 夢感黑帝而生, 故曰玄聖。³²

Confucius' mother Zhengzai ["The Omen is Present"] dreamed of being stimulated by the Black Emperor, and then gave birth to [Confucius]. Therefore, he is called the "dark sage."

His miraculous conception associates him with the color black, representing the phase of Water in the theory. Since the Zhou house, the dynasty he lived under, represented the phase of Wood, he could not receive the mandate of Heaven based on the sequence. The term "dark sage" comes as a pair with "uncrowned king" in *Zhuangzi*.³³ Unlike the latter designation, the former one was not commonly used to refer to Confucius until apocrypha appeared.³⁴ Apocryphal texts tacitly appropriate the pairing to link Confucius with the "dark sage," and frame the term in the context of the theory of the Five Phases. Apocryphal texts state Confucius' fate even more clearly in the following:

丘為制法之主, 黑綠不代蒼黃。³⁵

Confucius was the lord of standard making. Black-green did not replace green-brown.

Green-brown, the color of the phase of Wood, indicates the Zhou dynasty. This sentence then makes it plain that Confucius would not replace the Zhou dynasty. Instead, his mission was to setup a standard for the world.

This does not make Confucius less special. For apocrypha, he in fact played the most important role in helping the upcoming dynasty, the Han dynasty:

黑龍生為赤, 必告示象, 使知命。³⁶

The black dragon was born for the red. It had to show the portents and make [people] know the mandate.

丘水精, 制法為赤制功。³⁷

Qiu [Confucius] was the essence of Water. He set up the standard to plan for the red's achievements.

丘攬史記。援引古圖。推集天變。為漢帝制法, 陳敘圖錄。³⁸

Qiu perused historical records and cited old diagrams. He deduced and compiled the changes of Heaven. He made principles for the Han emperor and set in order the diagrams and records.

Red, the color for the phase of Fire, indicates the Han dynasty. Black dragon refers to Confucius. The standard he made was not just for anyone or anyone representing the red, but very specifically for the Liu imperial family of the Han dynasty. Confucius' mission was to inform the Han dynasty about the mandate of Heaven as well as standards of ruling to help the Liu to achieve their kingly undertaking.

Apocrypha depict Confucius as a prophet who deciphered the will of Heaven, predicted the future dynasty, and transmitted his teaching to that dynasty. In answering the series of questions mentioned above, they confirm that Heaven is not arbitrary and that Confucius was a great sage. Furthermore, they state that his failed political career was due to nothing but the framework of the Five Phases. This does not make him less special or less sagely than the ancient sage kings. Engaged in the political culture of the first century CE, apocryphal texts believe that he was particularly special to the Han because he prophesized the founding of the dynasty with the Han people living out his prophecies.

Confucius' Authorship of the Annals in Apocrypha

In apocryphal texts, Confucius is marked by his special connection with Heaven. This is especially so for his composition of the *Annals*. In apocrypha, Heaven reveals its will at a city gate called the "Duan Gate" of the State of Lu:

孔子謂子夏曰:"得麟之月，天當有血書魯端門: '孔聖沒，周室亡'。"³⁹
Confucius told Zixia: "In the month of obtaining the *qilin*, Heaven will write on the Duan Gate of Lu with blood: 'the sage Confucius will be deceased, and the Zhou house will become extinct.'"

The following incident verified Confucius' prediction:

得麟之後，天下血書魯端門曰: 趨作法，孔聖沒，周姬亡。彗東出。秦政起，胡破術。書紀散，孔不絕。⁴⁰
After obtaining the *qilin*, Heaven sent writing in blood on the Duan gate of the state of Lu, saying "Set up the standard quickly! The sage Kong will die, and the Zhou dynasty's house of Ji will perish. A comet will appear in the east. [Ying] Zheng of Qin will arise. Hu Hai will break the way [of ruling]. Books and records will scatter, but [the teaching of] Kong will not become extinct."

"Obtaining the *qilin*" alludes to the last event in the fourteenth year of Duke Ai 哀 of Lu (481 BCE) in the *Annals*. In the Gongyang tradition, one of the commentaries of the *Annals* popular in the Han dynasty, this event marks the end of the Spring and Autumn epoch and the completion of the *Annals*. It signifies the end of Confucius' way.[41] In the apocryphal version of this event, Heaven then sends down a prophecy written in blood. It predicts the death of Confucius, the fall of the Zhou dynasty, the rise of the Qin dynasty, and the endangerment of the way of Confucius.[42] In the Gongyang tradition, Confucius does try to extrapolate Heaven's message from the capture of the *qilin* and the death of his two disciples, Zilu and Yan Yuan. Nevertheless, Heaven never explicitly expresses its will. In contrast, in the apocryphal passage, Heaven unequivocally presents its ideas via an explicit method (writing), commanding Confucius to set up the standard for later generations.

The reception of the prophecy from Heaven is not the end of the story; the message in blood reveals itself to Zixia, one of Confucius' major disciples, and turns into a text:

子夏明日往視之，血書飛為赤鳥。化為白書。署曰演孔圖。中有作圖制法之狀。[43]

The next day, Zixia went there to look at it. The blood writing flew up and became a red crow. It then transformed into a white text, entitled: *Diagrams Elaborating Confucius*. It contains descriptions for making diagrams and setting up standards.

The title *Diagrams Elaborating Confucius* is actually the title of the apocryphal text from which this passage is taken. The prophecy claims that the text contains instructions for setting up standards of good government, which allude to Heaven's command, "set up the standard quickly" (*qu zuo fa* 趣作法), in the prophecy.

The *Annals* is thus the product of this mandate:

昔孔子受端門之命,制春秋之義， 使子夏等十四人求周史記。得百二十國寶書，九月經立。[44]

In the past, Confucius received the mandate of the Duan gate, and he created the principles of the *Annals of Spring and Autumn*. He made fourteen people, including Zixia, seek the historical records of Zhou. They obtained precious writings of one hundred twenty states. The classic was established after nine months.

Apocryphal texts present Confucius' composition as his own plan. But behind this plan, Heaven guided Confucius on every step of his mission. It not only revealed to him what he needed to do, but also the knowledge of how to do it, which is contained in this very apocryphal text. The apocrypha transform this human sage into a heavenly prophet. In apocryphal texts, his greatness lies in his heavenly nature as well as his capability to perceive and follow Heaven's will.

This rather outlandish revelation might surprise modern readers, especially those who focus on the *Analects* as the credible record of Confucius' life and teaching. Nevertheless, in the first two centuries BCE, his sagehood manifests in various ways and often involves strange phenomena.[45] For example, in an anecdote from the *Records of the Grand Historian*, the state of Wu found a piece of bone in Kuaiji as long as a chariot. They sent an envoy to meet Confucius to inquire about this odd object. As if his reputation as a knowledgeable sage was not obvious enough, the envoy of Wu tried to trick Confucius. Instead of filling him in, he asked Confucius who had the longest bones in history. Confucius answered: "When Yu 禹 [a legendary sage king] summoned spirits at Mount Kuaiji, Fangfeng 防風 came late. Yu killed him and exposed his body, whose bones were as long as a chariot. They are the longest." His answer precisely covered both what the envoy did and did not know. After grinding him on a few more questions, the envoy finally yielded and exclaimed: "What a sage!"[46]

In fact, Confucius identifying odd objects is a trope in the Western Han. In another anecdote, Ji Huanzi 季桓子 (?–492 BCE), a noble from Confucius' motherland Lu, brought another puzzle to Confucius. In drilling a well, Ji found an earth jar with a goat-like creature inside it. Tricking Confucius again, Ji lied that they found a dog in the jar. Not being misled, Confucius said that it should be a goat, and stated his reason: "*kui* 夔 [a one leg creature] and *wangliang* 魍魎 are the odd creatures of wood and stones; dragons and *wangxiang* 罔象 are the odd creatures of water, and goats are the odd creatures of earth."[47] Once again, Confucius successfully evades the trap, identifies the object, and explains the origin of the strange phenomenon.

The Duan Gate incident in apocrypha borrows many ingredients from this trope. In all of the stories, Confucius encounters bizarre phenomena: an extraordinary long bone, a goat in a jar, or blood writing on the Duan Gate. He never witnesses these objects himself; either someone, such as the Wu envoy or Ji Huanzi brings the issue to him, or the issue itself draws his attention. In these stories, none of these phenomena, no matter how bizarre they are, surprises Confucius. He always unmistakably deciphers the meaning of them, and his reading is always successfully attested. This trope introduces Confucius as an erudite who always correctly understands the world.

Nevertheless, unlike the other stories, the apocrypha bring Heaven into the Duan Gate story. While Confucius acts omnisciently in all the three stories, only in the Duan Gate one does he interact with Heaven. In the other two stories, he knows even the most obscure parts of history (longest bone in history) and nature (odd creature derived from certain natural environments). In the Duan

Gate story, he knows Heaven—an active agent. When he predicts the blood writing and its content, he does not give any rationale like he does in the other two stories. Without relying on any forms of divination or oracles, he precisely knows what this agent is going to announce almost verbatim.[48] His prediction of Heaven's acts requires more than just knowledge he learned from oral transmission or written documents. It suggests a special connection between him and Heaven.

This connection is also obvious from the side of Heaven, for it builds the whole plan around Confucius. In the apocryphal story, Heaven assigns the mission of composing the *Annals* to Confucius and meticulously foretells his death as well as the perishing of the Zhou dynasty, despite the fact that in the story Confucius seems to already telepathically know its will. It then even reveals a text with his name in the title. Indeed, the agenda of this apocryphal story is starkly different from the other two anecdotes. In apocrypha, Confucius is no longer an independent human sage, whose human knowledge could help his contemporaries. With Heaven taking over his fate, he becomes a heavenly prophet, whose agency shrinks to following Heaven's mandate. He is still wise, but the wisdom comes from his special connection with Heaven.

With our modern point of view, we might lament Confucius' shriveled free will in such a portrayal. However, first-century CE readers did not find his free will appealing, especially when it did not stop him from struggling. Moreover, apocryphal texts depict him based on a common understanding in the first century CE: Heaven is the ultimate agent of the world, and thus comprehending its will or principles is one of the most crucial tasks to achieve the welfare of a government or an individual.[49] In this context, Confucius' special connection with Heaven does not compromise but promotes his sagehood. In answering the aforementioned question "Since he failed in officialdom, was Confucius sagacious enough?" apocryphal texts answer: yes, he is as sagacious as Heaven. Following this logic, his *Annals*, which sets up standards for the upcoming Liu family, is also of heavenly nature, and thus reveals Heaven's will and principles. In this way, apocryphal texts tie Heaven, Confucius, and the Liu imperial family together, legitimizing the Liu's rule.

The Heavenly Sage

Indeed, in apocryphal texts, Confucius has a special relationship with Heaven. In this section, I will further pin down this relationship, where he became an offspring of Heaven in a literal sense. He even physically resembles his "father."

We can trace his miraculous birth as well as his physiognomic features back to tropes and images dedicated to sage kings in apocrypha and earlier texts. While breaking away from earlier records, the apocryphal Confucius still develops from a common understanding of the sage kings of that time.

As mentioned above, in apocrypha the black emperor impregnated Confucius' mother. This conception differs from the one mentioned in *Records of the Grand Historian*, which depicts Confucius as a human child:

[叔梁]紇與顏氏女野合而生孔子，禱於尼丘得孔子。魯襄公二十二年而孔子生。生而首上圩頂，故因名曰丘云。字仲尼，姓孔氏。 50

A woman of Yan had intercourse with Shuliang He in the wild and gave birth to Confucius.[51] They prayed to Mount Ni and conceived Confucius. Confucius was born in the 22nd year of Duke Xiang of Lu [551 BCE]. Because he had a concave forehead when he was born, he was named after a "mountain [Qiu 丘]."[52] His style name was Zhongni, and surname Kong.

Shuliang He was not the dark emperor by any means; he was a remote descendent of the ruling house of the state of Song and a minor noble from the State of Lu. Because he died soon after Confucius' birth, Confucius grew up fatherless. In fact, among pre-imperial texts, Confucius' parents were never emphasized. In this narrative, there is nothing extraordinary about Confucius other than his concave forehead and his conception in the wild.

In contrast, apocryphal texts narrate Confucius' conception with miraculous details:

孔子母徵在游大澤之陂，睡夢黑帝使，請已已往夢交。語曰：汝乳必於空桑之中。覺則若感，生丘於空桑。 53

When Confucius' mother Zhengzai travelled to a water margin, she dreamed of an envoy of the dark emperor, who invited her to go to a dream to have intercourse with him [the dark emperor]. [The dark emperor] said: "you must deliver at Kongsang [a hollow mulberry tree]. When she woke up, she seemed pregnant. She gave birth to Confucius at Kongsang."

Confucius' human father disappears in this story. Instead, the dark emperor takes over the whole process: he sends a messenger to invite Zhengzai, has intercourse with her, and commands her to deliver at a hollow mulberry tree. This series of actions sends an unambiguous message to Zhengzai as well as the readers that Confucius was an offspring of the black emperor.

If readers of the first century CE encountered this unconventional, if not alien, apocryphal story without any context, they would be just as surprised as we are. But they did have some background knowledge to draw from; this story is in fact a blending of two legends. The first one concerns Liu Bang 劉邦 (256–195 BCE), the founder of the Han dynasty:

其先劉媼嘗息大澤之陂，夢與神遇。是時雷電晦冥，太公往視，則見蛟龍於其上。已而有身，遂產高祖。⁵⁴

    Previously old lady Liu was used to resting on water margin, and she dreamed of encountering a spirit. At that time, it was dark and there was thunder and lightning. Taigong [Liu Bang's father] went to check, and he saw a dragon on top of her. Then she was pregnant and gave birth to Gaozu [Liu Bang].

Impregnated by a dragon, a symbol of a ruler, the story presents Liu Bang as half human half divine. His divine origin preludes his establishment of the Han empire. Both Liu Bang and Confucius' conceptions take place in a dream, in which the spirits interact with their mothers. The dreams also occur at the "water margin." While "water margin" describes a rather generic place, *da ze zhi bei* is a rather distinct combination of words. It is not a coincidence that *da ze zhi bei* appears in both Liu Bang and Confucius' birth stories. These similar flavors tie Liu Bang and Confucius together: via this particular style of conception, both are the chosen ones by Heaven.

The other legend regards a legendary minster Yi Yin 伊尹, who assisted Tang 湯 to defeat the Xia dynasty and establish the Shang dynasty (ca. 17–11 century BCE).⁵⁵ In the *Chronicle of Master Lü* (*Lüshi chunqiu* 呂氏春秋) (ca. 239 BCE), Yi Yin's birth was associated with Kongsang, the hollow mulberry tree. In the story, a woman found the infant Yi Yin in a hollow mulberry and brought him to her lord. They later found out that Yi Yin's mother lived by the Yin water. When she became pregnant, a spirit appeared in her dream and warned her to run when water came out of her rice mortar. When this happened, she followed the spirits' words. Running more than six miles, she turned around and found out that water flooded her village. Witnessing this disaster, she turned into a hollow mulberry tree.⁵⁶

Although the moral of this story is rather opaque, Yi Yin's miraculous birth is obvious. In line with Liu Bang and Confucius' conceptions, we again find pregnancy by the water and an oracle in a dream. Moreover, the birthplace becomes significant in the Yi Yin story, for the human womb transformed into a supernatural one. The hollow mulberry, just as where Yi Yin came from, thus symbolizes his supernatural origin. Borrowing this birthplace for Confucius' story, apocrypha associate Confucius with Yi Yin: they were both worthy subjects and came from the same place.

Apocryphal texts' frequent allusions to miraculous birth situate Confucius in the universe of the ancient sages.⁵⁷ In this universe, the heroes were often fatherless. According to the *Records of the Grand Historian*, for instance, the mythic ancestor of the Shang people Xie 契 was conceived after his mother swallowed an egg from a dark bird; a giant footprint impregnated Jiang Yuan 姜原, who then bore Hou Ji 后稷, the ancestor of the Zhou people.[58] Apocrypha substitute Confucius' father with the miraculous conception, which is uncanny, but particular to sage kings. In this way, Confucius became one of the chosen ones in human history.

Apocrypha further string Confucius with other sage kings by applying a single set of rationales to explain their conceptions. Based on the theory of the Five Phases, apocryphal texts claim that there are five emperors, the red emperor Wenzu 文祖, the yellow emperor Shendou 神斗, the white emperor Xianji 顯紀, the black emperor Xuanju 玄矩, and the green emperor Lingfu 靈府, corresponding to Fire, Earth, Metal, Water, and Wood respectively. Confucius' real father, the dark emperor, thus refers to the black emperor of water. These heavenly emperors are located in the constellation Taiwei 太微, and the human sage kings' conceptions were due to their mothers' correspondence (*gan* 感) with these emperors' "essence," or *jing* 精.[59] For example, Yu was the "essence of the white emperor," or *baidi jing* 白帝精,[60] and King Wen was the "essence of the green emperor," or *cangdi jing* 蒼帝精.[61] Yao was the "essence of Fire," or *huo jing* 火精,[62] and Confucius was the "essence of Water," or *shui jing* 水精.[63] Therefore, for apocrypha, the dark bird's egg, giant footprint, or the dreams are various ways of transmitting the essence from Heaven.

In apocrypha, Confucius' heavenly nature also manifests through his physical features:

孔子長十尺，大九圍。坐如蹲龍，立如牽牛。就之如昴，望之如斗。[64]

Confucius was ten *chi* (2.31 m) tall.[65] He was nine *wei* around.[66] He looked like a squatting dragon when he sat, and like a driven ox when he stood. He looked like [the constellation] Mao when one approached him, and the Big-Dipper when one looked at him from a distance.

More than being a giant man, Confucius looked literally heavenly. Apocrypha go into details: he had a dragon-like forehead (*long sang* 龍顙), moon-like sides of the forehead (*yue jiao* 月角), a sun-like nose (*ri zhun* 日準), Yellow-River-like eyes (*He mu* 河目), Big-Dipper-like lips (*Dou chun* 斗唇), and a constellation "Flourishing Literature" (*Wenchang* 文昌)-like face (昌顏).[67] For apocryphal texts, Confucius accorded with Heaven and earth to such an extreme extent that he even looked like his "biological" father.

In the first few centuries BCE, Confucius' unusual appearance was a well-accepted assumption. But the principles behind them differ from that of the apocryphal description. One of the greatest thinkers in the third century BCE, Xunzi 荀子 (ca. 310–238 BCE) mentioned that Confucius had a rather undesirable face. According to him, Confucius looked like a *meng qi* 蒙倛, a phrase that also refers to a type of mask terrifying enough for exorcists to wear in order to drive demons away.[68] Xunzi uses Confucius' appearance to critique physiognomy. He believes if we were to assume facial features reflected one's intelligence and achievements, we would greatly underestimate Confucius. Xunzi's larger point is that the physical appearance of a person, whether desirable or not, has nothing to do with his mind or behavior.[69]

In the *Records of the Grand Historian*, Sima Qian mentions Confucius' unusual concave forehead and 6'3" height, which are similar to that in apocrypha.[70] Does his appearance indicate his internal qualities or are they nothing but noticeable traits? The *Records* captures this nuance in an anecdote:

孔子適鄭，　與弟子相失，　孔子獨立郭東門。鄭人或謂子貢曰：" 東門有人，其顙似堯，其項類皋陶，其肩類子產，然自要以下不及禹三寸。纍纍若喪家之狗。" 子貢以實告孔子。孔子欣然笑曰：" 形狀，　末也。而謂似喪家之狗，然哉！然哉！"[71]

Confucius [and his disciples] went to the state of Zheng, and they lost each other. Confucius was standing alone by the east gate of the outer city wall. Some people of Zheng told [his disciple] Zigong: "There is a person at the east gate. His forehead looks like that of Yao, the back of his neck looks like that of Gao Yao, and his shoulders look like that of Zichan. However, down from his waist, he is two and a quarter inch shorter than Yu. Exhausted, he looks like a homeless dog." Zigong told Confucius that. Confucius smiled delightfully and said: "Figures and shapes are the most trivial. But as for looking like a homeless dog, yes, yes!"

Two conflicting views surround Confucius' appearance. On the one hand, the Zheng people provide a physiognomic reading of Confucius.[72] In this reading, his resemblance to the sage king Yao, legendary minister Gao Yao, and worthy official Zichan implies Confucius' sagehood. His shorter height than the sage king Yu suggests that he is quite close to, but a few inches short from becoming a ruler. This reading obviously takes advantage of a retrospective view of Confucius' life as a talented man with a failed political career. On the other hand, Confucius tacitly disputed the Zheng people's theory. While admitting the resemblance between his life and that of a homeless dog, he completely dismisses the physiognomic reading. In line with Xunzi's point, he believes that his height has nothing to do with talent or fate.

Apocryphal texts go down the same path as the Zheng people, especially in comparing Confucius to ancient sages. In the apocryphal universe, sage kings' idiosyncratic features prelude their virtues: Cang Jie 倉頡 had four eyes because he was "doubly insightful (*bing ming* 並明)"; Yao's eyebrows had eight colors because he was "comprehensively insightful (*tong ming* 通明)"; King Wen had four breasts because he was "nurturing of the worthies (*han liang* 含良)."[73] Like Confucius, many of their features resemble Heaven. For example, the Yellow Emperor "had a dragon face, and had [a resemblance to] the [constellation] North of Heavenly Court (黃帝龍顏, 得天庭陽)."[74] The North of Heavenly Court indicates the celestial constellation Privy Council, or Taiwei 太微, which symbolizes the imperial house.[75] Di Ku had overlapped teeth, "imitating the moon and the constellation Triplet above (上法月參)."[76]

Again, from his origin to physical appearance, apocryphal texts exhibit Confucius' heavenly nature along with a roster of ancient sage kings. Through such exhibition, he was no longer a human sage traveling on earth to solve the crises of his time. Instead, he was a heavenly offspring descended from Heaven rescuing the world in the far future. Apocryphal texts prove to his contemporaries that Confucius was as sagacious as other sage kings; his wisdom was not just superb, but heavenly superb. Ironically, even though his teaching was still obtainable, his level of wisdom and talent were far beyond the grasp of ordinary human beings. He became a distant, shining star people worshiped, not a day-to-day role model one could hope to emulate.

Concluding Remarks

The prophet Confucius enjoyed its heyday together with the apocryphal corpus in the first two centuries CE China. The early Eastern Han (25–220 CE) emperors were politically invested in the texts as well as Confucius' undertaking. The second emperor of the Eastern Han, Emperor Ming (57–75 CE) not only sacrificed to Confucius for the first time in Chinese history, but also compared himself to Confucius.[77] Under his son Emperor Zhang's (75–88 CE) sanction, Confucius along with the ancient sage kings and Han dynasty rulers became the only sages who were able to receive the mandate of Heaven.[78] This meant that the officials in the court could no longer guide their emperor like Confucius did for the warlords. Instead, they were, at best, equivalent to Confucius' disciples who assisted the sage.

While the Han fell in 220 CE, the prophet Confucius did not fall with it. Many scholars through Imperial China considered the prophet Confucius part of the larger inventory of images of Confucius. They cited apocryphal entries about

Confucius in their commentaries on the Five Classics or compiled them in their imperial encyclopedia projects. Before being swept into the "superstition" garbage can along with "feudal China" in the twentieth century, the prophet Confucius had been a large part of the cultural memory of Confucius. For example, the "Ultimate Sage" (*zhisheng* 至聖), one of his posthumous titles ubiquitous in China from the eleventh to early twentieth century, originated as the Dark Sage (*xuansheng* 玄聖) in 1008 CE. The Song dynasty emperor Zhenzong 真宗 (r. 997–1022 CE) entitled him as *xuansheng* particularly by citing the very same miraculous conception story we saw in apocrypha.[79] When Kang Youwei 康有為 (1858–1927 CE) composed his *Examination of Confucius' Reform* (*Kongzi gai zhi kao* 孔子改制考) to advocate his constitutional monarchy, one of the first things he mentioned was Confucius as the essence of the dark emperor.[80]

However, this prophet Confucius has always been the eccentric counterpart of the Confucius who kept a distance from the divine in the *Analects*. One of the reasons is obviously its political implications which were particular to the Han dynasty. But there might have been another reason. Born with a path set by heaven, Confucius saved himself from earthly struggles. This heavenly savior also came to rescue a dynasty. His teaching would help a dynasty to bring the ideal state of society to the world. But as long as this state was not realized on earth, he left individuals, many of whom were struggling just like the human Confucius himself in the wilderness of human life. In the next chapter, we will follow the thread of Confucius' engagement with the supernatural and turn to an image that was more connected to the individual concerns of the literati.

2

Confucius as Ghostbuster

Early medieval China (220–581 CE) has long been a stomping ground for bizarre creatures. This is a time period when all heaven and hell broke loose: demons lured people into their schemes, the living were invited into the world of the dead, and deities saved individuals because of their good deeds. Confucius' moral teachings and his prophecies for a new dynasty no longer seemed like enough for surviving against gods and ghosts, as mentioned in the last chapter. We find this bizarre territory in a literary genre called "records of the strange" (*zhiguai* 志怪), which includes short stories about strange occurrences and events. While supernatural stories can be found sporadically in earlier writings, it was during this time period that they gathered into one, vigorous stream, which involved Daoism, Buddhism, and other religious practices.[1] And Confucius came to the rescue for people's anxiety about the supernatural and the unseen world.

Modern scholars have taken several approaches to the relationship between these religions and the supernatural: some of them closely trace certain beliefs in records of the strange, some look at the borrowing of ideas across these religions, and some perceive these stories as the battlefield of different beliefs.[2] In these standard approaches, scholars treat Confucianism, or more specifically, teachings and people related to Confucius and the Five Classics (*wujing* 五經) as a hazy background.[3]

In this chapter, I will argue that Confucius and the teachings of the Confucian classics were more than relevant to the world within records of the strange. As the main consumers and producers of these records of the strange stories, the early medieval literati were often trained in the classics. They had a shared understanding of the premises of this world, where ghosts and demons lurked around the human realm and their power was beyond the reach of an ordinary living soul.[4] To cope with this menace, the literati integrated the learning of the Confucian classics with this world: Confucius possessed supernatural powers and if one chanted the classics, it could ward off demons. While scholars in early medieval China often labeled themselves in distinctive ways and attributed pejorative features to the labels of their rivals, they shared the same culture, in which so-called Daoism, Buddhism, and Confucianism were all actively involved. And individuals in fact moved from one label to another in their social lives. Stories from records of the strange manifest this culture, which was later divided into distinct categories by clear-cut "-isms." The image of Confucius in these stories well reflects such convergence.

In the following, we will discuss two types of records of the strange stories concerning Confucius and the Confucian classics. The first type involves the adventures of Confucius and his disciples, in which Confucius displays extraordinary knowledge in the identification of bizarre objects. The second type concerns the chanting of the Confucian classics, usually the *Classic of Filial Piety* (*Xiaojing* 孝經). In this type of story, chanting could ward off demons. Both kinds of stories have parallels in records of the strange tales that have Buddhist or Daoist ingredients, and both types can be traced back to earlier traditions of Confucius.

Confucius and His Strange Adventures with His Disciples

From traditional to contemporary China, one sanctioned image of Confucius has been his distance from anything supernatural. Sayings from the *Analects* (*Lunyu* 論語) have frequently served as the *locus classicus*: "Confucius did not talk about the strange, forces, disturbances, and wonders," or "Confucius said: 'respect the spirits and ghosts but distance yourself from them.'" Later on, the title of Yuan Mei's 袁枚 (1716–1797) compilation of bizarre stories, *Confucius Did Not Say* (*Zi bu yu* 子不語) was based on this reading of Confucius. Through this narrative, Confucius in contemporary China has become a philosopher who promoted rationality and scorned superstition.[5]

In early medieval China, however, other images of Confucius were more dominant, and many of these images held precedence beginning in the Han dynasty (205 BCE–220 CE). As we have seen in the previous chapter, Confucius was of half divine origin in Han dynasty apocrypha (*chenwei* 讖緯). According to these texts, Confucius wrote his *magnum opus*, the *Annals of Spring and Autumn* based on heavenly revelations, and the *Annals* itself served as a prophecy, which named the upcoming ruling family.[6] In the *Records of the Grand Historian*, Sima Qian included several anecdotes in which Confucius had uncanny knowledge about the world. In these stories, he identified the spirits of earth as well the biggest bone in the world from legendary times.⁷ In these narratives, Confucius kept no distance from the strange.

The Strange Birth and Death of Confucius

In one of the records of the strange stories from Wang Jia's 王嘉 (?–390 CE) *Records of the Left-out* (*Shiyi ji* 拾遺記), Confucius came into the world surrounded by heavenly happenings:

> 周靈王立二十一年，孔子生於魯襄公之世。夜有二蒼龍自天而下，來附徵在之房，因夢而生夫子。有二神女，擎香露於空中而來，以沐浴徵在。天帝下奏鈞天之樂，列以顏氏之房。空中有聲，言天感生聖子，故降以和樂笙鏞之音，異於俗世也。又有五老列於徵在之庭，則五星之精也。⁸

> In the 21st year of King Ling of the Zhou dynasty, Confucius was born under the rule of Duke Xiang of Lu. One night, two green dragons came down from Heaven and into Zhengzai's room. Zhengzai thus had a dream and conceived Confucius. Two divine maidens, holding fragrant dew, descended from the sky and gave Zhengzai a bath. The heavenly emperor sent down the music of the central Heaven to Zhengzai's room. There was a voice in the sky saying: Heaven stimulated [you] to give birth to the sagacious son, therefore it sends down the harmonious and happy music of pipes and bells, in order to distinguish him from the ordinary. There were also the Five Elders who lined up in the hallway of Zhengzai. They were the essences of the Five Stars.

In the above description, almost every sentence involves otherworldly powers. As Heaven mentions, these supernatural manifestations are supposed to separate Confucius from those in the ordinary world.

As miraculous as it is, most of the readers in early medieval China would not find this birth of Confucius too outlandish; the miraculous conception of Confucius was included in the apocryphal texts beginning in the first century CE as we have seen in the previous chapter. For example, apocrypha mention how the envoy of the dark emperor came to the dream of Confucius' mother Zhengzai and invited her to have intercourse with the dark emperor.⁹ These stories share many elements: the dream, the correspondence (*gan* 感), and the name of Confucius' mother, Zhengzai, which rarely appeared in any other texts before apocrypha.¹⁰

Meanwhile, the story in the *Records of the Left-out* added a nativity scene to his miraculous conception. Confucius' mother no longer gave birth in the wilderness; she lay comfortably in her room, accompanied by heavenly music and various deities. If the apocryphal conception of Confucius is aimed at linking him to a heavenly origin, the nativity scene in the *zhiguai* literature celebrates this link.[11]

In records of the strange, Confucius' death was also filled with strangeness:

孔子冢在魯城北,塋中樹以百數,皆異種。魯人世世無能名者,傳言孔子弟子,既皆異國之人,各持其國樹來種之,孔子塋中,至今不生荊棘草木。[12]

Confucius' tomb was located in the north of the city in the state of Lu. At his cemetery, there were hundreds of trees, which were all of alien origins. From generation to generation, no one from the state of Lu could name them. It was said that Confucius' disciples were all foreigners and they planted there the trees of their own countries. Even now, at his cemetery, no brambles or thorns can grow.

In this story, the word *yi* 異 paints an exotic color to Confucius' tomb and his disciples: it first indicates the strangeness of the trees in Confucius' cemetery, and then the foreignness of his disciples. The story further adds a bizarre feature to his cemetery; only worthy plants could grow, not weeds. Unsurprisingly, this story is included in the "Recording the Strange" ("Zhiguai" 志怪) chapter in Xiao Yi's 蕭繹 (508–554 CE) the *Master of the Golden Mansion* (*Jinlouzi* 金樓子). The rest of the chapter also concerns a huge turtle with writing on the bottom of its feet, people who do not have bellies from the Country of the Belly-less (Wufu guo 無腹國), the lake that can impregnate women from the Country of Women (Nü guo 女國), and other exotic anecdotes about lands outside of China. In contrast with the heavenly realm in the nativity scene, here Confucius' tomb is connected to foreign realms to highlight the strangeness of him and his disciples.[13]

Confucius' prophecy in his tomb adds a gruesome layer to his powers even after his death:

秦世有謠云:"秦始皇,何強梁!開吾戶,據吾床;飲吾漿,唾吾裳;飡吾飯,以為糧;張吾弓,射東牆;前至沙丘當滅亡。"始皇既焚書坑儒,乃發孔子墓,欲取經傳。墓既啟,遂見此謠文刊在冢壁,始皇甚惡之。及東游,乃遠沙丘而循別路,忽見群小兒攢沙為阜,問之:"何為? 答云:"此為沙丘也。"從此得病而亡。[14]

There was a ballad during the Qin dynasty: "How aggressive is the First Emperor of Qin! He opens my door and occupies my bed; he drinks my drink and spits on my clothes; he eats my rice as if it were his food; he draws my bow and shoots the eastern wall; and when he arrives on the Sand Hill, he will perish." After he burned the books and buried the literati, the First Emperor opened Confucius' tomb in order to obtain the classics and commentaries. When the tomb was opened, he saw the ballad written on the tomb wall. The First Emperor was deeply troubled by it. When he traveled to the east, he avoided the place called Sand Hill and sought another route. Suddenly he saw several children accumulating sand to make a mound. He asked them: "What are you making?" They said, "A sand hill." Then he was ill and eventually died.

This story might contradict Confucius' image in the *Analects*, in which he refrains from mentioning supernatural occurrences and even death.[15] Nevertheless, his vision of his own demise did occur in the *Records of the Grand Historian* of the first century CE. In the *Records*, Confucius had a dream that he sat between two pillars, just like deceased Shang people to whom sacrifices were being offered. As a Shang descendant, Confucius took the dream as the sign of his death, and after seven days, he indeed passed away.[16]

Different from the vision of his own death, this records of the strange story from the *Minor Sayings* (*Xiaoshuo* 小說) demonstrates the otherworldly power of Confucius. The story introduces the founding emperor of the Qin dynasty, the First Emperor (260–210 CE). Often depicted as a tyrant in traditional historiography, the First Emperor symbolizes the greatest power in the human world. In the story, Confucius not only predicted the First Emperor's transgression toward his tomb, an event that happened 200 years after his own death, but Confucius could even predict the First Emperor's death. The power of his prediction was so strong to the extent that the First Emperor could not escape from the "sand hill." From his nativity to his death, records of the strange show the power of Confucius and his disciples beyond the human realm.

Perceiving the Future

This prophecy touches on one of the recurring themes in records of the strange stories, the prediction of the future. Certain scholars have argued that records of the strange shaped this image of Confucius, as if outside this literature, a this-worldly and secular sage was Confucius' only normative image.[17] However, as we have seen in the previous chapter, Confucius as a prophet was a popular image in the first two centuries CE China. The records of the strange continued with this tradition of Confucius as a person who could perceive the future.

In the Han dynasty, one of Confucius' main identities was as the author of the *Annals of Spring and Autumn*, originally a chronicle of the state of Lu, recording its state affairs from 722 to 481 BCE. However, as we have seen in the previous chapter, most Han literati did not just read the chronicle as lessons from history, but as a prophetic book that legitimated the rule of the Han dynasty. An apocryphal story specifically mentions that Confucius received the mandate at the Duan gate, which told him to compose the *Annals of Spring and Autumn*. It alludes to Confucius' reception of the blood writing (*xie shu* 血書) from Heaven. In the story, the blood writing predicted the death of Confucius and the subsequent dynastic changes: the end of the Zhou dynasty and the rise of the Qin.[18] In the apocryphal narrative, the *Annals* also reveals what happened after the fall of the evil Qin dynasty: the rise of the Han dynasty and the Han ruling family, with the Liu's reception of the heavenly mandate.[19] Confucius thus became a prophet who could perceive the future of the human world, especially dynastic changes. Within this context, the aforementioned ballad about the First Emperor becomes even more relevant: because Confucius could predict dynastic changes, he could also foresee the death of important political figures.

The difference between the apocryphal narrative and the records of the strange stories lies in what Confucius' visions were for. In apocrypha, his supernatural visions are aimed at legitimating the Han dynasty's rule. These records of the strange stories, on the other hand, focus on Confucius; he was the hero of the story, and his uncanny prediction was the point. The records of the strange stories emphasize personal revenge and retribution instead of inevitable dynastic changes—the First Emperor transgressed into Confucius' tomb in order to eliminate the Confucian classics and records of the ancient sages, and Confucius' prophecy reacted to this personal offense: "he drinks *my* drink and spits on *my* clothes." As we will see in other cases from records of the strange, knowledge about the future was more often tied to personal welfare than the fate of dynasties.

In line with being a prophet, in records of the strange stories, Confucius could divine the future, using the *Book of Changes*:

孔子嘗使子貢出，久而不返。占之，遇鼎。弟子皆言無足不來。顏回掩口而笑。孔子曰："回笑，是謂賜必來也。"因問回："何以知賜來？"對曰："無足者，蓋乘舟而來，賜且至矣。"果然，明旦，子貢乘潮至。[20]

Once Confucius sent [his disciple] Zigong out, and for a long time Zigong did not come back. Confucius made a divination and received the hexagram Tripod (Ding). His disciples all said that because there was "no feet" [as an interpretation of the hexagram], Zigong would not come back. Yan Hui [Yan Yuan] giggled with his mouth covered. Confucius said: "Hui is giggling; this means Zigong will definitely be back." Then the disciples asked: "How do you know that Zigong will come back?" Confucius said: "'No feet' means that he will come back by boat. Zigong will arrive."[21] As it was said, the next morning, Zigong came back by following the tide.

Here Confucius and his disciples practice a divination based on one of the Five Classics, the *Changes* (*Yi* 易), and they receive one of the sixty-four hexagram results, Tripod (Ding 鼎). "No feet" comes from the interpretation of the hexagram lines, more specifically, the third line from the top. In the received version of the *Changes*, the interpretation of this line states that the tripod's feet are broken (*Ding zhe zu* 鼎折足), and it is inauspicious. Following this interpretation at face value, most of Confucius' disciples believe that Zigong has no feet to return. Confucius, however, goes around the "no foot" part, stating that Zigong could come back without *using* his feet, which would be by boat. The successful return of Zigong verifies Confucius and his disciple Yan Yuan's more superior divinatory skills.

The story develops from several elements in the *Analects* and other earlier sources. First, it is well testified that Confucius was fond of the *Changes*. In the *Analects*, Confucius said that if he could have several more years to learn the *Changes*, at the age of fifty he would not make big mistakes.[22] In the *Records of the Grand Historian*, Confucius read the *Changes* so diligently that he broke the leather bindings of the text three times.[23] Second, in the *Analects*, Yan Yuan was Confucius' favorite student and his intellectual heir. Zigong was a disciple who was talented in worldly affairs, such as trade and diplomacy.[24] This story depicts Yan Yuan and Zigong in a similar manner, where Zigong travels away for certain business, and Yan Yuan is the only person besides Confucius to understand the result of the divination. Third, this story from *Minor Sayings* already appeared in a text from the second century CE, the *External Tradition of Han's Book of Poetry* (*Han shi waizhuan* 韓詩外傳).[25] The reincorporation of this story into records of the strange further reinforces Confucius' power beyond the human realm.

Confucius and his Disciples as "Ghostbusters"

Going along with their supernatural halo, Confucius and his disciples also encountered ghosts and monsters in records of the strange. This is not surprising, for ghost stories form the most common theme in the genre. But certain stories unfold in a way that reminds readers of Confucius' life and teachings in earlier traditions. For example, in Gan Bao's 干寶 (?–336 CE) *Records of Searching the Wondrous* (*Soushen ji* 搜神記):

孔子厄於陳, 絃歌於館, 中夜, 有一人長九尺餘, 著皂衣, 高冠, 大吒, 聲動左右。子貢進問 "何人耶?" 便提子貢而挾之。子路引出與戰於庭有頃, 未勝。孔子察之, 見其甲車間時時開如掌, 孔子曰: "何不探其甲車, 引而奮登?" 子路引之, 沒手仆於地。乃是大鯷魚也。長九尺餘。孔子曰: "此物也, 何為來哉? 吾聞物老, 則群精依之。因衰而至此。其來也, 豈以吾遇厄, 絕糧, 從者病乎! 夫六畜之物, 及龜蛇魚鱉草木之屬, 久者神皆憑依, 能為妖怪, 故謂之'五酉。"五酉'者, 五行之方, 皆有其物, 酉者, 老也, 物老則為怪, 殺之則已, 夫何患焉。"[26]

When Confucius was stuck in the state of Chen, he sang with string music at his guest house. In the middle of the night, a person, more than 6.5 feet tall, wearing black clothes and a tall hat, was shouting loudly. The sound shook the people around. Zigong approached him and asked, "Who are you?" The person then grabbed Zigong and tried to kidnap him. Zilu came out and fought with him in the courtyard for a while, but he did not win. Confucius observed him and saw his chariot frequently opening up like palms. Confucius then said: "Why don't you pull him near and step onto his chariot to explore it?" Zilu pulled him, and out of control,[27] the figure fell on the ground. It was [actually] a big catfish, more than 6.5 feet long. Confucius said: "Why does this thing come [to us]? I have heard that when creatures become old, various spirits will attach [themselves] to them. They follow the decline [of the creature] to come here. Isn't its appearance because I am stuck here, with no food, and my followers are sick? The creatures of the six domestic animals belong to the categories of tortoises, snakes, fish, turtles, grass, and trees. After [living] a long time, spirits come to attach [themselves] to them, and [the creatures] would be able to become anomaly. That is why they are called the 'five *You*.' 'Five *You*' means that they exist in all the places of the Five Phases. *You* means 'old.' When a creature grows old, it would act in a strange way. Killing it will be the end. Why would there be any worry?"

In short, a catfish spirit was trying to attack Confucius and his disciples, but it was defeated by Confucius' disciple Zilu. After explaining why it appeared, Confucius provided a solution to this kind of situation: kill the strange creature. Once again, several elements in the story come from earlier traditions, but *Records of Searching the Wondrous* gives a new spin.

The story appears to be in the middle of Confucius' journey in the state of Chen, a well-known trip in the *Analects* and the *Records of the Grand Historian*. In order to connect to the more mainstream narratives, it even quotes these texts verbatim such as "stuck in the state of Chen" (*e yu Chen* 厄於陳), "with no food" (*jue liang* 絕糧), and "the followers are sick" (*congzhe bing* 從者病).[28] Confucius' disciples also resemble their conventional portraits: Zigong was a diplomat who handled conversations but was not physically strong, and Zilu was the martial and hotheaded one.

In this temporary "ghostbuster" squad, everyone seems to have a role: Zigong is in charge of the talking, Zilu is the muscle, and Confucius is the explainer.

In fact, this is not the first time Confucius took this role. As mentioned in the previous chapter, the second-century BCE *Records of the Grand Historian* includes a bundle of such stories. A few decades later, Liu Xiang 劉向 (77–6 BCE) compiled several similar stories in his *Garden of Persuasions* (*Shui yuan* 說苑). In one of them, Confucius was busy with two inquiries into strange subjects:

> 楚昭王渡江，有物大如斗，直觸王舟，止於舟中。昭王大怪之，使聘問孔子。孔子曰：" 此名萍實。"令剖而食之："惟霸者能獲之，此吉祥也。"其後齊有飛鳥一足來下，止於殿前，舒翅而跳。齊侯大怪之，又使聘問孔子。孔子曰："此名商羊，急告民趣治溝渠，天將大雨。"於是如之，天果大雨，諸國皆水，齊獨以安。²⁹
>
> When King Zhao of Chu was crossing a river, a thing as big as a gourd ladle directly hit the king's boat and stayed in the boat. King Zhao found it very strange. He then sent people to ask Confucius [about it]. Confucius said: "That is the fruit of duckweed." He asked them to open and eat it, [saying:] "Only people who will become hegemon can receive it; it is auspicious." After a while, a flying bird with one foot came and landed in the state of Qi. It stayed in front of the palace hall [of Qi], spreading its wings and hopping. The Marquis of Qi found it very strange. Likewise, he then sent people to ask Confucius [about it]. Confucius said: "This is called 'Shangyang.' It urgently warns people to build ditches, [because] there is going to be heavy rain from the sky." Qi then followed it [the advice.] Indeed, it rained heavily, which flooded every other state, and only Qi was safe.

Others might be puzzled by the fruit of duckweed hitting the boat or a one-footed bird dancing, but not Confucius.

In the story, Confucius went further to explain how he obtained this knowledge:

> 孔子歸，弟子請問。孔子曰："異時小兒謠曰：楚王渡江得萍實，大如拳，赤如日，剖而食之，美如蜜。此楚之應也。兒又有兩兩相牽，屈一足而跳，曰：天將大雨，商羊起舞。今齊獲之，亦其應也。夫謠之後，未嘗不有應隨者也。"故聖人非獨守道而已也，睹物記也，即得其應矣。³⁰
>
> Confucius came back, and his disciples asked [about the answers]. Confucius said: "Earlier on, there was a ballad from children saying: 'The king of Chu receives a duckweed fruit when he crosses the river. It is as big as a fist and as red as the sun. When you open and eat it, it is as tasty as honey.' This is the portent for Chu. There were also kids holding each other in pairs, hopping with one foot, saying: 'It will rain heavily, and Shangyang will dance.' Now Qi received it, so this is the portent. After a ballad, there are always follow-up correspondences." Therefore, sages do not just stick to their own way; they observe the things and keep them in mind. That is how they see the correspondences.

In the story, Confucius admitted that his knowledge came from observing the children and their ballads, which were considered prophetic throughout Imperial China. More explicitly, the compiler of the story, Liu Xiang, made the moral clear: even the sages need to observe the world and learn from it. Liu also put this story and the earthen jar story together with similar ones in the chapter called "Distinguishing Things" ("Bian wu" 辨物). Clearly to Liu, one of Confucius' main traits was his uncanny ability to identify strange phenomena. Therefore, it is not a surprise to early medieval Chinese readers that Confucius could give an explanation of the strange situation in the catfish story from the *Records of Searching the Wondrous*.

Records of the strange provide a new spin by adding the theme of ghost fighting with identification of the strange. In another story from the *Minor Sayings*, Confucius' "ghostbuster" squad is on the defense:

顏淵子路共坐於門, 有鬼魅求見孔子, 其目若日, 其形甚偉。子路失魄口噤, 顏淵乃納屨拔劍而前, 捲扯其腰, 於是化為蛇, 遂斬之。孔子出觀, 歎曰: "勇者不懼, 知者不惑; 仁者有勇, 勇者不必有仁。"[31]

Yan Yuan and Zilu sat together at the doorway [of Confucius' dwelling]. A ghost asked to see Confucius. Its eyes were like the sun, and its body was grand. Zilu was dumbfounded. Yan Yuan then put on his shoes, took out his sword, and approached it. When he grasped and pulled its waist, it transformed into a snake. He then severed it. Confucius came out and witnessed [the incident]. He sighed, saying: "The courageous are not afraid, and the intelligent are not confused. The benevolent have courage, but the courageous are not necessarily benevolent."

Again, the squad members are consistent with their portrayal in the *Analects*: while Zilu was martial, he did not have much to offer beyond his physical strength; Yan Yuan as Confucius' favorite disciple embodied Confucius' teaching on benevolence; and Confucius' comments were verbatim from the *Analects*.[32] Even though the first half ("The courageous are not afraid, and the intelligent are not confused") and the second half ("The benevolent have courage, but the courageous are not necessarily benevolent") come from two different passages, the story tries to unify them under the same context, namely, the confrontation of otherworldly danger.

Most importantly, the new spin of these records of the strange stories reveals a new role for Confucius. In records of the strange, the nonhuman realm is no longer far away and ambiguous, waiting for Confucius to clarify it for his fellow contemporaries; it instead invades the human society, as shown by the transgression of the snake spirit and the catfish spirit's attempted kidnapping of Zigong. Confucius here differs from in the *Analects*, where he teaches his disciples how to live an ethical life in human society, or from in the apocryphal texts, where he brings legitimacy to the Han rule. Instead, Confucius was trying to tell his readers how to live in a world where creatures from the other realm approach you. The good, old teachings from the *Analects* still help, but it means something else this time: if you are intelligent and benevolent like Yan Yuan, you will be able to spot a monster and kill it.

The haunting threat of ghosts was a general concern in records of the strange and the medieval Chinese intellectual world by and large. For example, with a Buddhist touch, demonic retribution was a common theme in the *Records of the Hidden and Visible Realms* (*Youming lu* 幽明錄) of the fourth century. The moral of many of these stories was to commit good deeds and avoid bad deeds in order to deal with karmic consequences.[33] One of the Daoist scriptures of the time, the *Scripture of Divine Incantations of the Abyssal Caverns* (*Taishang dongyuan shenzhou jing* 太上洞淵神咒經) expresses the constant fear of ghosts, who cast diseases and disasters upon the human world.[34] Faced with the ghosts, the scripture suggests that readers chant the scripture and the names of demons in order to tame them or ward them off.

Confucius and his disciples in records of the strange took on the same mission: they tell people why the strange phenomena take place and how to avoid undesirable consequences.[35] The stories from this tradition equip them to do so as well. Not only could Confucius identify the lurking dangers, spot their weakness, and sense the future, but he even possessed a divine halo because of his heavenly origin. Combined with the more classical image, this new superpowered Confucius was designed to help the readers of early medieval China cope with their anxieties about otherworldly beings.

The Power of Chanting

If Confucius possessed powers to ward off otherworldly threats, could we somehow borrow his powers? As mentioned above, Daoist practitioners used chanting to ward off demons. Similarly, in many of the Buddhist stories from records of the strange, chanting sutras or Avalokiteśvara's (Guanyin) name could also call up miraculous effects when someone was in danger.[36] In records of the strange and older traditions, there are stories about how the literati chanted the Five Classics to cleanse themselves and ward off demons. In this section, we will see how borrowing the words from Confucius was imagined to be protective against the otherworldly menace.

Previous studies on chanting in early medieval China give us the impression that only Daoists and Buddhists emphasized the supernatural power behind chanting.[37] Although chanting the classics was never as popular among the literati of early medieval China as it was among circles of Daoist practitioners or Buddhist monks, the practice itself seems to be shared by people of various communities. Just like the transformation of the image of Confucius in records of the strange, I believe the practice of chanting exemplifies the various ways early medieval Chinese literati engaged in the contemporary discourse of supernatural threats, wherein the normative division between Daoism, Buddhism, and Confucianism melted down.

Chanting in general was a way of learning written words from early China on.[38] As Xunzi (ca. 313–238 BCE) mentioned, reciting the classics was the starting point for becoming a gentleman. If we understand chanting as the repetition of someone's words, chanting can be seen as an activity of imitation. As Mencius (ca. 372–289 BCE) mentioned, if one recited the words of the sage kings Yao and Shun and dressed like Yao and Shun, he would become Yao and Shun. A sense of devotion and concentration often comes from an immersive action of chanting, with "reciting it for a life time" (*zhong shen song zhi* 終身誦之) as a common expression for such devotion and learning. Zilu was a good example, who for his lifetime recited Confucius' comment on detachment ("He dislikes none, he covets nothing—what can he do but what is good!" 不忮不求, 何用不臧).[39] Just as learning can lead to new knowledge, chanting can make one become someone else through a concentrated embodiment of knowledge.

In the process of chanting, concentration and embodiment could bring transforming effects. The *Spring and Autumn Annals of Master Lü* states the connection between concentration and chanting: "One thinks about it [the sayings] day and night. He serves his heart and lets his concentration take charge. When he gets up, he recites it; when he lies down, he dreams about it." (日夜思之, 事心任精, 起則誦之, 臥則夢之)[40] The concentrated mind would stimulate (*gan* 感) either spirits or the *qi*, which in turn would affect the physical world. As *Huainanzi* mentions, when the concentrated mind stimulates one's body, it moves the *qi* in Heaven, and auspicious omens such as the yellow dragon (*huang long* 黃龍) and auspicious phoenix (*xiang feng* 祥鳳) arrive.[41]

The transforming power of chanting could also protect one from curses:

武帝時迷於鬼神, 尤信越巫, 董仲舒數以為言。武帝欲驗其道, 令巫詛仲舒, 仲舒朝服南面, 誦詠經論, 不能傷害, 而巫者忽死。[42]

During Emperor Wu's time, the emperor was obsessed with ghosts and deities. He especially believed in Yue exorcists (*wu*). Dong Zhongshu spoke against it several times. Emperor Wu wanted to test the methods of Dong Zhongshu, so he asked the exorcist to curse him. Dong wore court dress and faced the South. He [then] recited and chanted the classics and commentaries to the exorcist. He could not be harmed, and the exorcist suddenly died.

By the first century CE, we already see depictions of Emperor Wu as a seeker of longevity and his official Dong Zhongshu as a great classicist.[43] Collected by Ying Shao 應劭 (153–196 CE) in the second century CE, this story further amplifies their images: Emperor Wu becomes an enthusiast of spiritual power, and Dong Zhongshu becomes a possessor of super powers. In the story, Emperor Wu simply wants to find out, between the exorcist and Dong, who is more powerful. Our classicist does not disappoint us; he uses chanting not only to protect himself from the curse, but also bounces it back to the exorcist. The chanting of the classics was not just a way to learn, but also a numinous skill that counters invisible harms in the human realm.

Fan Ye 范曄 (398–445 CE) also included an anecdote about the protective power of chanting the classics in this dynastic history of the Eastern Han (25–220 CE):

公沙穆字文乂，北海膠東人也。家貧賤。自為兒童不好戲弄，長習韓詩、公羊春秋，尤銳思河洛推步之術。居建成山中，依林阻為室，獨宿無侶。時暴風震雷，有聲於外呼穆者三，穆不與語。有頃，呼者自牖而入，音狀甚怪，穆誦經自若，終亦無它妖異，時人奇之。後遂隱居東萊山，學者自遠而至。[44]

Gongsha Mu's (fl. 155 CE) style name was Wenyi, a native of Jiaodong, Beihai. He came from a poor family. Since he was a child, Gongsha was not fond of playing. When he grew up, he learned the Han tradition of the *Book of Poetry* and the Gongyang tradition of the *Annals*. He especially concentrated on the method of astrological calculation of the *River Chart* [*He tu* 河圖] and *Luo Writing* [*Luo shu* 洛書]. He lived in the mountains by Jiancheng. Using the woods as shelter, he built a house and lived without any companions. One day it was stormy with thunder, and a voice called Gongsha's name three times. But Gongsha did not respond. After a little while, the source of the voice came in through the window, and its shape and voice were very strange. Gongsha calmly chanted the classics. Eventually, there was no other bizarre strangeness. His contemporaries were impressed by him. Afterwards he retreated to Mount Donglai, and people who wanted to learn from him came from a distance.

The anecdote sets Gongsha in a typical horror movie scene: alone, in the middle of nowhere in the mountains, with heavy rain and strange sounds. He is clearly not just paranoid, however, after a strange-shaped creature calls his name three times and then breaks into his room. Thanks to chanting the classics, he does not end up like a victim in a horror movie, and in contrast to facing the Yue exorcist, the classicist Gongsha was even faced with an otherworldly creature. Here, chanting the classics reaches out from within human society to ward off danger from outside of it.

From the second century CE on, chanting as an extraordinary skill to cope with dangers became part of the literati's arsenal to deal with supernatural threats. Influenced by Buddhism or not, the image of the classicists merged with that of the exorcists when coping with threats from outside the human realm, especially if one was in an isolated position. In early medieval China, when traveling was necessary, mountains became increasingly accessible, and people were forced to immigrate to new and strange areas, so self-protection, and hence chanting, was greatly needed.[45]

Chanting the Classics in Records of the Strange

The need to ward off strange creatures might have prompted Gan Bao to incorporate a second-century CE story into his *Records of Searching the Wondrous*:

北部督郵西平郅伯夷，年三十許，大有才決，長沙太守郅若章孫也，日晡時，到亭，敕前導人：「且止」。錄事掾曰：「今尚早，可至前亭。」曰：「欲作文書。」便留，吏卒惶怖，言當解去。傳云：「督郵欲於樓上觀望，亟掃除。」須臾，便上。未暝，樓鐙、階下復有火。敕云：「我思道，不可見火，滅去。」吏知必有變，當用赴照，但藏置壺中。日既暝，整服坐，誦《六甲》、《孝經》、《易本》訖，臥。有頃，更轉東首，以拏巾結兩足，[以]幘冠之，密拔劍解帶。夜時，有正黑者四五尺，稍高，走至屋柱，因覆伯夷。伯夷持被掩之，足跣脫，幾失，再三。以劍帶擊魅腳，呼下火照上。視之，老狐，正赤，略無衣毛。持下燒殺。明旦，發樓屋，得所髡人髻百餘。因此遂絕。[46]

North Regional Investigator of Transgressions Zhi Boyi of Xiping was more than thirty years old, and he was very decisive. He was the grandson of Zhi Ruozhang, the Grand Administrator of Changsha. He and his entourage arrived at a post around three in the afternoon. He commanded the tour guide: "Stop." His Head for Managing Affairs said: "It is still early; we can get to the next post." Boyi said: "I want to write some documents." Then they stayed. The clerks and soldiers were terrified [of the place], and they said that they would leave. Boyi announced to them: "The Investigator would like to go up to the canton building to observe. Clean the building immediately." After a little while, he climbed into the building. It was not dark yet; there was fire in lamps in the attic and under the stairs. Boyi announced: "I am meditating on the Way and should not see fire. Put it out." The clerks knew that something would happen, and they were going to need to use the lights. Therefore, they hid the lights in their vases. When it became dark, Boyi dressed formally and sat. He recited the *Six Jia*, the *Classic of Filial Piety*, and the "Origin of the *Changes*."[47] After he finished, he lay down. After a while, he turned to the east side of the top of the canton. He wrapped his feet with broad headbands and capped them with conical hairbands. He secretly drew his sword out and untied his sash. At night, a black creature, four feet or taller, ran from the pillars of the room and tried to tackle Boyi. Boyi covered it with a sheet. With bare feet, it ran out of the sheet. After going back and forth three times, he used the sash of the sword to hit the feet of the bizarre [creature] and asked the people from downstairs to light the attic. They looked at it, and it was an old, red fox without clothes and fur. He took it down and burnt it to death. The next morning, they searched the rooms of the canton, and found hundreds of topknots that it had shaved off of people. The strange things then disappeared.

In the story, the hero Zhi Boyi and his clerks are on a business trip, as many Han local officials often were. The post, originally set up by the Han empire, becomes an intersection between human society and the wild, as many of them were located in the countryside and not frequently used. In contrast with his oblivious staff members, Zhi calmly identifies the killer fox, demobilizes it, and kills it, a rare image for a classicist. Chanting here has the dual function of calming our hero's mind as well as revealing the bizarre creature. This is similar to how a concentrated mind could make otherworldly, auspicious animals appear as mentioned in *Huainanzi*, but this time it is used on ominous creatures.

One of the texts Zhi chanted, the *Classic of Filial Piety* had a tradition of being used for exorcism in the second century CE. It is not entirely clear why this text on filial piety stood out for exorcism, but filial piety was believed to bring divine help and provoke miraculous happenings in early medieval China. In addition, the text elaborates the social and cosmic significance of filial piety through the putative sayings of Confucius.[48] The total of 1,903 characters in *Filial Piety* also makes it a suitable length for chanting, while the other classics of the time were above 10,000 characters. It is likely that the potency of Confucius' words combined with the cosmic power of filial piety gave the text power to ward off danger.

For example, Wang Yun 王允 (137–192 CE) told Emperor Xian (r. 181–234 CE) that reciting the *Classic of Filial Piety* could "dissolve the disasters and ward off the deviant" (*xiao zai que xie* 消災卻邪). Accepted by the Emperor, Wang and his colleague came into the court every day to chant the text.[49] Similarly, the classicist Xiang Xu 向栩 (fl. 180 CE) indulged in the magical power of the *Filial Piety*. When the religious leader Zhang Jiao 張角 (?–180 CE) rebelled, Xiang

Xu advised against the court's military campaign, but instead advised "sending generals onto the Yellow River and reciting the *Classic of Filial Piety* to the north." In this way, he believed, the "bandits will vanish on their own."[50]

In another records of the strange story from the *Records of Searching the Wondrous*, a student of the classics (*shusheng* 書生) similarly uses chanting to reveal as well as to ward off monsters.[51] The story also takes place at an ominous post, where the traveling student seeks accommodation for one night. Aware of being surrounded by a sow spirit, an old cock spirit, and an old scorpion spirit, the student silently chanted his books (*min bian song shu* 密便誦書) the whole night. Unlike the previous visitors, he survived the monsters—he found the sow, cock, and scorpion in the morning and killed them.[52] Once again, chanting becomes a shelter to protect the student from outside harm.

Both stories from the *Records of Searching the Wondrous* have a demonology that was similar to Confucius' statement mentioned earlier in the chapter: "when creatures turn old, they become strange." This is especially the case for the old cock and the old scorpion, which according to the story, are as big as a guitar. In both stories, the strangeness takes place at night, when human society falls asleep and the wild wakes up. The stories imply that the threat does not even need to come from otherworldly deities or ghosts; they can come from the domestic animals one raises. In records of the strange of early medieval China, the sentient danger was much more imminent, constantly ready to invade human society.

The chanting of the classics does differ from Buddhist and Daoist chanting in several ways. Among all the examples we have seen, the recitation of the classics never provoked any supernatural agency, at least not in an obvious way. In the case of chanting Buddhist sutras or Daoist scriptures, either Avalokiteśvara, the Buddha, inner gods, or other deities sitting high in the heavenly bureaucracy would respond to the requests and manifest their powers.[53] In the cases of the classics, Confucius and his disciples did not come to the rescue, nor did Heaven directly interfere with human affairs. The classics were not covenants between humans and deities, the articulation of which would call their attention; the classics were the relics of ancient sages' words. It is this extension to Confucius' power that could strike awe in strange creatures.

Concluding Remarks

In this chapter, we have seen yet another unusual presentation of Confucius, his disciples, and the classics. In records of the strange, Confucius was not just the worldly sage who kept his teaching in the human realm, he was also of divine origin erudite whose knowledge covered human society and beyond. This kind of knowledge allows both him and his disciples to ward off danger, especially ghosts and spirits. This representation speaks to the literati of early medieval China, who were concerned with threats from outside the human world. In dealing with these threats, the classics, as the legacy of Confucius, also became numinous. The recitation of them fit into the common practice of incantation among various religious communities. Similar to other traditions, the recitation of the classics provided protection and even the power to fend off vicious spirits. Unlike other traditions, however, it did not call out for help from a higher sentient being. Like Confucius' knowledge about strange creatures, the power of the classics comes from sagely knowledge.

When we speak of Confucius and his disciples, we often consider them the "sane" ones for their time. This image comes from contrasting them with other traditions: if Buddhists argue for the existence of ghosts, the anti-ghost interlocutors become "Confucian"; if Daoists argue for immortality, the believers of natural life span become "Confucian"; if Buddhists and Daoists concentrate on otherworldly business, the writings about worldly affairs become "Confucian." However, it was the *individuals* who had the potential to develop into various tenets of thought, labelled as "Buddhist," "Daoist," "Confucian," or not. They derived ideas from existing knowledge, but also reshaped them in order to cope with the concerns of their time. In this way, in records of the strange, the strange Confucius and his teachings became only natural.

3

Confucius as Diviner

In the previous two chapters, we have seen representations of Confucius especially among the literati. What about the people who did not identify themselves as literati? Or to put it another way, would people still care about Confucius in their daily lives if they did not need to worry about the mandate of Heaven for a dynasty or ghosts haunting them on a long trip? In this chapter, we will turn to these questions by focusing on a town called Dunhuang 敦煌 in the tenth century CE. In such a metropolitan place as Dunhuang, we will have a rare peek into what the local residents needed from Confucius other than the Five Classics that he putatively edited.

Perhaps surprisingly to some modern readers, Confucius appeared in the Dunhuang documents as a great diviner, an occupation that was seemingly different, if not at odds with, his image as a teacher and thinker. Derived from the earlier depiction of Confucius as well-versed in the *Changes* and the classics in general, this diviner image responded to an audience who was anxious about their futures instead of moralities and who sought for expeditious means of coping with them. Their anxieties concentrated on practical daily activities, and so did this diviner Confucius: he foretold the fortunes of dwelling spaces through rocks, rivers, or wells; he gave a clear yes or no answer to the arrival of travelers; he even designed a divinatory method that was simplified from the *Changes* for instant use. He was not just a sage who was worshiped in the temple; he was the wise man in the neighborhood who could provide you with immediate help.

In this chapter, we will make sense of this representation from two directions: on the one hand, divination resonated with a more mainstream image of Confucius that existed since early Imperial China; on the other hand, Dunhuang residents expected a great sage like Confucius to know the future. We will start with an introduction to the region of Dunhuang and why this region is ideal for our endeavor. Then we will examine the divination manuals from this region, in both Literary Chinese and in Tibetan. Putting these manuals into the larger textual world of Dunhuang, we will explore how divination and diviners were presented in Dunhuang texts and then move to a more general issue: the conception of sages. I argue that people in Dunhuang imagined sages as individuals who could foresee the future, and the local image of Confucius exemplified such imagination. This image in turn illustrates how divination and foreknowledge are related to sagehood in Dunhuang and late Tang society in general.

Dunhuang and its Textual World in Medieval China

Geographical location and history

Located in northwest China, Dunhuang might seem to be a random frontier area for the Chinese dynasties at first glance. Yet its geographical surroundings made it an essential traffic point, as it is centrally located in an area that spans from the western boundary of Gansu 甘肅 province to the most western part of the Hexi Corridor, a narrow plateau sheltered by several mountains: Wushao 烏鞘 Mountain in the southeast, Qilian 祁連 mountain and Altyn-Tagh in the southwest, as well as Mazong 馬鬃, Heli 合黎, and Longshou 龍首 mountains in the northeast. The two series of mountains run roughly parallel to each other from northwest to southeast, creating a corridor. While the climate is mainly desert, several oases are found along the corridor, which makes it a viable route for traveling.[1]

Popularly referred to as the Silk Road, Dunhuang and this corridor became an essential part of the trade routes that connected China with Central Asia.[2] For the better part of the first millennium CE, the route started in Chang'an 長安, crossed the Hexi Corridor, and then split into three branches. Two of them went to the north and south of the Taklamakan Desert, respectively, and converged at Kashgar. The third one passed north of the Tian Shan mountains through Turpan, Talgar, and Almaty. With several other splits and convergences again, two of the branches terminated at Merv, Turkmenistan, and the other one passed the Aral Sea and went on to the Black Sea. Because Dunhuang was the entrance to this narrow corridor, all the branches converged there. Dunhuang thus became China's western gate.[3]

As a crucial travel station since the first century BCE, Dunhuang grew into a trading center and metropolitan area, which further led to a blossoming of education and religious practices. After the collapse of the Han dynasty (205

BCE–220 CE), central China went through frequent power shifts over the next 300 years. In contrast, the Dunhuang region remained under the reign of the five Liang 凉 dynasties (301–421 CE), most of which protected trade and encouraged education.[4] Buddhism also flourished due to the general prosperity.[5] Meanwhile, because of the turmoil in southern China, Dunhuang attracted many southern literati immigrants.

After the Sui dynasty's (581–618 CE) reunification of the north and the south, Dunhuang blossomed as a metropolitan city. It served as a common stopping point for the main commercial routes through the corridor. Under the expansion of the Tang territory and its political relations, Dunhuang attracted goods and travelers from China as well as Central Asia. When the number of inhabitants in Dunhuang increased, cultural activities were boosted as well. On the one hand, the city hosted schools at the provincial and county levels with a curriculum based on the Confucian classics. On the other hand, it also welcomed Daoism, Zoroastrianism, Manicheism, and Christianity, which all became localized.[6]

Among all the religions, Buddhism enjoyed exceeding popularity during the Sui and Tang. Thanks to the two Sui emperors, more than seventy Buddhist grottoes were built in Mogao 莫高 in less than thirty years. From that point on, building grottoes became a fashion in Buddhist worship. By Empress Wu's reign (690–705 CE), the number of grottoes at the Mogao Caves exceeded 1,000, with many donated by individual families. Further, the Tang dynasty also encouraged the building of Buddhist temples, such as Dayun Temple 大雲寺, Longxing Temple 龍興寺, and Kaiyuan Temple 開元寺. These temples not only transmitted Buddhist scriptures, but also served as locales to teach and entertain local communities.[7]

From 786 to 848 CE, Tibet occupied Dunhuang. During this period, Buddhism became the only accepted religion and continued to flourish. In seizing Dunhuang, the Tibetans did not invade the city, but encamped around it for ten years (776–786 CE) until the local people surrendered. This nonviolent tactic left local people and facilities intact.[8] Under Tibetan rule, however, local schools and Daoist temples disappeared, and Manicheism was banned.[9] In contrast, the number of Buddhist temples in the Dunhuang area increased from thirteen to seventeen, and the number of registered monks and nuns skyrocketed from 300 to several thousand. Tibetan occupation also protected local Buddhism from the Great Anti-Buddhist Persecution in 845 CE, which swept most parts of the Tang dynasty.[10]

After Zhang Yichao 張議潮 (c.a. 799–872 CE) and his Guiyi Circuit (Guiyi jun 歸義軍) took control of Dunhuang in 848 CE, Buddhism continued to flourish and other religious and cultural activities were revived.[11] Many of Zhang's alliances came from powerful Buddhist communities that took shape during the Tibetan occupation. The Zhang family and their successors, the Cao 曹 family, continued to build grottoes in Mogao and Yulin 榆林, among other places.[12] Dunhuang continued to host monks, envoys, and travelers going in and out of China. Meanwhile, the Guiyi Circuit adopted the Tang administrative system, and local schools were revived to teach Confucian classics with curricula common in Tang dynasty proper. Moreover, Zoroastrianism, Manicheism, and Christianity reappeared in Dunhuang. Dunhuang continued to enjoy its pivotal position until the eleventh century, when the Western Xia 西夏 empire took control of the region and overseas trading developed from the Song onwards.[13]

Dunhuang texts and a world larger than Buddhism

If it were not for the Mogao caves, we would not have a peek into the metropolitan culture of Dunhuang in the second half of the first millennium CE. One cave is especially of interest: cave no. 17, which contained more than 30,000 manuscripts from the fifth century to the eleventh century.[14] This cave and cave no. 16 were built around 852 CE in homage to the monk-supervisor Hongbian 洪辯 (?-862 CE).[15] It was likely sealed shortly after 1002 CE, around the time when the Islamic Kara-Khanid Khanate dynasty conquered the Buddhist kingdom of Khotan (1006 CE). Perhaps in fear of a similar extermination of Buddhism as during the Tang, the monks sealed cave no. 17 together with the manuscripts they owned. This accidentally preserved the manuscripts until 1900.[16]

The manuscripts belonged to the library of the Three Realms Monastery (Sanjie si 三界寺) of the late Tang, which was close to cave no. 17 then.[17] Dated 405 CE to 1002 CE,[18] the majority of the manuscripts, or more precisely, 80 percent of the Chinese language texts are related to Buddhism.[19] This is hardly surprising since they came from a monastery library. Meanwhile, the rest of the manuscripts reflect the monastery's multiple functions:[20] for education, there are Confucian classics, dynastic histories, and primers for children; for daily use, there are practical documents like calendars and accounting books; and for entertainment, there are literary texts ranging from the most highbrow verses to rather popular and even coarse stories. They tell a rather different story from what scholars often assume about the textual and intellectual segregation between different religions, between the religious and the secular, and between different socio-economic strata.

Confucius and his Disciples in Dunhuang Divination

While we expect to see Confucius in texts for learning the classics, it is surprising to find him in divination texts. Often referred as "methods of numbers" (*shushu* 數術) in traditional China, these were techniques of predicting the future or finding unknown knowledge.[21] This is particularly because the *Analects* famously claims Confucius' silence toward the strange and wonders.[22] And divination could easily appear to be a "wonder" to many literati, who were suspicious of the practice.[23]

Nevertheless, divination manuals are not a negligible part of the Dunhuang texts and the world of knowledge behind them.[24] The proportion of them (ca. 0.5 percent) certainly cannot compare to Buddhist texts or literature (ca. 3.7 percent), but it does not trail far behind Confucian classics (ca. 0.74 percent) or primers (ca. 0.61 percent). It is bigger than the proportion of medicine, calendar, and astronomy texts combined (ca. 0.34 percent), and surpasses legal texts (ca. 0.1 percent) as well as historical and geographical works together (ca. 0.24 percent in total).[25] Some of the divination manuals belonged to students of local schools in Dunhuang because, by the tenth century, the provincial schools (*zhouxue* 州學) in Dunhuang offered the study of divination (or literally, Yinyang 陰陽).[26] That is to say, these divination manuals had official affiliations. More interestingly, many of these manuscripts, otherwise lost or unheard of, depict Confucius and his disciples as masters of divinatory arts, largely unknown to the *Analects* or even Confucius' biography in the *Records of the Grand Historian*.

Confucius as a divination interpreter

One might object to the claim that Confucius kept a distance from divination. It is true that according to the *Analects* and the *Records of the Grand Historian*, Confucius was familiar with the *Book of Changes* (*Yijing* 易經), originally a divinatory text. For example, in the *Analects*, Confucius said that learning the *Changes* could help him avoid serious wrongdoings. The *Records of the Grand Historian* also adds that Confucius was so fond of reading the *Changes* that he broke the binding of the text multiple times.[27] However, neither of the texts specify that he practiced the *Changes* as a divinatory technique. On the contrary, they hint that Confucius had a moral reading of the text. And more importantly, the depiction of Confucius' teaching in the *Analects* and *Records* almost always emphasized human relations and the moral calculations behind them.[28]

However, the Dunhuang divination manuals understood Confucius' familiarity with the *Changes* more literally. For example, he and his disciples, especially Zixia 子夏 (507 BCE?–?) and Yan Yuan 顏淵 (521 BCE?–481 BCE?), have a lot to say in a divinatory manual called the *Three Completions of the Changes* (*Yi sanbei* 易三備).[29] This text reveals the fortunes of dwellings and burial places through the hexagrams from the *Changes*. In the text, Confucius and Zixia comment on the results:

剝, 坤下艮上。乾家五世。剝, 九月卦。世在五, 應在二。占世爻定, 穿井深八尺, 得蚯蚓, 長六寸, 似蛇。子夏云: 居得此宅, 絕滅, 凶。孔子云: 此宅出孤寡。[30]

The hexagram Bo 剝 has the trigram Kun ☷ below and Gen ☶ above. It is the fifth generation of the Qian trigram family.[31] Bo is the hexagram of the ninth month. Its generation lies in five,[32] and correspondence in two.[33] In the divination, if the generation line is decided [as such], one will find out that after drilling eight *chi* (8×29.6 cm) [at the burial place], he will obtain an earthworm that is six *cun* long (6×2.96 cm) and looks like a snake. Zixia said: living in this house will lead to the elimination of the family. It is inauspicious. Confucius said: this house produces orphans and widows.

Divining on the auspiciousness of a living or burial place, this entry is typical of the text, containing three parts. It first introduces the hexagram that results from a divinatory procedure, which is unfortunately not included in the manuscript.[34] This part also elaborates on the technical details of the hexagram based on the so-called Jing Fang 京房 (77–37 BCE) tradition of the *Changes*, shown by the appearance of terms like "the Qian family," "generation," and "correspondence."[35] The entry then moves on to the physical phenomena that can be predicted based on the line features of the hexagram, in this case a snake-like earthworm. Last, it quotes Confucius and his disciple Zixia to reveal the auspiciousness of the dwelling or burial site, giving meaning to the place.

This structure is used for the entries of all the hexagrams in the *Three Completions of the Changes*, and Confucius and his disciples' comments consistently occupy the last part of each entry. For example, after Bo, the text proceeds to Jin 晉:

占世爻定, 穿井深七尺, 得銅。此地水美。孔子云: 居得此宅, 君子吉, 小人自如, 先富後貧。[36]

In the divination, if the generation line is decided [as such], then one can obtain copper by digging a seven *chi* well. Here the water is good. Confucius said: Living at this house will be auspicious for gentlemen and the petty people will be at ease. They will become rich first and then poor.

Then to Dayou 大有:

> 占世爻定, 此地舊有龍道, 不可居, 絕嗣。子夏云: 此地葬, 出三公, 大吉, 宜子孫。
>
> In the divination, if the generation line is decided [as such], then this place used to have a dragon pathway. One cannot dwell here, [otherwise] they will have no descendants. Zixia said: Burial here will produce the three dukes. This is greatly auspicious and good for offspring.

The same pattern continues. The structure suggests that the technical explanations of hexagrams together with the corresponding geomantic features are not enough to tell the readers the fortune of a place. Therefore, more explanation is needed. This is particularly the case for the Dayou entry. In medieval China, dragon pathways were believed to attract unpleasant, harmful phenomena such as storms or landslides, and thus dangerous to live nearby.[37] A reader from the eighth century would take this geomantic feature as a bad sign, especially with the explicit warning right after the feature is mentioned. However, Zixia reveals the counterintuitive information that this place is in fact auspicious as a burial site. In other words, Confucius and Zixia are used in this text to discern the hidden meanings of the divinatory patterns that the technical readings do not render apparent.

While modern scholars might find it odd for Confucius and his disciples to give geomantic advice in a divinatory manual, the residents in Dunhuang might not have thought so. In fact, the *Three Completions* does not present itself as just a divination text, but as a complete version of the classic, the *Book of Changes*. As the preface announces:

> 《三備》者, 經云: 上備, 天也; 中備, 筮人中宅舍吉凶也; 下備, 筮【地】下盤石、涌泉深淺吉凶安葬地也。[38]
>
> As for the *Three Completions* [*of the Changes*],[39] the classic[40] says: The upper completion is Heaven, the middle completion prognosticates the auspiciousness of dwellings among people, and the lower completion prognosticates the depth and auspiciousness of bedrocks and wells underground as well as burial places.

This preface does not directly precede the so-called upper completion, but the middle completion, which contains the hexagram segments quoted above. This is likely because, as Zhang Zhiqing 張志清 and Lin Shitian 林世天田 speculate, the upper completion is simply the text of the *Book of Changes*.[41]

Indeed, piggy backing on more famous texts was a common practice in medieval China. For example, one of the earliest Daoist scriptures, the *Inner Scripture of Laozi* (*Laozi zhong jing* 老子中經) manipulates its name so that it appears to be a volume of the more famous text *Laozi* 老子.⁴² Since early China, the *Laozi* text was often more specifically divided into two parts and thus referred as "upper" and "lower" (*shang xia* 上下).⁴³ Claiming to be the middle part (*zhong* 中) then inserts the *Inner Scripture* into the *Laozi* corpus.

The *Three Completions* deploys the same strategy to claim to be part of the classics. The "upper," "middle," and "lower" sections create a sequence in which the *Changes* is only one part of a bigger corpus. And only with the middle and lower parts is the corpus "complete," or as the title indicates, *bei* 備. The preface to the text does not boast to be more essential than the *Changes*, or even as important.⁴⁴ It is comfortable ranking the text literally lower than the *Changes*. The contemporary readers of the text might not see this divinatory manual as equal to the *Changes*, but they would recognize the continuity between them.

Confucius and his disciples, especially Zixia, fit right into the narrative about the *Changes*. From the time of the Han dynasty, Confucius was seen as a key transmitter of the *Changes*. As mentioned before, the *Records of the Grand Historian* already claimed that Confucius made a series of commentaries on the core of the text.⁴⁵ The bibliographical work "Seven Epitomes" ("Qi lue" 七略) from the late first century BCE constructed a genealogy of the *Changes*: the primordial sage Fuxi 伏羲 invented the eight trigrams, then King Wen of Zhou (1152–1056 BCE) elaborated the trigrams into sixty-four hexagrams, and then Confucius made ten commentaries on the hexagrams in order to reveal the meaning of the symbols.⁴⁶ In this narrative, Confucius not only completed the *Changes* as a text, but he also served as a commentator who revealed the hidden meaning of the ancient sages' undertaking.

A similar situation applies to Zixia. As one of Confucius' main disciples, Zixia's name was gradually associated with the *Changes* starting in the sixth century. The exegetical dictionary *Textual Explanations of Classics and Canons* (*Jingdian shiwen* 經典釋文, ca. 582–589 CE) by Lu Deming 陸德明 (556–627 CE) listed a previously lesser-known work called *Zixia's Commentary on the Changes* (*Zixia Yi zhuan* 子夏易傳). It identified this "Zixia" as the one who studied with Confucius.⁴⁷ Despite the obscure origin, many Tang scholars further confirmed that this work belonged to Confucius' disciple Zixia.⁴⁸ Accordingly, the genealogical narrative evolved: "Confucius made 'Commentary on the Judgement,' 'Commentary on the Images,' 'Commentary on the Appended Phrases,' 'Commentary on the Words,' the 'Sequence of the Hexagrams,' the 'Explanation of the Trigrams,' and 'Miscellany on Hexagrams.' Then Zixia made commentaries on them."⁴⁹ In other words, Confucius completed the body text of the *Changes*, and his disciple Zixia then became the very first commentator of his teacher's work.

Indeed, the *Three Completions* appears as not just any divinatory manual, but as a continuation of the sages' words. Only this time the sages' teachings are particularly relevant to the reader's daily concern: living and burial location. This concern was in many families' mind in medieval China because the location for both the living and the dead was believed to affect the fate of the whole household.⁵⁰ Therefore, Confucius and his disciples' advice would be welcomed, particularly because it was specific to *what topographical condition yields what kind of fortune*. In other words, by creating such specific geomantic guidance, Confucius and his disciples attended to the daily needs of the people in Dunhuang.

Yan Yuan's commentaries

Confucius' favorite student in the *Analects*, Yan Yuan was also featured in the Dunhuang divinatory manuals. In the previous chapter, we already saw him assisting Confucius in the ghost stories of early medieval China. By the Tang dynasty, the government had placed his name in the Confucius Temple (Kong Miao 孔廟) right next to his teacher, before the other disciples. But because of his premature death, the literati of Imperial China did not attribute to him the transmission of any classics or commentaries. It is thus surprising that his name as a commentator appears not only in a Dunhuang text, but more specifically in a divinatory manual.⁵¹

This divination manual is called the *Divinatory Method [Using] the Sublime Tokens* (*Lingqi bufa* 靈棋卜法, P.3782), and it emerged in the late fourth century CE.⁵² Originally attributed to a monk named Fawei 法味 (fl. 373–375 CE),⁵³ its core method is straightforward: the diviner needs twelve tokens, each with a character on one side and blank on the other. Four of them should have the character *shang* 上, or "above," four should have *zhong* 中, or "middle," and four should have *xia* 下, or "below." The diviner tosses all the tokens at once, and the result is a combination of "aboves," "middles," "belows," and blanks on each of the twelve tokens.⁵⁴ This randomized method yields a total of 125 possible results, each of which corresponds to a distinctive judgment with commentaries.

The entries for each of the 125 potential outcomes have the same structure: they start with a result, which vertically lists the numbers of the character *shang* 上 on top, *zhong* 中 in the middle, and *xia* 下 below.⁵⁵ Then they go into a four-character verse judgment that resembles the responses of many temple oracles in later periods.⁵⁶ After the rather opaque judgment are the more illustrative commentaries. A typical entry looks like the following:

上上上/中中中中/下下下下 賢君在上, 下有讒臣, 雖有聰明, 終見暗塵。 注曰: 事在主暗, 凡事不果, 當叩下人, 和則叩上, 叩下史告。 顏淵曰: 上雖高明, 下蔽者多, 徒抱其智, 殆于危矣。 賢名蓋假稱耳, 亦猶之《詩》云"哲者成城", ⁵⁷《離騷》云"哲王不悟" 矣。 ⁵⁸此卦百事有悔, 求仕進弥非, 婚姻小吉, 陰陽頗應, 故言也。 ⁵⁹

Above, above, above/middle, middle, middle, middle/below, below, below, below

> The worthy lord is on top, but there are fawning officials below. Even if one has talents, he will [still] eventually be in the murky dusts.
>
> The commentary says: when the affair takes place and the lord is uninformed, the affair will not be fruitful. [In this case,] one should ask the people below. If it is harmonious, one should inquire with the people above. When one inquires with the lower officials (?), they will talk.⁶⁰
>
> Yan Yuan said: Even if the one above is bright, there are many people below who blind him. If one only holds on to his talents, he will [still] end up in danger. A worthy reputation is just a borrowed name. This is like in the *Book of Poetry*, which says "The wise people make a city," or in "Encountering Sorrow," which says "The wise king does not wake up." For this symbol, everything will be regretful. Searching for official advances will be especially bad. It is slightly auspicious for marriage. This is because the *yin* and *yang* correspond well.

In the manuscript, a one-character space proceeds both the "Commentary says" and "Yan Yuan says." The space suggests these two parts are independent from each other as well as from the initial verse judgment.

In the second commentary, "Yan Yuan" provides divinatory interpretation as well as moral teachings through classical precedents. He first provides a quadrisyllabic verse commentary that paraphrases each line of the initial judgment. Then, he turns to the topic of reputation and supports his view with two quotations from classical works, one from "Looking Up" ("Zhan Yang" 瞻卬) in the Great Odes ("Da ya" 大雅) section of the *Book of Poetry* (*Shijing* 詩經) and the other from "Encountering Sorrow" by Qu Yuan 屈原 (ca. 340–ca. 278 BCE), who was born around 150 years after Yan Yuan's time.⁶¹ After lingering on moral teachings and classics, our "Yan Yuan" goes back to prediction and further links the result to the auspiciousness in conducting daily activities.

The historical inaccuracy of this attribution to Yan Yuan is easy to detect. In the *Daoist Canon of the Zhengtong Reign* (*Zhengtong Daozang* 正統道藏,

1444 CE), the received *Sublime Tokens* contains two commentaries: one from Yan Youming 顏幼明 of the Jin dynasty (265–420 CE) and the other from He Chengtian 何承天 (370–447 CE) from the Liu Song dynasty (420–479 CE).[62] The text quotes them with "Yan said" (*Yan yun* 顏云) and "He said" (*He yun* 何云), respectively. This is the same case in several other Dunhuang copies of the *Sublime Tokens*, such as P.4984V. In contrast, the copy we are examining, P.3782, elaborates "Yan" as "Yan Yuan."[63] That is to say, interpreting "Yan" as "Yan Yuan" is a distinctive textual change made by the textual tradition that P.3782 represents.[64]

As we have seen in the previous chapter, this divination expert image of Yan Yuan was not completely outlandish for the medieval Chinese literati. In the previous chapter, we already saw the story where Confucius and his disciples divined the return of the disciple Zigong. In the story, only Yan Yuan successfully predicted his return.[65] This story continued circulating in the official compilations in medieval China, such as in *Book Excerpts from the Northern Hall* (*Beitang shuchao* 北堂書鈔) in the early seventh century, the *Categorized Collection of Literary Texts* (*Yiwen leiju* 藝文類聚) in 624 CE, and the *Imperial Reader of the Taiping Reign* (*Taiping yulan* 太平御覽) in 984 CE.[66]

While the classical sources and Six dynasties stories about Confucius and his disciples already prelude their expertise in divination, the uniqueness of the Dunhuang divinatory manuals lies in their sense of practicality. The manuals neither solely present conventional moral knowledge nor entertaining stories about the marvelous Confucius. They specify what daily activities will occur, how they will develop, and what one should do. For example, the *Three Completions* focuses on the common concerns of living and burial spaces, identifies the objects in these places, illustrates their meanings, and reveals the auspiciousness of the spaces. Similarly, the *Sublime Tokens* not only explains broad general future visions, but also links the results to the concerns that were common to the local communities, such as marriage and careers. Here the sage and his disciples did not just have bookish knowledge, they came down to help people with their daily problems.

The physical format of the two manuals also suggests this sense of practicality. The Dunhuang copies are in a book format that is designed to allow readers to quickly look up information.[67] Up until the seventh century CE, the most common form of bookbinding in China had been scrolls. The paper scrolls were modeled on bamboo scrolls and were easy to wrap. However, the longer they became, the harder it was to pinpoint a certain part of the text.[68] With paper being a rather fragile material, the scrolls, especially the beginnings of them, were easily damaged by frequent rolling and unrolling. During the Tang dynasty, a new form of bookbinding appeared to solve this problem. Scrolls were made by binding one piece of paper next to another on a long backing paper, which could then be rolled up and stored. Derived from scrolls, this form instead put one page above another (sometimes in decreasing lengths) and then bound the left margins of all the pages together to a bottom backing paper that served as a protective cover. This so-called "whirlwind binding" (*xuanfeng zhuang* 旋風裝) then could be rolled up like a scroll but flipped like a codex book.[69] It is not a surprise that divinatory manuals like the two texts we saw adopted this booklike form, since the format facilitates frequent lookup. From content to format, Confucius and his disciples were linked to practicality.

Confucius and his methods

According to Dunhuang divinatory manuals, Confucius could not only interpret divination, he could also design it. The manual *A Divinatory Method of Confucius [Leaning toward] the Horse Head* (*Kongzi ma tou zhanfa* 孔子馬頭占法) introduces the origin of its name as the following:[70]

> 昔者孔子因行逐急,看疑決事,坐馬。馬上坐,臨馬頭上卜事,故曰馬頭占。[71]
>
> In the past, Confucius was traveling in a rush. He observed doubts and decided on affairs. He sat on a horse and leaned toward the horse's head to divine on affairs. This is why it is called "divination from the horse head."

Here the introduction sells the method as an expeditious one that Confucius created and used. Sitting on the horse without dismounting enhances the sense of urgency for the reader. Another introduction of the same divination further explains why Confucius invented the method:

> 凡陰陽卜筮,《易》道為宗。文義甚多,猶如江海。非聖不裁,豈凡能決。所以孔子造此卜法 ... 孔子因行,馬上坐,定心啟願,如卜,不得亂。心有疑事者,立馬便上,故曰孔子馬頭占。徧與後世。[72]
>
> As for the matters of *yin* and *yang* as well as divination, the way of the *Changes* is the mainstream. [However,] it has too many words and interpretations, just like the rivers and the seas. Without a sage, no one can adjudicate; how can ordinary people decide? Therefore, Confucius made this divinatory method ... When Confucius was on the road, he sat on his horse, concentrated his mind, and pledged his vows. During the divination, he should not be disturbed. If one has doubts in their mind, they can stop the horse and cast the divination immediately. This is why it is called "*A Divinatory Method of Confucius [Leaning toward] the Horse Head.*" It is to be spread in later generations.

Here Confucius did not just use the method, he actually invented it. His motivation behind inventing the method was speed: because the epitomic divination in the *Book of Changes* is too complex for the ordinary person to navigate through, Confucius designed this easier method for everyone to use. In this introduction, Confucius still appears as a transmitter of the *Changes*, but this time he does not transmit the textual form of it, he transmits its divinatory essence. This is why, as the introduction assures its audience, this expeditious method is still perfectly accurate: "it hits every affair" (*shi wu bu zhong* 事無不中).[73]

The method is indeed straightforward to practice. It uses nine tokens and a bamboo cylinder: each of the tokens has a number from one to nine, and they are placed inside the cylinder. The cylinder has one small opening to let the tokens out. In performing the divination, one simply concentrates on what one wishes to know and shakes a token out of the cylinder. A number between one and nine will be the result.[74] Methodologically speaking, the procedure is much simpler than that of the *Changes*, where one needs to divide fifty-one yarrow stalks multiple times to generate a result. Nor does it require any specific symbols like the hexagrams from the *Changes*; simple numbers would do.[75]

Expediency also runs through the divinatory results. For example, in divining the arrival time of travelers, the manual states:

占行人何日來: 一, 二日來; 二, 日在道; 三, 日有消息, 三日至; 四, 即至; 五, 在道; 六, 未到; 七, 有書, 未到; 八, 在道; 九, 發來。[76]

In divining on which day the travelers will arrive: "One" means they will arrive in two days. "Two" means they are on the way each day. "Three" means that you will hear from them every day, and they will arrive in three days. "Four" means they will arrive immediately. "Five" means that they are on the way. "Six" means that they have not arrived yet. "Seven" means that there is a letter but they have not arrived yet. "Eight" means that they are on the way. "Nine" means that they are sent to be here.

Unlike the *Three Completions* or the *Sublime Tokens*, there are no examples, precedents, classical allusions, or moral teachings to illustrate the results. Corresponding to each number, the results go straight to particular scenarios of daily life. In this way, the manual does not require a diviner as the middleman; the inquirers can directly follow the manual and practice the method by themselves, which fits its design for emergency use.

Following this DIY sentiment, the two Dunhuang copies of the manual cover more than twenty topics that are specific, mundane concerns. Regarding family life, it includes the auspicious locations of housing, illnesses of family members, success in finding a wife, and the gender of a soon-to-be-born baby. When it comes to livelihood, the manual mentions hunting, trading, the likelihood of rain, and the prosperity of business ventures. For social life, it covers lawsuits, the arrival of travelers, success in borrowing money, auspiciousness in praying to deities, and success in fighting rebels.[77] The two copies not only render the orders of the topics differently, each of them also includes unique topics, showing the customizability of the manual.[78]

Who was the audience of this "Confucius" method? Its topics reveals a rather wide target audience. Farmers and hunters would most likely need to know if rain would fall or whether one would run into a tiger while hunting. Merchants would pay attention to the predictions on trading and business success. More commonly, Dunhuang residents asked about basic concerns related to a family's wellbeing and the arrival of travelers. And given Dunhuang's frontier location, they would also care greatly about fighting rebels, no matter whether they were soldiers, military leaders, or civilians. While these vocations were not mutually exclusive, the manual did try to reach out to the daily concerns that were deeply rooted in a diverse spectrum of Dunhuang social lives.

Historically speaking, this *Divinatory Method of Confucius [Leaning toward] the Horse Head* was not invented by Confucius, but most likely a literatus named Lin Xiaogong 臨孝恭 (fl. 581–618 CE). As an erudite of the Sui dynasty (581–618 CE),[79] Lin received an audience with Emperor Wen 文 (r. 581–604 CE) because of his expertise in calendar making and astrology. Lin's works include the design of timers, earthquake detectors, and complex divinatory methods such as the *Classic of the Grand Unity Board Divination* (*Taiyi shi jing* 太一式經). The *Divinatory Method of Confucius* is listed in between his highbrow works and only the title of it survived in official records.[80] But the excavated Dunhuang copies testify to the popularity of "Confucius'" help among the general public.

The method of Confucius and the Duke of Zhou

A similarly expedient divinatory manual from Dunhuang also has Confucius in its title: the *Divinatory Method of the Duke of Zhou and Confucius*.[81] Without any explanation of the title, it depicts a rather straightforward method: the numbers one, two, and three alternate through the twelve double hours of a day. For example, according to the manual, the first double hour *zi* (11 p.m.–1 a.m.) of the first month is one, then the next hour will be two, the next three, and the fourth double hour goes back to one again (Table 2).[82] Accordingly, the *zi* hour of the second month is two, that of the third month is three, and that of the fourth month goes back to one. The manual helps the readers by including a visual aid:

Table 2 The distribution of 1 to 3 through the yearly cycle.

chou	zi	hai	xu	you	shen	wei	wu	si	chen	mao	yin	
2	1	3	2	1	3	2	1	3	2	1	3	1st month
3	2	1	3	2	1	3	2	1	3	2	1	2nd month
1	3	2	1	3	2	1	3	2	1	3	2	3rd month
2	1	3	2	1	3	2	1	3	2	1	3	4th month
3	2	1	3	2	1	3	2	1	3	2	1	5th month
1	3	2	1	3	2	1	3	2	1	3	2	6th month
2	1	3	2	1	3	2	1	3	2	1	3	7th month
3	2	1	3	2	1	3	2	1	3	2	1	8th month
1	3	2	1	3	2	1	3	2	1	3	2	9th month
2	1	3	2	1	3	2	1	3	2	1	3	10th month
3	2	1	3	2	1	3	2	1	3	2	1	11th month
1	3	2	1	3	2	1	3	2	1	3	2	12th month

From right to left in the top row, the sequence of the earthly branches marks the double hours of a day. From top to bottom in the right column, the sequence of the twelve months marks the whole year cycle.

The technical core of this method can be traced back to the hemerological tradition in early China, or the so-called "day books" (*rishu* 日書). This type of divinatory method often correlates a sequence of symbols with a certain sequence of time units. For example, the most common system employs a sequence of twelve symbols, namely *jian* 建, *chu* 除, *man* 滿, *ping* 平, *ding* 定, *zhi* 執, *po* 破, *wei* 危, *cheng* 成, *shou* 收, *kai* 開, and *bi* 閉. Following this specific order, these symbols correspond to the first through the twelfth days of a month, respectively. From the thirteenth day on, the sequence repeats itself. Each of the symbols indicates specific fortunes for certain social activities. Among different day books from early China, technical details of this so-called *jian chu* 建除 system differ, but the core of this method always hinges on the correspondence between two sequences.[83]

The *Divinatory Method of the Duke of Zhou and Confucius* is a simplified version of this hemerological tradition, made accessible to the more general public in Dunhuang. It uses three numbers to replace the more specialized twelve-symbol-*jian chu* system. Therefore, the readers can follow the very commonly used numbers and do not need to learn the meaning of the *jian chu* symbols. Meanwhile, the manual also uses a chart to illustrate the correspondence between the sequence and the time. This visual aid further lifts the burden of calculation: the readers can simply use their time at the moment to locate the resulting number instead of making correspondences in their minds. Clearly, the manual presents the method as accessible as it can afford.

After the chart, the manual explains the meaning of each number for various social activities, where it is also noticeably straightforward:

凡時下得二: 注官事, 和了不成。占家, 憂小口, 兇。占盜賊, 不來。占聞口舌, 有。占遠行人, 在道未至。占求妻財, 損財, 得。占奸惡, 有。占戰鬥, 不如也。占失財, 得半。占養蠶, 得平。占所居宅, 多有夢。占造作, 不如意。占欲市易, 利以。占聞憂, 有, 不吉。占主人有酒, 不與。占杖, 豎, 其杖小取。[84]

For the hours with "two" under them: on official business, it will be reconciliation without accomplishment. Divining on family, be worried about the minors; inauspicious. Divining on burglars, they will not come. Divining on scandals, they will happen. Divining on travelers, they are on the way but have not arrived yet. Divining on seeking wife and fortune, there will be loss in fortune, but there will be gain. Divining on evil, it will appear. Divining on fights and battles, there will be no match to [the opponents]. Divining on lost fortune, you will gain half back. Divining on sericulture, it will be normal. Divining on dwellings, there will be many dreams. Divining on building and producing, it will be wayward. Divining on trading, there will be profit. Divining on worries, they will happen and be inauspicious. Divining on the masters owning wine, they will not share. Divining on canes, it is vertical and slightly crooked (?).[85]

Unsurprisingly, the topics all involve daily activities and provide a clear, specific answer. There are no verses, riddles, or anything else that opens the text to multiple interpretations.

In the title, Confucius was associated with another ancient sage and his personal hero, the Duke of Zhou (1042–1035 BCE). For Dunhuang residents during the Tang dynasty, he was the most important cultural hero to live before Confucius. He was important to them not only because he was the advisor of the sage king King Wu, who established the Zhou dynasty, but because he was also the designer of the blueprints for an ideal society called the Great Peace (*taiping* 太平), as recorded in the *Rites of Zhou* (*Zhou li* 周禮).[86] Meanwhile, The Duke of Zhou also appears as a master diviner in Dunhuang, as we can find his name in divinatory manuals such as *The Duke of Zhou Interpreting Dreams* (*Zhougong jie meng* 周公解夢) and the *Chart of the Duke of Zhou Traveling through Eight Days* (*Zhougong ba tian chuxing tu* 周公八天出行圖).[87] In fact, his reputation as a diviner lasted through the rest of Imperial China right alongside his reputation as a sage.[88]

The Twelve Coins Divination and its creators

In another case, Confucius was accompanied by other famous sages as the creator of a divination method called "Twelve Coins Divination," or *shier qian bu fa* 十二錢卜法. This method involves tossing twelve coins and receiving a resulting number of heads and tails. It then converts the numbers into two trigrams. Based on the "Explanation of the Trigrams" ("Shuogua" 說卦) chapter of the *Changes*, it then determines the relationship between the two trigrams. This relationship finally yields divinatory judgments on certain daily activities, such as traveling, theft, loss, childbirth, etc.[89] More than six different copies of the method from Dunhuang attributed the creation of it to three names, respectively.

One of the names is the Duke of Zhou. The preface to one of the copies states: "In the past, the Duke of Zhou was assisting King Cheng of Zhou. He wanted to hide himself and avoid the vicious words of Guanshu 管叔 and Caishu 蔡叔, so he used the twelve coins to decide on auspiciousness and doubts." Attributing the method to the Duke of Zhou, this statement taps into a narrative about his life based on the classical texts, where he was being attacked by others and doubted by the young king.[90] Instead of considering him a powerful diviner as in other texts, the statement here portrays him as a human sage in a predicament, and the method was thus born out of urgency, a common origin story for Dunhuang divination methods.

Another name is Laozi, as the title of one copy suggests: *The Twelve Coins Divination Method of the* Book of Changes *by Lord Li of Lao* (*Li Laojun* Zhouyi *shier qian bu fa* 李老君周易十二錢卜法).[91] The preface of it states that "This is the method from which Laozi made the *Changes* divination. It uses twelves coins tossed on a plate. One knows the fortune just by looking at the heads and tails. Among ten thousand tosses, not even once will it miss."[92] Like the *Three Completions* and the *Horse Head* divinations, this text also links the method to the tradition of the *Changes*. But instead of Confucius, this time it was Laozi's design.

Residents in tenth-century Dunhuang would be familiar with Laozi as a teacher and a Daoist deity. From the fourth century BCE, Laozi appeared as a reclusive teacher, who left his teaching in the *Dao de jing* 道德經. Legends from the second century BCE stated that Confucius paid homage to Laozi, asking him about rites.[93] Laozi was the Buddha and even founded Buddhism according to the fourth-century Daoist scripture the *Scripture of Laozi Converting the Barbarians* (*Laozi hua Hu jing* 老子化胡經). Meanwhile, he was also a focus of worship both in the imperial court in the second century CE and later in various Daoist sects, which produced several scriptures attributed to him. All of these aforementioned texts were available in Dunhuang by the tenth century.[94] The Dunhuang residents might not have read them, but most likely were aware of his teacher-deity image.[95]

Confucius also appears as the inventor of the method, but in a Tibetan version. The preface of it states:

> gnam dang po kong tshe 'phrul kyi bu/ gcug lag mang po zhig mdor bsdus te/ gtan la phab pa/ … /dkong tse 'phrul gyis mdzad pa'i dong tse bcu gnyis kyi mo// brdzogs so//
>
> [By?] supernatural ('phrul) son Kong tshe, originally (dang po) [of] heaven [gnam], much wisdom summarized, edited (gtan la phab) … Composed by Dkong-tse, the supernatural, the 'Coins-twelve mo' is finished.[96]

"Kong tshe" and "Dkong-tse" are different renderings for Confucius. Here the passage not only claims Confucius was the inventor of the method, but also gives him the epithet "supernatural," meaning he was of heavenly origin. In this way, the source of the power for this "twelve-coins mo" divination comes from the heavenly power of Confucius. This contrasts with the previous invention narratives, where Confucius' own agency or his knowledge of the *Changes* created the divination methods.

This representation of a divine Confucius might be derived from his apocryphal image as a son of Heaven. As mentioned in Chapter 1, the newly established Eastern Han dynasty (25–220 CE) perpetuated the narrative that Confucius was of heavenly origin and was born into the human world to prophesize the rise of the Liu family as the imperial house. This half-human, half-divine Confucius together with his miraculous birth formed an eminent tradition in the imperial houses and among the literati in medieval China.[97] Occupying the Dunhuang region, the diviner communities of the Tibetan Empire (618–842 CE) absorbed this image of Confucius as a divine prognosticator.[98] This Tibetan adaptation further demonstrates the predominance of Confucius as a diviner in the Dunhuang region of the time.

What does Confucius share with the Duke of Zhou and Laozi in this context? One obvious similarity is that none of them were primarily considered as diviners in literati culture. Instead, they appeared as ancient sages who possessed supreme wisdom. Their wisdom helped them to make enlightened judgments, ranging from governing a dynasty to understanding the universe.[99] If they could do so, how much more helpful would their judgments be for helping with people's daily troubles? In addition, the three of them had reputations as teachers or advisors. This reputation led to the narrative that they invented simplified methods for the ordinary people to make good judgments. In this sense, the appeal of Confucius and sages like him was not only because of their knowledge about making judgments, but also because of how they could transmit the knowledge in an approachable, expedient way.

Perceptions of Sages and Divination in Dunhuang Texts

Indeed, people in Dunhuang might not separate divination from Confucius, but saw it as derivative of his powers. Since, in the *Analects*, he could guide the nobles on state affairs, he could certainly help more ordinary people on individual, minor, daily decisions. In fact, for many people living in Dunhuang then, being a sage meant that one could perceive the present and future better than ordinary people, either with supreme knowledge or what we would categorize as divinatory skills. This view extends to any extraordinary person, or, as Dunhuang texts refer to them, "worthies" (*xian* 賢).[100] In the last part of this chapter, we will explore a few types of popular storytelling from Dunhuang to see how storytellers and their audiences understood the worthies and divination. This was the context in which our diviner Confucius was celebrated.

Divination and visions about the future are common themes in stories from Dunhuang. The love story of Han Peng 韓朋 and his wife Zhenfu 貞夫 in the "Rhapsody of Han Peng" ("Han Peng fu" 韓朋賦) exemplifies the ubiquitous appearance of divination. In the beginning of the story, Han leaves his beloved wife at home for an official position under the King of Song. The King is attracted to Zhenfu because of her well-composed letter. In order to trick her into marrying him, the King sends his official Liang Bo to her. Before the arrival of Liang, the wife has an ominous dream about three birds flying together and two of them fighting, which turns out to be a vision of the future. Then, the King, anxiously waiting at his palace for the result of the trickery, asks his grand historian to perform a divination. The result is "certain," which also turns out to be true.[101] Even in just the first part of this story, prediction of the future repeatedly appears as a story telling device.

Divinatory activities can also tie into the plots of the stories in order to increase dramatic effect. In the "Biography of the Liu Family Heir of the Former Han" ("Qian Han Liujia taizi zhuan" 前漢劉家太子傳), the heir of the former Han escapes from the usurper Wang Mang 王莽 (45 BCE–23 CE) before eventually restoring the Han dynasty.[102] During his escape, the climax comes when the heir is chased by Wang's troops. Luckily, a clever farmer helps our hero: he buries him underground for seven days, leaving a bamboo straw in his mouth for breathing and seven grains of rice. Failing to find him, the court asks the villainous grand historian to use divination to locate the heir. The historian does locate him, but the divination shows the heir lying underground with bamboo shooting out of his eyes and maggots coming out of his mouth.[103] The historian then takes his vision to mean that the heir is dead. Cheating the divinatory detection is the turning point of the story, and after successfully escaping the chase, the heir finally manages to restore the Han dynasty.

Divination is abundantly featured in the so-called transformation texts (*bian wen* 變文) from Dunhuang, a storytelling form based on pictorial representations combined with prose in vernacular language and heptasyllabic verses. Designed to be entertaining, these were elaborations of existing stories. Even though in their written forms the texts were intended to be read, they were undoubtedly derived from earlier oral forms and were performed in front of people with varying levels of literacy. Therefore, the transformation texts covered a wide range of audiences, from people who could barely read to the ones who gained pleasure from reading literary works.[104]

For example, in the "Transformation Text of Li Ling" ("Li Ling bianwen" 李陵變文, 786 CE or later), the hero Li Ling 李陵 (ca. second century–74 BCE) is besieged by the Xiongnu 匈奴 troops.[105] In addition to being outnumbered, Li Ling also finds out that his battle drums are somehow mute. Facing these predicaments, a turning point reveals itself when he notices three lines of black ether rising from his cousins' carts. He immediately recognizes the ether as a suspicious sign and asks his people to search the carts. As a result, they seize two sixteen-year-old girls and execute them. The moment they die, the drums start beating loudly by themselves. The drum beat unifies Li's troops and turns the battle around.[106]

This image of an observant Li Ling differs from the one in the earlier dynastic histories. The *Book of Han* (*Han shu* 漢書) of the first century CE records this military campaign against Xiongnu in 99 BCE, where he and his fellow 5,000 infantrymen encountered some 10,000 Xiongnu cavalry in Jujishan 浚稽山. After resisting, he and his men eventually surrendered. The surrender enraged Emperor Wu 武 (r. 141–87 BCE) of the Han dynasty: he executed Li's family and even castrated Sima Qian (ca. 145 or 135–86 BCE) who defended Li's surrender.[107] The transformation text version in general follows the same storyline as the *Book of Han*, but it adds more dramatic details, such as the observation of omens. Following the dynastic history, the transformation text still sticks to Li Ling's tragic defeat as the ending of the campaign, but it also emphasizes Li Ling as a general who was able to escape from a predicament through extraordinary judgment.

The drumming incident is an illuminating example of how to make an extraordinary judgment. The *Book of Han* tells the incident by making a straightforward inference: upon being besieged, Li Ling wondered, "The morale of my men has deteriorated and cannot be drummed up; why is this so? Perhaps there are women in the troops?" (吾士氣少衰而鼓不起者, 何也? 軍中豈有女子乎?) He then found the women whom his solders had hidden in the carts and executed them. This led to a boost of morale and hence a victory against the Xiongnu.[108] In this context, the Literary Chinese phrase "cannot be drummed up" (*gu bu qi* 鼓不起) means that the soldiers cannot be efficiently rallied, not that the drums do not work.[109] In the original narrative, Li Ling was an experienced general who understood the psychology of his soldiers.

While maintaining a similar plot line, the transformation text version looks beyond human behaviors. The *gu bu qi* part becomes more literal: the drums cannot be drummed up, indicating that the drums do not make any sound. Li Ling's remarks on the malfunction guide the story further in a more mystical direction: "Heaven is going to eliminate us!" (天喪我等). The three lines of black ether also add to this supernatural context, not to mention the automatic drumming after the execution of the women.

Faced with these mystically opaque predicaments, Li Ling's divinatory observation turns the situation around. In medieval China, black ether and black clouds in general are inauspicious signs in weather divination. In the civil context, black clouds often point to thefts and robbers; in the military context, they indicate ambush and other plots by the enemy.[110] The general principle behind these interpretations is that black ethers signify intruders, and thus finding the hidden women is the result of searching for intruders. In this new narrative, Li Ling becomes an observant diviner who could detect inauspiciousness as well as exorcise it.

In another story, a divination battle between the ancient hero Wu Zixu 伍子胥 (sixth century–484 BCE) and his nephews resembles dueling scenes from modern martial art movies. The "Transformation Text of Wu Zixu" ("Wu Zixu bianwen" 伍子胥變文) features one of the most famous vendetta stories in Chinese history, where King Ping of Chu unjustly murders Wu Zixu's father and brother, and Zixu eventually takes revenge on the king with an army from the State of Wu. In the text, the king hunts down Zixu after the execution of his father and brother.[111] While trying to escape, Zixu feels that his eyes are watery and ears hot. Recognizing these as strange signs, he conducts a divination and discovers that his nephews are coming to seize him. He then disguises himself through a seemingly bizarre routine: he splashes water over his head, wears bamboo slips over his waist, and puts on his wooden slippers backwards. He then draws the heavenly door and earthly gate on the ground, lies in the reeds, and chants: "The one who catches me will be harmed, and the one who chases me will die. Quickly, quickly, as the statutes command" (捉我者殃, 趁我者亡, 急急如律令!).[112]

This sequence of actions tricks his nephews. One of them, Ziyong 子永, prognosticates to detect his uncle. He finds out that his uncle has water on top of his head, which could mean that he is under water; his waist is surrounded by bamboo, which could mean that he is among a neglected burial place; and he wears his slippers backwards, which could mean that he is in a disorganized situation. Combining the three pieces of the vision, the nephew concludes that his uncle Zixu is already dead and hastily buried. They thus stop chasing him, and Zixu finally manages to escape.

Like many manifestations of Wu Zixu's vendetta story, the transformation text depicts him as a worthy. Since pre-Imperial China, Zixu had been considered a moral paragon based on the story arc of his tragic life: he avenged the murder of his father and brother with the help of the King of Wu, and then he was tragically killed by the next King of Wu because of his upright loyalty.[113] His moral sense as an official and his determination for revenge as a filial pious man were celebrated in literati culture.[114] Zixu's name is also listed in a primer from Dunhuang called a *Collection of Ancient Worthies* (*Gu xian ji* 古賢集). The text considers him an ancient worthy and describes him as a loyal official who gave upright admonishments (*zhi jian zhongchen* 直諫忠臣).[115]

Adding to the basic story arc, divinatory practices take over the common chasing-escaping trope in the transformation text version, and Zixu's mantic visions reify his worthiness. Like Li Ling's recognition of the black ethers, Zixu is able to identify signs around him and mantically interpret them. Through divination, he not only accurately envisions the upcoming trouble, but also successfully counteracts it. Indeed, as David Johnson points out, here Zixu appears more like a diviner rather than the sophisticated scholar depicted in previous literary sources.[116] However, to many people in Dunhuang, a sophisticated scholar was exactly like a diviner.

Indeed, these literary stories tell us about how the Dunhuang residents in medieval China perceived the ancient worthies in general. From Confucius to the Duke of Zhou, from Li Ling to Wu Zixu, a sage or a knowledgeable person in general was supposed to be able to use their knowledge to perceive the future and make good judgments. Recognizing the signs and performing divinations naturally match this perception of what a sage is. If worthies like Li Ling and Wu Zixu could manage to do so, how much easier would it be for sages like Confucius?

Concluding Remarks

In this chapter, we have seen a more regional image of Confucius from eighth to tenth-century CE Dunhuang. If the apocryphal Confucius and ghostbuster Confucius from the previous two chapters served the literati circles, this diviner Confucius was available to the more ordinary people in Dunhuang. He was deliberately shaped to address the anxieties of ordinary people, ranging from family members' health to the success of their job. Indeed, the local residents needed less a moral paragon or a prophet of the dynastic fate, but a wise man who could help them navigate through their life, one full of mundane tasks. As a result, the diviner Confucius emerged in the divinatory manuals to fulfill this demand.

The diviner Confucius did speak about the strange and wonders, but he did not deviate much from the more classical image. According to the *Analects* and the *Records of the Grand Historian*, Confucius was indeed fond of and well versed in the *Changes*, the paramount divination manual. The literati also understood knowing and predicting came together in sagehood, as Wang Chong 王充 (27–97 CE) alluded to: "When the literati talked about the sages, they thought they knew things from a thousand years before as well as ten thousand generations later." (儒者論聖人, 以為前知千歲, 後知萬世)[117] Similarly in Dunhuang, these divinatory manuals were copied together with the Five Classics by students of the classics as part of official learning.[118]

Still, in looking at Confucius as a diviner, one might consider it somehow outlandish. Where does this feeling of outlandishness come from? It might be in fact rooted in our own peculiar categorization of prediction. Following the scholarly dichotomy between science and magic since the nineteenth century, we have isolated certain predictive practices by calling them "divination," "prognostication," "mantic arts," etc.[119] Through this action, they become categorically segregated from economic predictions, weather forecasting, and other predictive activities that we consider legitimate. Our modern view of Confucius shifted toward a "superstition" free image of Confucius, where his relationship with divination has thus been downplayed or even disregarded. Indeed, the modern representations of Confucius are weird in their own ways. And we will explore that in the next three chapters.

4

Confucius as Stereotype

In the previous chapters, we have seen weird Confucius in ancient China. From this chapter on, we will move into a larger and more contemporary world. Some of the presentations of Confucius will go beyond the Chinese borderland, as in this chapter. But more importantly, they have become much more international, incorporating or deriving from transregional tenets of thought, such as Christianity, Marxism, and consumerism. As the geographical and intellectual landscape expands, the images become even more diverse. For example, as outlandish as they might be, the first three chapters all portray Confucius in a respectful manner, which are in line with the imperial Chinese evaluation of the sage. In contrast, the modern portraits we will see range from playful and diminishing to blatantly disparaging. Meanwhile, as we enter modern times, the amount and forms of sources increased exponentially, allowing us to study both the representations and their audiences in a more pin-pointed and nuanced way. For example, in Chapter 6, we will dissect the audience's immediate comments—a luxury for historians—on the cute image of Confucius on YouTube.

The choice of the images for the modern world is, again, not meant to be comprehensive, but illustrative of transregional and global trends. In the past three chapters, we have seen Confucius as a unique individual, as well as a representative of a group, namely the ancient worthies. In this chapter, we will see how Confucius represented a much larger community of people, the Chinese; in the next chapter, we will see how Confucius represented an even larger unit, standing in for traditional Chinese history in 1970's Communist China; and in the last chapter, we will look at him as the representative of timeless Chinese culture in the current global market. These images crystalized the particular moments when the world adjusts to China and China reconciled with its past in the global context.

In this chapter, we will explore Confucius as a stereotype of the Chinese people in American newspapers during the debate of the Chinese Exclusion

Act (1882), when Chinese immigrant labor was accused of threatening the local labor market. American politicians vehemently debated on whether the USA should limit or even expel these Chinese immigrants, which eventually led to the passing of the Chinese Exclusion Act. During the debate, both the supporters and the opponents of the Act turned to Confucius, using him to signify, as well as to stereotype, the Chinese people as a whole. As words like "almond-eyed" and "heathen" were increasingly linked to Chinese immigrants, the stereotypes were also cemented around the image of Confucius. He even became the source and symbol of the heathen and of vile Chineseness in American newspapers. As apparently orientalist and racist as these stereotypes of Confucius were, they are still relevant to our time in the second decade of the twenty-first century.

We will start with one of the Christian missionary groups in China, the Jesuits, because they for the first time systematically conceptualized Confucius as a representative of China or Chinese civilization, naming him the "Chinese philosopher." Then we will trace the introduction of this representation to the USA in the late eighteenth century as part of the world philosopher pantheon, being grouped together with Socrates, Zoroaster, etc. In the third part of the chapter, we will examine how the image of heathen Chinese dominated the debate of the Chinese Exclusion Act and merged with the existing image of Confucius in the news media. I argue that using Confucius as an individual to stereotype the Chinese was an effective strategy to personify "national characteristics" and otherwise nameless and ineffable crowds of people.

The Jesuit Depiction of Confucius and its Impacts

American newspapers did not invent Confucius as a stereotype of Chinese, the Jesuits did, or at least laid a foundation. Founded in 1540, the Jesuits, or the Society of Jesus was part of the Catholic Church and was engaged in missionary and educational missions in more than 100 countries. In less than two decades of its founding, the Jesuit Francis Xavier (1506–52) already made attempts to visit then Ming China (1368–1644). Later, the Jesuits set foot in Macao in the 1660s and eventually established themselves in Guangdong by 1682. Like many missionary groups, the Jesuits emphasized the mastery of local languages and culture so that they could better understand the locals when proselytizing. Meanwhile, the Vatican supervised their progress and gave approval to their actions.[1]

In the early years, the Jesuits already discovered the importance of Confucius through the official learning of the Ming, and later the Qing dynasty

(1644–1912). They very much understood the gravity of official learning, because the success or even the survival of the mission depended on the sanction of the Chinese emperor and his officials. During Ming and Qing China, the Civil Examination was the primary way of selecting officials, and the key subject of the Examination was called the Eight-Legged Essay (*Bagu wen* 八股文), a highly stylized response to examination questions based on a collection called the *Collected Commentaries on the Chapters and Sentences of the Four Books* (*Sishu zhangju jizhu* 四書章句集注). The collection included four Confucian texts, or the Four Books (Sishu 四書): the *Analects* (*Lunyu* 論語), *Mencius* (*Mengzi* 孟子), the "Great Learning" ("Daxue" 大學) and the "Doctrine of the Mean" ("Zhongyong" 中庸). Equally important was the twelfth-century thinker Zhu Xi's 朱熹 (1130–1200) line-by-line commentary on the Four Books as the authoritative interpretation.[2] The *Analects* and Zhu Xi's interpretation thus laid the foundation for the Jesuits' understanding of Confucius.

This understanding was crystalized in the first Jesuit translation of the complete *Analects* published in 1687.[3] Attempts at translating the *Analects* and the rest of the Four Books started 100 years earlier around 1584, after the Italian Jesuit Michele Ruggieri (1543–1607) arrived in Macao in 1579. In 1593, Matteo Ricci (1552–1610) was ordered to continue with Ruggieri's unfinished work. While Ruggieri's project was aimed to reveal the linguistic and cultural aspects of the texts, Ricci was instructed to make the translation suitable to catechize the Christian message. After Ricci died, the Portuguese Jesuit Inàcio Da Costa (1603–66) carried on the mission and taught the incoming Jesuits the Four Books. Together with his trainees, they published *Chinese Wisdom* (*Sapientia Sinica*) in 1662, which included a Latin translation of the "Great Learning" and five chapters of the *Analects*. Meanwhile, their project was slowed down by the anti-Christian persecution in Qing China and objections from the Vatican because their translation was considered too accommodating to be accurate.[4]

Eventually, one of the trainees of Da Costa, Philippe Couplet (1623–93) managed to publish the first complete translation of the *Analects*. Because the translation was surrounded by controversy, Couplet was summoned to Europe as a delegate for the China mission in 1680 to defend the work. Fortunately, the translation of the Confucian texts attracted the attention of the librarian of the Bibliothèque Royale at the time, Melchisédech Thévenot (ca. 1620–92), who in turn convinced King Louis XIV (r. 1643–1715) to publish the texts in Paris instead of the Vatican Library in Rome. With the king's support, Couplet worked in Paris starting in 1686 to continue with the translation work and eventually published the entire Latin translation in 1687 with the title: *Confucius, the*

Philosopher of China, or the Knowledge of China Translated into Latin (*Confucius sinarum philosophus, sive, Scientia sinensis latine exposita*).[5]

The Chinese Philosopher

Confucius, the Philosopher of China set the tone for the Jesuits' understanding of Confucius, which later entered the Antebellum era United States.[6] The original intention of the translation was to prove to the Vatican that the ancient Chinese were neither deist nor superstitious, but recognizant of a personal God. Accordingly, it depicted Confucius as the Chinese philosopher, who was comparable with ancient Greek counterparts like Socrates and Plato.[7] Both the "Chinese" and "philosopher" parts of the image were new to the Ming and Qing dynasty literati, and they became the two pillars of the image of Confucius in the USA until the mid-nineteenth century.

What did the Jesuits mean by "philosopher"? They were referring to the ones who could reason, or "philosophize" as in the Socratic dialogues. When Ricci encountered the Chinese classics, he also witnessed the Chinese literati's worship of Confucius, including the imperial rituals and liturgies. He was acutely aware that such practices could be interpreted as religiously incompatible with the Catholic Church, and thus opposed by the Vatican. At the same time, it would also be an uphill battle to convince the Chinese imperial house to change their practices. To reach a compromise, Ricci carefully avoided depicting Confucius as a god sacrificed to by the Chinese, but focused on the moral philosophy of his teaching, portraying him as a pagan philosopher, comparable to respectable Greek philosophers, such as Plato and Aristotle. Through his translations and commentaries, Ricci further argued that Confucian teaching was in accordance with the Christian faith, even though they failed to discover God.[8]

At that time, there was no Chinese equivalent term that could exactly convey "Chinese philosopher." In Imperial China, Confucius' main titles included "sage," as in the "Ultimate Sage" (Zhisheng 至聖), and "teacher," as in the "Previous Teacher" (Xianshi 先師). The latter spoke to the moral and political guidance he provided to his disciples and contemporaries, and the former referred to how much his guidance was in accordance with the mandate of Heaven.[9] Neither of them emphasized "reasoning," particularly because it was not an apparent category in the literati discourse. The predominant discourse during that time was how to understand the rightful "principle" (*li* 理) that permeated in the cosmos through *qi* 氣 and how to embrace it through the cultivation of the thinking-organ, the heart (*xin* 心). This discourse, often labelled as Neo-Confucianism, was represented by both the authoritative commentator Zhu Xi and the Ming literatus Wang Yangming 王陽明 (1472–1529).[10]

Jesuits thus worked around the Confucian discourse of the time with their hermeneutic strategies. *Confucius, the Philosopher of China*, in particular establishes the sense of philosophical dialectic through interpreting the title of the *Analects*, or *Lunyu*. It adopts the Ming official Zhang Juzheng's 張居正 (1525–82) glossing of the title as "discussions" (*lun* 論) and "answers and elaborations" (*yu* 語). Putting this glossary together, the book states that "it is entitled *Lunyu*, because it records in a simple way the discussion between people who are reasoning and philosophizing."[11] This implies that *Lunyu* contains dialectics toward reaching an opinion, rather than simply assertions of already established theories. Following this assumption, the book also translates "love of learning" (*haoxue* 好學) as "philosopher," since the ancient Greek etymology of the word literally indicates "love for wisdom."

What kind of philosophy, then, did Confucius practice? *Confucius, the Philosopher of China* states that the *Analects* contains "moral sayings," in other words, moral philosophy. The Jesuits in fact tried to avoid diving too deep into Neo-Confucians' cosmology of "principle" and "*qi*" because it might render too atheist or pantheist an interpretation. For example, Zhu Xi explained the word Heaven (*tian* 天) in the *Analects* as the impersonal principle. Instead, the Jesuits turned to Zhang Juzheng's commentary, which interpreted Heaven as the most honored existence, implying a sense of personal God. Based on Zhang's commentary, they understood the most important virtue in the *Analects*, "humanity" (*ren* 仁) as "the inner and firm perfection of the mind, by which we constantly follow the natural light endowed by heaven." Driving home the strong Christian connotation, they argued that "universal charity and love" was the main goal of Confucius' philosophy.[12]

A less surprising part of the Jesuit invention of Confucius is the "Chinese" part, yet it was still just as impactful. It is natural that Ming or Qing dynasty literati would not refer to Confucius as the *Chinese* sage just like they would not refer to their food as *Chinese* food. It is reversely natural for the Jesuits to denote Confucius using the country name. Therefore, they not only entitled the book as *Confucius, the Chinese Philosopher*, but in the book, they also included a portrait of Confucius standing in front of the so-called *Imperii Gymnasium* (Guoxue 國學), or Imperial Academy. Furthermore, Couplet as the editor of the book, placed the *Analects*, the "Great Leaning," and "Doctrine of the Mean" all under the name of Confucius, making him the representative of the *ru* 儒 tradition.

Confucius thus was not just from China, located in the center of the imperial academy, he also represented the learning of China, or China in general.[13]

The Universal Philosopher in Antebellum America

This Chinese philosopher Confucius image entered Antebellum America and stayed stable until Americans started interacting more frequently with Chinese immigrants in the 1850s. The first group of Chinese immigrants, mostly from Canton province, went to California in 1849 for the Gold Rush. They received hostility from the local European immigrant population, especially because of the potential competition over mining business. This soon led to the Foreign Miners' Tax Act of 1850, which charged foreign miners with higher taxes. The act did drive many Chinese immigrants away from mining, but they stayed in the USA and went into construction instead. In the mid-1860s, the Central Pacific Railroad (CPRR) company faced a shortage of European immigrant construction workers for their ambitious "transcontinental railroad" project, so they started hiring Chinese immigrants. Renewing earlier hostilities over mining, this further spurred resentment from the local European settlers against the Chinese. This resentment spread through American media from the 1870s to 1880s and developed into the legislative exclusion of the Chinese population, despite the fact that the United States of America and Qing China (1636–1911) had an agreement on the importation of Chinese labor under the Burlingame Treaty (1868).[14]

This resentment needed justification, and Confucius became part of it. In this section, we will trace how the resentment created a new and more negative image of Confucius to justify the exclusion of the Chinese workers. Meanwhile, the defenders of the Chinese workers, despite being in the minority, stuck to the Jesuits' version of Confucius to argue in support of the Chinese workers. Both sides built upon the Jesuits' legacy and further developed Confucius into a stereotype of the Chinese population as a whole. They did, however, differ regarding the universal values of Confucius: while the opponents of the exclusion embraced them, the supporters hinged their argument on the uniqueness of the Chinese sage. This tension between universality and uniqueness was born from the contemporary political beliefs that universality was best represented by Christian values, and that uniqueness equaled inferiority and heathenism.[15] As a result, Confucius emerged from the Chinese exclusion debate as a peculiar representative who taught heathen behaviors, which were unacceptable in American society.

Confucius arrives in the United States

Confucius was introduced to the Americas as a universal philosopher before the USA became independent. After the publication of the Jesuits' *Confucius, the Philosopher of China*, it was soon translated into English in 1691 with the title *The Morals of Confucius, a Chinese Philosopher*. The translation was advertised in the *Boston Evening-Post*, and part of it was serialized in *New York Weekly Journal* from January to February in 1737. Newspapers at this time reached a wide range of audiences in the colonies, including both aristocratic elites and their servants. Thus, the Jesuits' work formed the basic understanding of Confucius throughout the colonies.[16]

This understanding of a universal philosopher Confucius continued after the USA gained independence. For example, in his *Moral Reasoning*, the revolutionary and philosopher Thomas Paine (1737–1809), compared Confucius with other great thinkers in history. In the book, Paine took a theological position called deism, where our empirical knowledge and observation of the natural world were sufficient enough to understand the supreme being of the universe. He went on to state that Christian theology, e.g., the miracles and the trinity of God still contained the "idolatry of the ancient mythologists," and awaited "reason and philosophy to abolish the amphibious fraud" like what Jesus Christ preached. He thus argued that Jesus indeed preached amiable morality, which was also comparable to Confucius, some of the ancient Greek philosophers, Quakers, and "many good men in all ages."[17] In other words, Confucius was as good as Jesus on the universal scale of rational thinking.

Paine's position was shared among many of the founding fathers of the United States, and Confucius was part of this universal pantheon. Based on this universalist position, one could argue that Confucius could be supplementary to Christianity. For example, the Vermont based *Christian Messenger* in 1817 published a letter from Reverend J. C. Supper in Java, which claimed to have successfully converted a rich Chinese man to Christianity through the "doctrines of Confucius." Reverend Supper did say that the Chinese man already preferred Christianity to Confucius' doctrine. But this conversion strategy shows that to Supper, Confucius and Jesus were mutually intelligible and knowing Confucius' doctrine would even be beneficial for the spread of the gospel.[18]

According to a short biography of Confucius from the *Christian Messenger* in 1819, the Chinese sage's life even paved the road to the Christian mission. The biography narrates that Confucius was born "about 556 years before Christ," and in propagating his "maxims," he "sent no less than 600 missionaries into different parts of the empire to effect a reformation in the manners of the people." This, as the biography claims, "should be a powerful excitement to Christians." With a Protestant ring to it, Confucius' disciples became the apostles, followers became missionaries, and his endeavor became a demonstration of the Chinese openness to Christianity. To avoid any link to idolatry or pagan worship, the biography insists in referring to Confucius as a "philosopher" and celebrated how his "transcendent virtue" had been revered by the Chinese people.[19] In this biography, Confucius was the ancient wiseman laying the groundwork for the gospel.

Chinese turning heathen

This universal philosopher image of Confucius gradually gave in to a much more negative one: heathen. Related to "pagan," the origin of the word referred to ones who were unbaptized in the "heath" as opposed to the Christians in cities and towns. In nineteenth-century America, "heathen" suggested not just pagan, but also uncivilized and barbaric. To Christian missionaries in particular, all heathen people were on the wrong path of government and lifestyle—the physical decay, hideous looks, and vulgar customs of the non-Christian communities around the world were the results of their heathen beliefs. Many of them thus desperately needed guidance out of heathenism to save them from both physical and cultural demise. Moreover, there is rank inside heathenism; for example, in her *Dictionary of All Religions and Religious Denominations* (1817), Hannah Adams (1755–1831) ranked Greeks and Romans as the highest heathen group, then other ancient nations such as Chaldeans and Phoenicians, then the Chinese, Hindus, and Japanese, and then Indians of America and the Negroes of Africa as the lowest Barbarians.[20]

Starting in the mid-nineteenth century, Chinese became increasingly connected with heathenism in the USA. In the 1848 survey on Qing China, *The Middle Kingdom*, the American missionary and sinologist Samuel Wells Williams (1812–84) documented the predominance of Confucius' moral teaching throughout the country. He stated that "this civilization is Asiatic and not European, pagan and not Christian." This is because, according to Williams, the "government of a heathen nation" was greatly affected by powerful individuals, and the oscillation between good laws and bad rulers rendered "the utter impossibility of securing the due administration of justice without higher moral principles than heathenism can teach." With heathenism, Williams concluded that China was not capable of "improvement," because it was "founded on wrong principles."[21]

During this time, the deficiencies of heathenism expanded from the Chinese government to Chinese people, especially immigrants. Some missionaries described Chinese immigrants as "poor, self-righteous, unprincipled, opium-eating heathen," or "an army of heathen, selfish, cruel, corrupt and corrupting." Other African American-led newspapers also embraced the same rhetoric, denouncing the Chinese as "foreigners, unacquainted with our system of government, adhering to their own habits and customs, and of heathen or idolatrous faith."[22] Here the attacks followed the same logic as Williams: since Chinese built their customs on heathenism, a wrong foundation, they inevitably behaved wrongfully.

The application of "heathen" was a way to justify the unequal treatment of different non-white groups domestically. In 1854, the California Supreme Court delivered a verdict on the appeal of the murder case of the Chinese miner Ling Sing, prohibiting Chinese to testify against whites in court, because they "are incapable of progress or intellectual development beyond a certain point."[23] This ruling, practically speaking, put Chinese in the same legal category as African Americans and Native Americans.[24] In contrast to the Chinese situation, Mexican Americans were allowed to choose their citizenship between the Mexican Republic and the USA because of the Treaty of Guadalupe Hidalgo (1848). Over time, it became increasingly difficult to explain the unequal rights of non-white people, especially after the Fifteenth Amendment passed Congress in 1869, which normatively granted voting rights to males of any race. Therefore, the Democrats and Republicans embraced the narrative that African Americans were also allowed to have voting rights because they had transformed from being pagan to Christian, they could speak English, and they were integrated into the society. This same religious-cultural reasoning applied against Native Americans and Chinese, labeling them as heathen and hence incapable of integration.[25]

While being "heathen" was linked to non-Christian religious beliefs, the application of the label to the Chinese was not a solely religious matter. For example, atheists and the Jewish were not considered to be heathen as long as they were of European descent.[26] Another obvious sign for heathenism beyond religiosity was the argument that Chinese immigrants were unable to be converted. For example, with the completion of the transcontinental railroad in 1869, California became more connected to the rest of the States, and Chinese immigrants saw greater mobility. Seeking better treatment, many Chinese realized that since the main obstacle was their "heathenism," converting to Christianity could solve the problem. However, soon the critics blocked this conversion strategy by denouncing the ability of Chinese: "inferiority and unfitness; mental and physical incapacity," or "incapable of assimilation with our own race."[27] Critique expanded to the capability of the Chinese, suggesting that even if they were to convert to Christianity, it would not be successful. Once again, just as Williams denied Qing China's progress due to heathenism, these critics denied the Chinese people's capability to change and adapt.

The Rise of the Heathen Confucius

In the coming decades, Chinese immigrants' situation only became worse in the USA. The growth of the Chinese population, especially in California, spurred even more resentment. They were being further described as cheap, unexperienced laborers, or "coolies," who unfairly competed with the European workers. Newspapers, with few exceptions, increasingly asked the "Chinese Question": whether the Chinese immigrants' customs, religion, and living and working habits posed a danger to American life. The question was hotly debated in Congress. Democrats and western Republicans argued for exclusion, and some of the eastern Republicans, together with presidents such as Chester Arthur (1829–86), sought for a more moderate approach. In fact, all of them shared the anxiety that the Chinese immigrants posed a threat to American society, but the latter was more concerned with breaking treaties with Qing China and hurting trade between the two countries. With the back and forth on the specific terms of the act, President Arthur on May 6, 1882 signed the bill now referred to as the Chinese Exclusion Act with its original name: "An Act to exclude certain treaty stipulations relating to Chinese." Behind this act was a shared answer to the Chinese question: they do pose danger to the republic.[28]

This answer brought devastating consequences for Chinese immigrants. The Constitution of the State of California in 1879 banned the Chinese from being employed by corporations as well as state, county, and municipal governments; the Angell Treaty in 1880 between the USA and China allowed the former to suspend Chinese immigration; the Chinese Exclusion Act passed in 1882 prohibited the immigration of Chinese laborers for ten years; its amendment two years later and the Scott Act of 1888 targeted ethnic Chinese regardless of their country of origin and banned them from reentering the USA, practically revoking their US citizenship as soon as they left the country. In 1888, the Supreme Court case *Chae Chan Ping v. United States* cemented the Acts, ruling that the Congress had absolute power to exclude aliens. As a result, the Chinese population in the USA dropped from approximately 105,000 in 1880 to 61,000 in 1920.[29]

The heathen Confucius

During the debate of the exclusion, Confucius increasingly became a focus of attention. Since the debate concerned Chinese immigrants as a whole, both supporters and opponents of exclusion sought a blanket reference for the group, and the more specific and personified the reference the better. Confucius, as the most well-known "Chinese" person in American newspapers, became a fitting choice. This was enhanced by the literary style of journalism; rhetorically speaking, news tended to use epithets for the Chinese immigrants to avoid repetition. For example, in introducing Chinese New Year, a short piece initially uses the label "Chinaman" to refer to the local Chinese, and then switches to "almond-eyed and innocent citizens from the land of Confucius." The piece itself does not assert any political orientation, but this rhetorical reference is stereotyping, giving a sense that everyone from China was a follower of Confucius.[30]

Beyond rhetoric, the idea of a "Confucian" nation already had well founded roots at this time. The Jesuits' *The Morals of Confucius* and Williams' the *Middle Kingdom* had already lay a foundation for the American elite readers' understanding of Confucius' role in China. Later works like *Confucius and the Chinese Classics; or Readings in Chinese Literature* by the Presbyterian missionary A.W. Loomis (1816–91) systematically introduced what texts the Qing Chinese read, where works related to Confucius took a central role. Meanwhile, the importance of Confucius' teaching was also being proven by Chinese immigrants or people from China.[31] For example, the celebrity and well-respected Zhan Shichai 詹世釵 (1841–93), referred to as "Chang, the Chinese giant" in American newspapers, still valued Confucius' teaching even after being baptized and compared it to the that of the Bible. This created the perception that Confucius was ubiquitous in China.[32]

As a result, Confucius was responsible for or linked to the vices of the Chinese people. In reporting street scenes in Papeet, Tahiti, *Chicago Daily Tribune* describes a "Chinaman with nothing on but a pair of big-legged breeches, leans against a door-post gazing into vacancy pondering on the wise sayings of

Confucius or planning a 5-cent swindle."[33] This description overtly stimulates the disparaging stereotype of the Chinese in the mind of the local readers of Chicago: half-nakedness meant he was uncivilized; "gazing into vacancy," laziness; the sayings of Confucius, heathen; and swindling people, cunning. Further, the "or" creates a connection between the pondering of Confucius' sayings and petty swindling, as if Confucius' wisdom was responsible for the cunningness of the Chinese.

Cunningness found Confucius in another story of the same newspaper. On Christmas Eve of 1879, a *Tribune* reporter went to a Chinese laundry and found out that "the disciples of Confucius were utterly regardless of the observance of the day." When the reporter asked a worker there whether he enjoyed any Christmas food, he answered yes because he went to the Methodist Episcopal Church on Wabash Avenue and Fourteenth Street. Meanwhile, he laughed at his fellow worker for going to another church and not getting any food. When the reporter pressed him on his belief in Christianity, he reportedly answered: "Oh yes; Clistianty goodee; gettee good supper to-night. He no gette, ha, ha; he go Farwell Ballee, ha, ha, ha!"[34] The moral of the report was that the followers of Confucius joined Christian churches only for the free meals rather than the religion. Tapping into the age-old stereotype of Chinese immigrants speaking broken English, the report provokes an alienizing and misguided cunningness among the "followers of Confucius."

The more someone was familiar with Confucius' teaching, the more cunning they might be. In the September 15, 1877 issue, *Boston Daily Globe* republished a report on the Feast of Confucius. In addition to complaining about the noise of the festival, it features "Wing Za-Sook, a theologian of recognized ability, preached an able discourse, based upon the doctrines of old Confuse-us." The report does not mention anything else regarding the preaching, except that the theologian advised the "faithful not to steal chickens in the full of the moon, as it displeased the gods and gave the owners of the chickens too many chances."[35] Similar to the last report, this one suggests that regardless how solemn an activity would be, the Chinese always had a sinister motivation for doing it. And this time, it was not a lone, ordinary Chinese worker who was cunning, but a scholar of Confucius who was responsible for teaching this behavior to his fellow Chinese. In other words, Confucius' wisdom was sinister cunningness in disguise that was spread among the Chinese population.

Sometimes Confucius was involved in more heinous activities. In American newspapers, Chinese immigrants were often associated with opium smoking and accused of bringing drug problems to the United States.[36] In this context, *Boston*

Daily Globe reported on Ah Bak, "the dead ex-disciple of Confucius." It laments that "Although Bak was a Christian, he was a Chinaman still, and he never gave up his opium habit." The report mentions that "He lived on opium and was a prodigy at 'tapping the pipe,' even to the Chinamen running the local dens."[37] Although he died a Christian, Ah Bak's association with Confucius was still one of his defining features. And the Christian vs. drug user contrast reenforced the sinister trope of Chinese: while they claimed to be assimilated into American culture, they still clung to their "Chineseness."

In addition to opium, gambling was another activity that was often associated with the Chinese. According to the *New York Times*, a local residence in Brooklyn was raided and "on the table there were several small sums of money, and the Chinamen were handling their strips of card covered with curious hieroglyphics as if engaged in some game." Apparently, the police deliberately planned to take out this gambling and opium smoking den; arresting fourteen people, they "put an end to the exercises in which the disciples of Confucius were engaged, and for a time the chatter of Chinese tongues made a din that was deafening." Another report from *Boston Daily Globe* investigates a gathering of more than a dozen "almond-eyed descendants of Confucius" playing Chinese chess. Admitting that the game was for intellectual people, it doubles down on the stereotype of gambling Chinese people and quotes a fellow player: "he had never seen a game of chess played unless there was a stake of some kind on the table, for all Chinamen are inveterate gamblers."[38] Just as all of them were descendants of Confucius, all Chinese were gamblers.

Occasionally, Confucius was even associated with murder. On April 17, 1877, *Boston Daily Globe* reported on a death sentence in California for a murderer "who is a very intelligent man and devout follower of Confucius." Facing death, he showed "perfect calmness and resignation," and the piece attributes this to "the support derived from religious belief," referring to Confucius' teaching.[39] Here the devotion to Confucius was associated with calmness, as well as the simple fact that he was a convicted murderer. From swindling to murder, these newspaper pieces do not overtly blame Confucius, but tacitly transform the Jesuits' representation of Confucius from a philosophical one to a more sinister one: Confucius' wisdom resulted in the cunningness of the Chinese, and his moral teaching served or even spurred baleful causes. Therefore, it is not a surprise to see statements of Confucius' influence as such: "the Chinaman's reverence for age is not founded on filial affection, but rather on superstition, a worship, to be accounted for by the exceptional and extraordinary influence of the teachings of Confucius for twenty-three centuries."[40]

To American readers, the ubiquity of Confucius went into the very blood of the Chinese people. In newspapers, the Chinese immigrants are commonly referred to as "the followers of Confucius," "the disciples of Confucius," "sons of Confucius," or "the descendants of Confucius."[41] The first two reflect the presence of Confucius either as a teacher or a religious leader, but the latter two claim a blood tie. The blood-relative metaphor not only assumes the Chinese people's familiarity with him, but more importantly hint that his teachings were innate to all the Chinese people. In some news reports, one could argue such a metaphor served nothing but an indexical purpose, but the repetition of this particular metaphor undoubtedly reinforced a "Confucian-nativist" view, assuming that the Chinese people were naturally bound to Confucius' teaching instead of Christianity.

This affinity with Confucius was so deep that many claimed Chinese were not convertible to Christianity or American culture in general. As we have seen, *Boston Daily Globe* was a stronghold of anti-Chinese sentiment, and in 1878 they published a comprehensive disparagement of the Chinese's behaviors, entitled: "The Chinese: Moon-Eyed Knights of the Wash-Tub and Sad-Iron." The piece lists the "peculiarities" of the Chinese, ranging from their coolie and corrupted nature to carrying leprosy and suffering from opium addiction. It believes that as far as the "national proclivities" of the Chinese are concerned, they "may be ranked AMONG THE MOST UNCONVERTABLE OF PAGANS, and likely to worship Joss [a Chinese deity], and obey Kong-Fu-Tsee [Confucius] for generations to come."[42] Arguing to exclude Chinese from the United States, the disparagement was written not just to point out the negative attributes of the Chinese, but also the fact that these attributes could not be changed. Employing a concept similar to "national characteristics," Confucian heathenism equaled nationality with ethnicity.

With the Chinese's incapability of change, there seems to be an answer to the "Chinese Question". On February 14, 1879, the US Senator James Blaine (1830–93) delivered a speech called "Chinese Immigration to the Pacific Slope" to the Senate, where he reiterated the heathen and coolie stereotypes of Chinese. While he supported white immigration from Europe and Black suffrage in the USA, he thought the Chinese was unfit for citizenship:

> The Asiatic cannot live with our population and make a homogeneous element. The idea of comparing European immigration with an immigration that has no regard to family, that does not recognize the relation of husband and wife, that does not observe the tie of parent and child, that does not feel in the slightest degree the humanizing and the ennobling influences of the hearthstone and the fireside![43]

Blaine made it clear to his more sympathetic colleagues that the situation was not a temporary one where the Chinese could be converted: "the conversion of Chinese is largely a failure; that the demoralization of the white race is a much more rapid result of the contact than the conversion of the Chinese race …"[44]

Blaine believed that the USA was facing an inevitable cultural and racial war, caused by the immigration of unchangeable Chinese. He provoked his colleagues with the sentiment of competition: "Either the Caucasian race will possess the Pacific slope or the Mongolian race will possess it." This mounts to the ultimate choice: "We have this day to choose whether shall have for the Pacific coast the civilization of Christ or the civilization of Confucius."[45] Here Confucius became the totality of the Chinese customs, characteristics, and race, each of which were inseparable with the other and unchangeable. To Blaine, such totality was not only worth condemning, but also completely at odds with Christianity. Behind Blaine's claim was the repeated belief that heathenism equaled vice. Through Blaine and his supporters, this belief consolidated the stereotype of the changeless and unchangeable Chinese, and Confucius was the ultimate source of it.

Defending the Universal Philosopher

Blaine and his allies were not without their opponents. For example, during Blaine's speech, his fellow Republican senators Thomas Stanley Matthews (1824–89) from Ohio and Hannibal Hamlin (1809–91) from Maine interjected several times, with the latter saying: "Treat them, I will not say like pagans, because Confucius would shame us if we go to his counsel—treat them like Christians, and they will become good American citizens." Among these opponents, some maintained that it was not economically and diplomatically beneficial to break the immigration agreement with Qing China, and more importantly, it was not constitutional to deny citizenship to Chinese, especially in light of Black suffrage.[46] While these opponents were the minority in number, they envisioned a more open empire than their colleagues.[47] Nevertheless, they similarly turned to Confucius to stereotype the Chinese. Once again, Confucius was *the* Chinese person, and his redeeming attributes or thought became the reason for Chinese immigrants to stay.

The Protestant church in the USA was a stronghold for supporting Chinese immigration. Since heathenism became the reason to deny the Chinese US citizenship, its leaders saw the opportunity to convert Chinese immigrants by helping them circumvent the situation. The American Missionary Association already possessed the expertise in Chinese language, and they worked with local congregational schools to establish English language schools for Chinese. This maneuver of assimilation not only happened in California, where some 87 percent of the 56,000 Chinese population in the USA were located, but they also reached out to New York and Portland.[48]

Behind the support was a universalist vision of God's Kingdom on earth. Many Protestant missionaries shared the optimism that people around the globe could be united through their evangelism. And some of the missionaries maintained that universal human equality was the foundation of such Godly unification. That is not to say that they had a high opinion of Chinese or other non-white communities, but viewed them as either "childlike" or "misguided," so that they could be changed through their evangelist education.[49] It was this logic that justified the opening of Sunday schools to Chinese, and Confucius was usefully part of the justification.

In this context, the go-to strategy was the time-honored one: Confucius was compatible to Christianity. In May 1878, *The New York Herald* published a piece called "Chinese Characteristics," which reported Methodist Reverend John Newman's (1826–99) lecture "Confucius and Confucianism." In the report, he stated that the Chinese sage not only taught the five virtues (faith, knowledge, propriety, righteousness, and benevolence), but also invented a negative form of the Golden Rule, as Confucius replied to the question: [A disciple asked] "Should injury be recompensed with kindness", [Confucius replied] "With what, then, will you recompense kindness? Recompense injury with justice and recompense kindness with kindness."[50] While acknowledging Confucius' contribution, Newman believed that it was inferior to Jesus' positive version: "Therefore all things whatever ye would that men should do to you do ye even so to them."[51]

Like the Jesuits, Newman made a lesser Jesus out of Confucius. As in the case of Golden Rule, he depicted Confucius as an honorable saint who had his own defects and was somehow waiting for the true teaching of Jesus. He listed more defective teachings of Confucius, such as "despotism," "subordination," and "degradation of woman," summarizing by saying that "Christ taught all that Confucius taught that was excellent, but in a purer, higher and completer form." In other words, Confucius' teaching was inferior to that of Jesus in two senses: the bad part of his teaching was flawed, and the good part was in the same direction of Jesus, but less developed. This evaluation of Confucius, in fact, matched the "childlike" and "misguided" image of Chinese, where they could correct their bad habits and further develop the good ones so they could become qualified Christians.[52]

Newman even reinterpreted a Buddhist narrative to reiterate this lesser Jesus version of Confucius. At the end of his lecture, Newman concluded that Confucius was actually aware of his imperfect teaching, so he prophesized that "A sage shall come from the west," referring to Jesus. According to Newman, the Chinese emperor in 60 CE did send an embassy "to Palestine to invite Christ to China," but the ambassadors went to India and were convinced by a Buddhist priest that the Buddha was the "sage." Originating from the Jesuits' *Confucius, the Philosopher of China*, this narrative patched together two separate records: one, in the third-century CE text *Liezi* 列子, Confucius says "there will be a sage coming from the west," when he comments on the ancient sage kings; two, according to the *History of the Later Han* (*Houhan shu* 後漢書) from the fifth century CE, Emperor Ming dreamed of golden statues and sent envoys to learn Buddhist teachings.⁵³ The Jesuits then replaced Buddhism with Christianity to claim that Confucius and his followers were in fact seeking Christian teaching.

Newman cited this then little-known legend to emphasize that the Chinese were misguided. He maintained that Confucius did prophesize the coming of Jesus, but later when the emperor sent the envoys, they were somehow tricked by Buddhism. This narrative suggests that Chinese people intended to convert to Christianity, but in the process were lost and distracted by heathen religions like Buddhism. In other words, they were capable of being brought back onto the right path. Even though Newman's lecture was aptly entitled "Confucius and Confucianism," *The New York Herald* published it with a title more telling of its readers' concerns: "Chinese Characteristics." To the readers, who Confucius was decided the nature of the Chinese people.

Some of the newspapers also published the Chinese's own words of comparing Confucius to Jesus or Christianity. For example, *Philadelphia Inquirer*, in February 1884, published an interview of Zhan Shichai, the "Chang, the Chinese Giant" mentioned above. Zhan was born in Fuzhou, Fujian Province and was reportedly 2.44m (8') tall. Taking advantage of his unusual height, he left China in 1865 and started his stage life in London, and from there he traveled to the rest of Europe, the USA, and Australia. His tours not only won him fame and money, but also led him to meeting his second wife, Catherine Santley (1847–93) from Liverpool, England. Familiar with Western cultures, Zhan was very positively depicted in English language newspapers as "gentle," "well-educated," and "speaking several languages."⁵⁴ His popularity and reputation made him a good candidate to talk about Confucius vs. Jesus in newspapers.

Like Reverend Newman, Zhan Shichai took a sympathetic view on Confucius and the Chinese. The *Philadelphia Inquirer* interview started by referring to

Zhan's book using Chinese characters, a common trope to exoticize Chinese. But Zhan immediately turned it around by pointing out it was in fact the Bible in Chinese. He then continued:

> Oh yes, I am Christian, because Christian takes his Bible from Chinaman. The political moral taught by our great philosopher. Confucius, or we say King fu-tse, and see how closely the Bible doctrines resemble the principles in which we are educated.[55]

According to Zhan, Confucius' thought is comparable to the teaching of the Bible to the extent that being a Confucian is like being a Christian. And it is not as Newman claimed that Confucius partially realized the Biblical teaching, but he inspired it. Turning the relationship around, Zhan went on to state that the Chinese not only shared similar moral teachings and mythology with Christianity, but they also had advanced technology, such as printing and silk making. To him, the civilization of Confucius was comparable to, and likely more advanced than, that of Christ.

It is rare to have Chinese individuals like Zhan featured in newspapers; most of the testimonies came from nameless and largely stereotypical shadows cast as "Chinese." For example, a short sketch from *New York Tribune* in May 1878 recounts a Chinese's answer to whether he believed in God: "Yes, me believe in Jesu Christie, me belleb in Confucie (Confucius) in China, alle samee."[56] In line with Zhan, the interlocutor also considered Jesus and Confucius to have shared the same teaching, but the stereotypical broken English suggests to the readers that such a statement is more out of ignorance than anything else. Fitting the stereotypical description, the interlocutor was given the name "John," after the generic name "John Chinaman" that was commonly used to refer to Chinese people.

Indeed, even for the defenders of the Chinese immigration, the individuals were often reduced and merged into a singular representation. In 1870, the writer Mark Twain (1835–1910) published the piece "John Chinaman in New York," to satirize such phenomena. In the piece, the narrator sympathizes with the hardship of a Chinese man standing outside of a tea store in New York, working as the store sign, who had a "quaint Chinese hat, with peaked roof and ball on top, and his long queue [hairstyle] dangling down his back …" Witnessing the stares from other pedestrians, the narrator humanizes this person, eulogizing his longing for his hometown, his feeling of sadness, and craving for happiness. But when they engage in a conversation, an Irish accent comes out of the

"Chinese" mouth: "Divil a cint but four dollars a week and find meself; but it's aisy, barrin' the troublesome furrin clothes that's so expinsive." As the narrator laments, "The New York tea merchants who need picturesque signs are not likely to run out of Chinamen." To many readers, this singular stereotype of "John Chinaman" was much larger than the lives of individual Chinese.[57]

The cartoonist Thomas Nast (1840–1902) made Confucius the face of "John Chinaman." As a radical Republican, Nast held a firm abolitionist position and supported universal citizenship. Serving as the cartoonist for *Harper's Weekly* from 1862 to 1886, he used his works to support Chinese immigration and satirize the Exclusion Act as well as its supporters. For that purpose, Nast created the character "John Confucius," who often appeared to be a Chinese diplomat in Qing dynasty fashion: winter Mandarin hat, Qing noble attire with a long gown and Mandarin jacket over it, and long mustache with a queue. This image was derived from Nast's earlier "John Chinaman" design, but with more official attire. And in contrast with the direct victim role that John Chinaman took, John Confucius mainly served as a witness observing the atrocity of American politics.[58]

Nast especially featured John Confucius' encounters with James Blaine. On the cover of the March issue of 1879's *Harper's Weekly*, he introduced Blaine in the center with one foot stepping on a slip of paper titled "Burlingame Treaty" and one arm holding an African American man who is laughing, while a Mandarin-looking man is left in the corner on a short platform with various pieces of porcelain and a banner saying "Teas, Silks, China Carvings" (Fig. 1). The caption reads "John Confucius: Am I not a man and a brother?" building on the saying from the famous Wedgwood medallion, which was known for its iconic abolitionist sentiment. These elements form the narrative that Blaine not only betrayed the treaty with China, he also hypocritically excluded Chinese from his abolitionist stance. Entitled "The Civilization of Blaine," this satire was obviously a response to Blaine's comment on the civilization of Christ vs. that of Confucius, where the civilization of Confucius was indeed personified through John Confucius.[59]

In another satirical piece about Blaine, Nast turned Confucius into the civilized one while Blaine and others were the savage ones. In the following April issue of *Harper's Weekly*, Nast published another satirical cartoon where John Confucius looks disgusted with two hands holding his stomach on the left side of the drawing, while on the wall behind him is a sheet of paper titled "The Anti-Chinese Bill" (Fig. 2). On the right side, Blaine and other presidential

Figure 1 The Civilization of Blaine. Courtesy of HathiTrust Digital Library.

candidates sit together and eat out of a big pot with the words "Mess Pottage (Sand-Lot)" in the "Kearney's Senatorial Restaurant." Behind them was another sheet on the wall, saying "Table Reserved for Presidential Candidates." "Kearney" refers to the California labor leader Denis Kearney, who was famous for his anti-Chinese agenda, especially the use of his rally call "Chinese Must Go!" in public squares and sandlots. With Confucius looking at the mouthful of sand in Blaine's spoon, the satire is captioned: "Confucius. 'How can Christians stomach such dirt.'"[60]

Figure 2 A Matter of Taste. Courtesy of HathiTrust Digital Library.

Entitled "A Matter of Taste," Nast played with the eating habits of the Chinese but with a twist. In line with "The Civilization of Blaine," Nast here continued to satirize the hypocrisy of Blaine's rhetoric on evangelical inclusiveness. He also went as far to state that in order to be considered as a presidential candidate, Blaine was even willing to eat messes from a sandlot, in other words, literally dirt, which even Confucius found disgusting. This only makes sense when we contextualize it with the age-old stereotype of Chinese eating foodstuffs that were repulsive to white Americans, such as rat, lizard, cat, and dog.[61] For example, Chin Shin Yin, the translator for the Chinese ambassador Chen Lanbin 陳蘭彬 (1816–95) had to answer the question of whether Chinese ate sewer rats, and he probably did not debunk this stereotype much by saying that "The rats that Chinese eat are what we call rice-field rats, or, more properly speaking, large mice …"[62] Invoking this stereotype, Nast means to say that Blaine's behavior was so vile that even the rat-eater John Confucius could not stomach it.

Indeed, perhaps constrained by the genre, Nast was more concerned with criticizing than building. His portrayal of Chinese was still largely stereotypical, with Confucius as the crown prince of this stereotype. The Qing style attire and queue sharply contrast with Blaine and others' suits and side-part hair style, as did his characteristic mustache where the ends droop down to the chin vs. either clean shaven faces or beards. As sympathetic to Chinese immigrants as Nast could be, John Confucius was decisively different and designed to provoke a sense of misplacedness and weirdness. Nast used this weird Confucius to caution his audience against the hypocrisy and harm of Blaine and supporters of Chinese exclusion. But in the process, this stereotyped John Confucius was accepted and even celebrated. Individual Chinese were once again reduced to a singular, stereotypical image.

Concluding Remarks

The Chinese Exclusion Act was in effect until 1943, and in between there were many more such stories.[63] In this chapter, we have only followed stories in the years surrounding the substantiation of the Exclusion Act. Indeed, Jesuits were the first to explicitly present Confucius as the representative of Chinese culture. But only in the context of a visibly growing number of Chinese immigrants in the USA was such a presentation reified in social life. The issue of citizenship tipped legislators, companies, and ordinary people toward generalizing communities of people, whether Chinese, Black, or Native American. News media, in order to inform and intrigue, accelerated this process by appointing Confucius as the forefather and prototype of the Chinese community as a whole. A clear advantage of such a strategy was that the audience could much better relate to a specific individual than an anonymous crowd. The disadvantage is that Confucius became the enormous generalization of the Chinese population or even Chinese civilization through history. Moral philosopher or sewer-rat eater, the space for individuality was extremely thin.

This Chinese-American Confucius is weird in two senses. Most literally, within the American politics of the 1870s, he was deliberately exoticized and, hence, out of place. As the paramount of vile habits and heathen beliefs, he was so deviant from the mainstream life or ideal of Americans to the extent that he and his followers should be denied citizenship. Beyond just the local politics, this image of Confucius is also weird because he is not one single person, but a representative of the entire Chinese community. The thought and acts attributed to him were somehow transmitted to all Chinese and justify their actions in a rather mystified way. Chinese individuals thus automatically became Confucian unless they took painstaking effort to demonstrate otherwise. This is not only contradictory to the social and intellectual diversity in China then, it even deviates from Confucius' own teaching on individual differences as mentioned in the *Analects*.[64]

While the first weirdness has been well recognized, the second still appears in different forms even up to today. At the time of writing this book, using Confucius or Confucianism to generalize China or East Asian countries is still largely in practice and taken for granted. In September 2021, *South China Morning Post* published an article called "How Pandemic Proves China's 'Digital Confucianism' is Superior to the West," in which the COVID policies in mainland China were celebrated as effective without explaining how they specifically link to Confucianism, especially given that the policies differed from region to region. I am also not sure whether the authors of the article have changed their view, because as I experienced the lockdown in Shanghai in 2022, it was neither digital nor Confucian. Either way, the article comes with an illuminating drawing where a blue-colored, digital-looked Confucius receives a bow from a jeans and T-shirt wearing person without eyes, symbolizing the younger and more modernized generations of Chinese. Once more, Chinese individuals with different opinions are reduced to a singular, unrecognizable, blind follower of Confucius.[65]

5

Confucius as Villain

In the previous chapter, Confucius was no longer just an extraordinary individual; he represented a community of people. When we move from North America back to China in the twentieth century, he was even conceptualized as a way to represent time, or more precisely, the Chinese past. Since China ended its last imperial rule and entered the Republican Era (1912–49), it had witnessed campaigns against Confucius that placed him as a symbol of the Chinese past. These campaigns reached their climax during the Cultural Revolution (1966–76), a radical iconoclastic movement led by the Chinese Communist Party (CCP) and its great leader Mao Zedong 毛澤東 (1893–1976). By 1973, Confucius had the No. 1 public enemy, who was associated with the oppressive slave-owning class of his time. More than just a historical figure, he represented the vile force that held back the development of Chinese history. The propaganda machine of the CCP made sure that everyone was on the same page through journal essays, newspaper articles, posters, and even comic books.

What is the use of turning the most revered historical figure into a hateful villain? And how can an individual be made to represent a historical period? This chapter will make sense of this image of Confucius as a defender of slavery. The first part of this chapter will trace the twentieth-century political atmosphere that gradually pushed Confucius to the dark side of history. The second part of the chapter will zoom in to the national anti-Confucius movement during the Cultural Revolution, where we will see how he was being theorized as a slavery defender and menace of the Chinese past. The last part of the chapter will examine this image of slavery defender Confucius during this movement by dissecting a particular comic book, namely the *Sinful Life of Kong the Second* (*Kong lao'er zui'e de yisheng* 孔老二罪惡的一生, 1973). We will especially focus on the textual base and the visual compositions of the comic book, through which Confucius was linked to not just a counter-revolutionary force of history, but also was the possessor of an unhealthy body with bad hygiene.

Revolutions toward the Cultural Revolution

Through imperial China (221 BCE–1911 CE), one feature of Confucius was consistent: he was venerated. The literati across this long 2,000 year period, for example, might not agree on their specific understanding of Confucius, but the overwhelming majority of them viewed him positively. This positive image undoubtedly resulted from imperial sponsorship. For example, as early as November of 195 BCE, the first emperor of the Han dynasty was already sacrificing to Confucius, and this tradition developed into a state cult through Imperial China;[1] as early as the second century BCE, the classics associated with Confucius were promoted in the Han court, and by the late sixth century CE, they had become the central subject matter for the so-called civil examination (*keju* 科舉), which was the most important system for selecting officials in imperial China.[2] On account of the imperial sponsorship, various communities looked up to him and even formed their unique narratives or traditions as we have seen in Chapters 2 and 3. Top down or bottom up, Confucius was worshipped.

This situation changed fundamentally in the beginning of the twentieth century. In 1905, the Qing government abolished the civil examination system, and by the end of 1911, the Qing government itself was overthrown. The newly established Republican China (Zhonghua minguo 中華民國) did not intend to install a new emperor, but pursued a vision of democracy. Behind this new polity was the Chinese elites' yearning for modernization, because they had witnessed the defeats of the Qing dynasty from the Opium War in 1842 to the more recent Sino-Japanese War in 1895. They painfully concluded that the success of Britain and Japan was due to their more advanced, or more "modernized" technology and polity. Therefore, they reasoned, China needed to be fundamentally transformed in order to strengthen itself.[3]

As an imperial symbol, Confucius at first appeared ambivalent, if not at the wrong end of this transformation. Since the beginning years of Republican China, students from the modern middle schools and universities no longer needed to learn through rote memorization the *Analects* and *Mencius*. By 1915, intellectuals like Hu Shi 胡適 (1891–1962) at Peking University promoted vernacular language in writing, marginalizing the Literary Chinese tradition that had been the core in any formal communication in imperial China. Together with the new direction of language was a revolution in culture, where modern science and democracy became the values that Chinese people as a community should embrace. Confucius in this context became more and more imperialistic and suppressive—many intellectuals believed that his teaching had served as a tool for the imperial rule.⁴

A spike of anti-Confucius sentiment took place in 1919, during the May Fourth Movement. Earlier that year, the Treaty of Versailles was negotiated between Germany on one side, and France, Great Britain, and the rest of the Allied Powers on the other side to conclude World War I. This peace treaty allowed Japan to retain the German colonized Qingdao, instead of returning it to China, enraging the Chinese public. Nation-wide protests broke out, including the student protests in Beijing on May 4, 1919. These protests were not only against imperialist power outside China; the protestors also blamed the weakness of their own government and attributed it to China's imperialist past. Confucius' teaching thus became the main culprit. Under the pen of Lu Xun 鲁迅 (1881–1936) and Wu Yu 吳虞 (1872–1949), his teaching together with the whole imperial tradition was nothing but human-devouring (*chiren* 吃人).⁵ To them, the Confucian tradition was not simply out of date, but anti-humanity.

Republican China in its early years then was caught in a predicament. On the one hand, it intended to join the contemporary world as a modernized nation-state; on the other hand, it had been repeatedly humiliated by the European and Japanese imperial power.⁶ These two sides created two opposing pulling powers, sometimes cancelling each other out—the humiliation could lead to the promotion of the Chinese past, and even the revival of imperial China; the longing to fit into the modern world could lead to the acceptance of and collaboration with the imperial powers.⁷ Many individuals and political institutions oscillated between these two sides, wanting to move away from China's past, but weary of full westernization, especially with its imperialist connotations.⁸

Was there a middle ground? Marxism provided an answer. Karl Marx (1818–83) derived social-economic theories from his critique of Western societies, especially Britain. His *Das Kapital* reveals the underlying relationship beneath the façade of the capitalist societies—the owners of the means of production, or the capitalists exploit the labor of their employees to maximize their surplus value. This engagement in the current world with a critique of the West found a ready audience in Republican China. Moreover, on November 7, 1917, the believers of Marxism, or Bolsheviks, overthrew the Provisional Government of Russia. For the first time, a communist government was established. This revolution demonstrated to the Chinese intellectuals that Marxism was not just a theory, but an action plan that could combat western imperialism.⁹

Four years after the Bolshevik Revolution, the Chinese Communist Party (CCP) was founded on July 1, 1921. With the support of Communist International (Comintern) in Moscow, the CCP grew into a competing power with the then leading party of Republican China, the Guomindang (GMD). After Chiang Kai-Shek (Jiang Jieshi 蔣介石, 1887–1975) took over the GMD in 1925, the CCP was no longer tolerated as a competitor and was persecuted from 1930 to 1934. In July 1937, Japan invaded China, forcing the GMD on the back foot. This gave the CCP a chance to breathe. Mao Zedong took the opportunity to assert his authority in the leadership of the CCP; the party also broke away from the control of Comintern. By the time Japan surrendered in 1945 and began retreating from China, the CCP had a firm grip in the countryside through its land reforms and better military strategies. In 1949, the CCP defeated the GMD, taking over China and founding the People's Republic of China (PRC).[10]

The image of Confucius fluctuated during the tug of war between the GMD and CCP. From the GMD perspective, Confucius was still a revered figure in the school system. In 1934, Chiang inaugurated a daily hygiene reform to modernize his citizens. In this so-called New Life Movement, Confucian teaching became an integral part of the values for the citizens to emulate.[11] During the Japanese invasion, Chiang also used Confucius as a unifier for the Chinese people. In other words, to the GMD and Chiang, Confucius and their vision of a modern nation-state could coexist.[12] The CCP on the other hand, was more ambivalent about Confucius, but not negative. This is partially because their mass mobilization targeted on peasants, where Confucius' teaching was less relevant. Meanwhile, overtly bashing Confucius as during the May Fourth Movement might alienate the intellectuals and further push them toward the GMD side. But the CCP's attitude soon became unambivalently negative once they took over China.[13]

The Confucian Shop in the new era

After the founding of the PRC on October 1, 1949, Confucius' teaching, if not the man himself, was condemned more and more. Borrowing legitimacy from the May Fourth Movement, the CCP party newspapers invoked and reinvented the expression "smashing down the Confucian Shop" (*dadao Kongjia dian* 打倒孔家店). The editor-in-chief of the party newspaper, the *People's Daily*, created a continuum between the May Fourth Movement and the CCP:

正因為五四運動是由共產主義者在政治上思想上領導的反帝反封建的偉大革命運動,因此,它才能夠同時成為徹底的反封建文化的運動。當年最勇猛地打倒孔家店、提倡文學革命、擁護民主和科學的仍然是共產主義的知識分子,而不是別人。[14]

Precisely because the May Fourth Movement was a great anti-imperialism and anti-feudalism revolutionary movement, led by communists politically and intellectually, it was able to at the same time become a full movement against feudal culture. It was none other than the communist intellectuals who most courageously smashed down the Confucian shop, promoted the literature revolution, and supported democracy and science.

In this continuum, the communists were the real force behind the May Fourth Movement. They championed in "smashing down the Confucian shop," which referred to not only Confucius' own teaching, but the Chinese imperial past in general. While rarely used verbatim during the May Fourth movement, this expression was crystalized as a main goal of the movement in the article. And the communists were cast as the supporters of the movement then and the heirs of it now.[15]

In the beginning years of the PRC, this emerging Chinese communist narrative of Chinese history provided a framework to villainize Confucianism. Applying Marxist ideas of class struggle and exploitation, it divided the Chinese past into four stages based on the main means of production during the time: the primitive commune society of the legendary Xia dynasty; the slavery society stretching from the Shang dynasty (c.1600–1046 BCE) to the beginning of the Western Zhou dynasty (1047–722 BCE); a feudal society from the Western Zhou until 1911 CE; and a mixture of capitalism and western imperialism from the start of Republican China up until 1949. These historical stages were considered necessary for the evolution of human society, but were filled with vicious exploitation after the initial commune society stage. Because of the different economic structures of each stage, the exploitation of labor also took on different forms. For example, in the slavery society, slaves were exploited by slave owners; in the feudal society, peasants were exploited by the land owners; and in the capitalist society, workers are exploited by factory owners or capitalists.[16]

According to this narrative of the Chinese past, exploitation was never explicit or outrageously naked, but sugarcoated with the ideology of the ruling class. Confucian thought thus served as the ideological backing of the Chinese feudal society, a product of Confucius' high social class. As mentioned in the previous chapter, early records like the *Records of the Grand Historian* note that Confucius was from the State of Lu and a descendant from the noble classes of the Shang dynasty.[17] This new Chinese communist narrative reinterpreted these traditional records using the class struggle framework, making Confucius a propagator of noble feudalism, who believed that the Zhou dynasty nobles should own the land and slaves. He then punched down the rising non-noble landlords and the peasants, ensuring that their labor could continue to be exploited.[18]

Confucius' thought accordingly represented and justified the sentiment of him and his class, the gentlemen (*shi* 士). His trust in the Mandate of Heaven (*tianming* 天命) became his faith in the absolute rule of the noble class (*junzhu zhuanzhi* 君主專制). And his famous saying of letting the lord be lord, subject be subject, father be father, and son be son unmistakably became a request of a constant, fixed noble hierarchy, instead of everyone behaving morally according to their social roles.[19] The virtues he promoted went through this new interpretation as well. Humanity (*ren* 仁) and filial piety (*xiao* 孝) represent his familyism (*jiating zhuyi* 家庭主義), where children cannot disobey their parents. Confucius' teaching of maintaining a balance, or *zhongyong* 中庸, also became a cowardly means of avoiding trouble and blame.[20]

All of these reinterpretations portrayed Confucius' thought as reactionary. Following the May Fourth tradition, the Communist narrative treats it as the ideology of feudalism. It further claims that the ups and downs of Confucianism in imperial China were directly linked to the dynastic cycles. For example, before a new dynasty seized power, they tended to disregard or even look down upon Confucianism because they were seen as rebels. But as soon as they established the new dynasty as legitimate, they needed to turn to Confucius to justify themselves. And the more a dynasty was in decline, the more they respected Confucius.[21] This claim locks Confucian thought and Chinese dynasties together into a vicious cycle of feudalism.

In the beginning of the PRC years, Confucius was not all bad. The Communist narrative considered his thought rich and complex; some of it should be completely thrown out, while the remainder could still be adapted to the new society. His view on learning, for example, would still be valuable for the contemporary world. Confucius was also still worthy of reverence as a teacher.[22] This narrative is in fact not much different from that of the May Fourth Movement, where many intellectuals intended to smash down Confucianism as an imperial ideology, but still considered Confucius' thought as relevant and helpful for the modern world.[23] The Communist narrative inherited this positive attitude toward Confucius, but it now confined him to the role of a great educator, instead of being a moral thinker or politician. Nevertheless, Confucius lost this last ground of respect in the coming years.

Revolutions gone too far

After the initial success of the socialist reforms, the PRC's policies became even more radical. At the end of 1953, Mao was determined to realize his socialist vision through completely nationalizing land and privately owned companies. The former spoke to China's "feudal" past, where agriculture was the main means of production, and land was controlled by the local gentry. The latter was a maneuver to eliminate capitalism. By the end of the 1956, this socialist transformation swept both urban and rural China. In an attempt to catch up with Western countries, the PRC also launched its ambitious industrialization and agricultural programs. In January of 1956, Mao produced the famously impractical slogan: "More, faster, better, and more economically," signaling the desired results of the programs. Accordingly, local governments projected even steeper indexes for agricultural and industrial production.[24]

This continuous pressure of producing more eventually developed into the Great Leap Forward movement from 1958 to 1960. Inspired by the then the First Secretary of the Soviet Union Nikita Khrushchev's (1894–1971) economic competition with the Britain and the USA, the leadership of the PRC decided to "catch up with Britain in ten years and the USA in fifteen." But catching up in what way? Mao and others decided to use the production of steel and grain. They took advantage of the previously successful nationalization of land and industries and mobilized the masses into the production process. Agriculturally, the PRC established the centralized people's communes (*renmin gongshe* 人民公社), where farmers collectively worked on the nationalized land and received living accommodation from the nation. Industrially, local governments coerced ordinary households into producing steel at home in order to hit the steep production index.[25]

The results were disastrous. The peoples' communes program eventually failed because the farmers lacked incentives to work on the land where their labor was not directly connected to their compensation. In addition, much of the harvest was collected prematurely for political display, which further hurt the agricultural cycle. Producing steel at home was even less feasible a mission because of the lack of both proper equipment and expertise. What is worse, residents were instructed to donate their property for this endeavor, such as their iron knives, pots, etc. The ending result was not just scrap steel, but also the citizens losing their tools. Perhaps exacerbated by weather conditions, the disregard of the agricultural cycle and mistreatment of tools formed the biggest famine since the founding of the PRC. Even the PRC official records report that from 1959 to 1961, at least 16.5 million people died an unnatural death.[26]

This failed movement did not thwart, but fueled, more radical movements that developed into the Cultural Revolution (*wenhua dageming* 文化大革命) in 1966. Given this failure, Mao's reputation took a big hit inside the party. To calm the dissatisfaction, Mao made a self-criticism on the Great Leap in front of over 7,000 party officials and temporarily took a semi-retired role in 1962. His experiences with the Soviet Union made him more paranoid. As early as February 25, 1956, Khrushchev formally criticized his predecessor Joseph Stalin (1878-1953) during a secret meeting at the 20th Congress of the Communist Party of the Soviet Union. In 1965, after driving Khrushchev out of power, a Soviet defense minister allegedly told a member of CCP delegation that "We've already got rid of Khrushchev; you ought to follow our example and get rid of Mao Zedong. That way we'll get on better." Knowing this, Mao greatly feared that he could end up like Stalin or Khrushchev, and increasingly perceived his fellow CCP leaders as potential enemies, whom he called the "revisionists" (*xiuzheng zhuyi zhe* 修正主義者), indicating the ones who take a different, or a "revisionist" path from the great leader.[27]

The Cultural Revolution practically started in May 1965, with the purge of the party first secretary and mayor of the capital Beijing, Peng Zhen 彭真 (1902-97). Many CCP leaders fell or were to fall: the then Chairman Liu Shaoqi 劉少奇 (1898-1969) in 1968; Vice Premier Deng Xiaoping 鄧小平 (1904-97); Vice Premier Tao Zhu 陶鑄 (1908-69); and Vice Chairman and Minister of National Defense Lin Biao 林彪 (1907-71), to name a few out of dozens. These leaders together with millions of people were publicly humiliated and beaten by the zealous devotees of Mao's mission. During the following ten years, labels like "feudal," "capitalist," or "revisionist" would grant the masses the license to dismiss the very existence of a person.[28] This existentially personal approach also found Confucius.

Confucius Could Be Anyone

Seemingly out of nowhere, Confucius came into the spotlight of the CCP propaganda again on August 7, 1973, the 7th year of the Cultural Revolution. He stayed there for a whole year, being disparaged on a very personal level, just as with the CCP leaders. More than just pejoratively historicizing him, the denouncements insisted that the phantom of this feudal villain was still among us. He could be the already demised Lin Biao, or anyone who dared to deviate from Mao's will. In this section, we will see how Mao's own anxiety propagated a specific image of Confucius, which in turn was used by his wife Jiang Qing 江青 (1914–91) and amplified through multiple mediums. While in line with the CCP tradition, this updated image of Confucius became both more cosmic and more villainous.

Mao's will and its amplifiers

By 1973, Mao had consolidated his absolute power inside and outside his political circle. In 1968, he had already purged his main political opponents, especially Liu Shaoqi. In 1971, his long-term protégé Lin Biao died in an air crash after allegedly attempting to have Mao assassinated. Thus, most of the leaders from the establishment of the PRC were ousted. Meanwhile, Mao's wife Jiang Qing 江青 (1914–91) filled the vacancy of power with her allies. Particularly in the ideological aspect, Mao was the absolute voice to be worshipped, and his messages would be delivered, amplified, or even distorted by Jiang's group, especially Yao Wenyuan 姚文元 (1931–2005), who oversaw the party propaganda. Thanks to the centralized system set up by the Cultural Revolution, Mao's messages would be univocally delivered to the ordinary households especially through radio and newspapers. An ordinary person in 1973 China could easily receive Mao's directives from *People's Daily*, from big-character posters (*dazi bao* 大字報) in their community, or the inescapable village broadcast.[29]

The criticism of Confucius originated from Mao's reading and thinking of the time. As an erudite reader, Mao frequently came back to traditional Chinese texts, especially dynastic history and Chinese philosophy. From August 1973 to July 1974, his reading list focused on the "reformers" in Chinese history, especially the *Book of Lord Shang* (*Shangjun shu* 商君書), *Han Feizi* 韓非子, and *Xunzi* 荀子. In Mao's view, the three texts from the Warring States period (476–221 BCE) represented the rising feudal society that evolved from a slave owning society. Categorizing them as "legalists" (*fajia* 法家), Mao believed that they were the progressive power in history and lumped in later historical figures like the First Emperor (259–210 BCE) and Wang Anshi 王安石 (1021–86), because of their radical reforms toward a centralized rule.[30] In this way, Mao transformed "legalists" from a generalized group to a cosmic force that generalized the positive, progressive force of history.

In Mao's opinion, the legalists met their enemies on the field of discourse: Confucius and his followers. On August 5, 1973, he wrote a poem for the Party intellectual Guo Moruo 郭沫若 (1892–1978):

> I hope you sir bash the First Emperor less; the incident of book burning and Confucian burying needs further discussion.
>
> The ancestral dragon [the First Emperor] might have died, but his undertaking is still here; the teaching of Confucius was reputable, but it indeed is rubbish.
>
> A hundred dynasties had practiced the Qin administration; the Ten Critiques are not good prose.
>
> Peruse the "Discussions of Feudalism" by the Tang people, but do not follow Zihou [Liu Zongyuan] to go back to [the time of] King Wen of Zhou.[31]

In a poetic form, Mao engages a debate with Guo, who wrote the *Ten Critiques* (*Shi pipan shu* 十批判書) in 1945.[32] He particularly disagrees with Guo's preference for Confucianism over Legalism and credits the First Emperor as a good practitioner of Legalism because of his accomplishments and legacy. At the end of the poem, he recommends to Guo the essay by the Tang dynasty literatus Liu Zongyuan 柳宗元 (773–819), the "Discussions of Feudalism." The essay argues that Zhou's enfeoffment system was institutionally flawed because it created states beyond the Zhou court's control. In contrast, it praises the First Emperor's centralized government as a better system. Using the essay to support his own vision, Mao hints that Confucianism was the reactionary power wishing to go back to the slave owning society of the Zhou dynasty. He thus warns Guo not to be on the wrong side of history.[33]

Mao's First Emperor and Confucius had contemporary reincarnations. On several occasions, he compared himself to the First Emperor, who started a new historical epoch. On the opposite side, he compared Confucius to the ones who were against him in the past, such as the GMD and especially Lin Biao.[34] Lin seems to be Mao's primary target in this narrative. Unlike the GMD, Lin used to be Mao's most trusted comrade and had played Mao's loyalist for years, including the famous brownnose: "Chairman Mao is a genius. Every single sentence of his is truth. One sentence of his is better than ten thousand of ours." Rising to be second to Mao in 1966, Lin officially became his successor in 1970. However, soon after this Lin sensed Mao's annoyance over his expansion of power and allegedly planned to assassinate Mao. Lin eventually died in an air crash, while fleeing from arrest following the failed assassination.[35] In Mao's eyes, his cosmic enemy could be among his closest alliances in disguise, and thus it was necessary to tell a cautionary tale of Confucius.

A Maoist Confucius

Mao's vision of Confucius was instantiated in front of the public in the newspaper *People's Daily* on August 7, 1973. Entitled "Confucius: The Thinker who Stubbornly Preserved Slavery" ("Kongzi: Wangu di weihu nulizhi de sixiangjia" 孔子——頑固地維護奴隸制的思想家), this biographical report uses the most common texts from traditional China to portray Confucius as the defender of slavery. It first describes Confucius' time as a transitional moment of history, where land ownership was transferred from the Zhou nobles to the individual landlords. When the Zhou nobles owned the land, they used their slaves as the labor, hence a slave-owning society. But once the land went into private hands, tenant farmers appeared, marking the rise of feudal society. Following the class theory framework, the report situates Confucius' background as a descendant of a decaying Shang dynasty slave-owning noble family.[36]

But did Confucius even mention the word "slave" in any way? The answer is no, but the report freely fills in the blanks with insertions of slavery. For example, *Xunzi* records Confucius' execution of Shaozheng Mao 少正卯 (?–500 BCE) with a list of accusations. The *People's Daily* report inserts slavery into these accusations:

二、不以奴隸制的正道而行,固執地走所謂革新之路的("行辟而堅")

Second, he does not practice the right way of slavery, and stubbornly takes the path to reforms ([*Xunzi*:] "He takes the deviant path and stick to it")

四、對奴隸制統治中所產生的一些腐朽不穩的現象,知道得非常之多的("記醜而博")

Fourth, he knows a lot about the decaying and shaky phenomena in the rule of slavery ([*Xunzi*:] "He remembers the ugly in erudition")

五、把反奴隸制的道理說得義正辭嚴似的("順非而澤")[37]

Fifth, he makes anti-slavery sound just and eloquent ([*Xunzi*:] "comply to the wrong things and justify them")

If we only read the original *Xunzi* text in the paratheses, it seems that the accusations are vaguely focused on the right verse the wrong way, through the words like "deviant," "ugly," and "wrong." The report then injects the word "slavery" into the Mandarin translation. Since most of Confucius' sayings in the received texts do not have a clear context, the report takes advantage of the vagueness and builds a concrete class-struggle framework around it.

Through this strategy of insertion, all of Confucius' behaviors became the testimony of his support for slavery. The morally advanced people, or the gentlemen (*junzi* 君子) become the slave-owning nobles, and the morally inferior, petty people (*xiaoren* 小人) become the slaves. Confucius' teachings on humanity, reciprocity, and filial piety unite the slave owners, while ideologically shackling the slaves. Everything he did, he did out of class struggle. For example, the report denounces his statement "The humane loves the others" (*renzhe ai ren* 仁者愛人) as "lying shenanigan" (*pianren de guihua* 騙人的鬼話) because Confucius did not mean to love everyone, but only the slave-owning class. With disparaging slurs like this, a sense of deceptiveness was also added to the image of Confucius.[38]

In this cruel world of class struggle, anyone Confucius was against was put on the right side of history. In the original *Xunzi* text, Shaozheng Mao only appears in the accusations of Confucius without any mention of his background. In the *People's Daily* report, he morphs into a reformer who formed a school of students in opposition to Confucius' teaching. Similarly, in the *Analects*, Confucius dismissed one of his disciples as a petty person because the disciple wanted to learn about agriculture. The *People's Daily* report interprets it as Confucius' contempt for manual work and by extension the working masses, who are the real force of history in Marxism. Confucius' choice of enemy demonstrates that he was on the opposite side of the masses and thus the progression of history.

We can easily imagine that such a polarizing piece came from none other than a propaganda department of the CCP in order to cater to Mao's agenda. But that is not the case. The report was written by a professor at Sun Yat-Sen University, Yang Rongguo 楊榮國 (1907–78), who had been sidelined and publicly humiliated during the Cultural Revolution. Influenced by the May Fourth and Communist movements, Yang was committed to Marxist historiography and applied it to early Chinese thought. We can already see this radical view of Confucius and traditional China in his book *The Thought of Confucius and Mozi* (*Kong Mo de sixiang* 孔墨的思想) in 1946 and more elaborately in *Intellectual History of Ancient China* (*Zhongguo gudai sixiang shi* 中國古代思想史) in 1954. Yang was one of the long-time Marxist historians before the PRC was established.[39]

Mao found his intellectual embodiment in Yang. As early as 1966, he mentioned Yang's name together with *Intellectual History of Ancient China* to his party leader colleagues.[40] Perhaps because of this, Yang was approached in 1972 to compile a textbook to help the worker-peasant-soldier students understand basic concepts in philosophy.[41] This was a significant shift. At the height of the Cultural Revolution, intellectuals like Yang had been re-educated, if not beaten up by the masses. Eventually, Yang received a secret invitation to write about Confucius from the *People's Daily* in mid-1973. Without any notice, his report suddenly appeared on August 7's *People's Daily*, the most popular and ideologically sanctioned newspaper during Mao's China. A few days before the publication, Mao read the draft of Yang' report and wrote: "Yang's essay is very good" (*Yang wen po hao* 楊文頗好).⁴²

Confucius is among us

Besides Mao and Yang, Jiang Qing and her allies also needed this image of Confucius, but for different reasons. While Mao intended to link Confucius to Lin Biao to make a statement about recent history, Jiang wanted to go further to link him to the current party leaders, so that she could replace them with her clique to expand her power in the CCP. Jiang reinvented herself from an actress and Mao's wife to a political player in 1966, when she was appointed as the vice head of the Central Cultural Revolution Group. This position granted her substantial power to sanction any artistic and cultural aspect of the PRC, but also to prosecute her political opponents. Being an outsider for so long, Jiang had to rely on Mao's authority, but now she could legitimately wield her own institutional power. In this case, her strategy was to develop Mao's visions into a movement.

The publication of Yang's report was thus an opportunity for Jiang. Receiving Mao's approval, Jiang and her allies formed a group in October 1973 at the two most prestigious universities in China, Tsinghua University and Peking University. Pen named as Liangxiao 梁效 (homophonic to "two schools" or *liangxiao* 兩校), this group's primary mission was to create a more specific link between the evil Confucius and Lin Biao. The members of the group, including established scholars like the historian Zhou Yiliang 周一良 (1913–2001) and intellectual historian Tang Yijie 湯一介, examined Lin Biao's residence, then already under police quarantine. They not only scrutinized Lin and his wife's personal items, but also screened every comment and note of Lin's in his collection of traditional Chinese texts to find any evidence of Lin praising Confucius.⁴³

For better or worse, the group members' academic training paid off. Inside a porcelain vessel at Lin Biao's residence, they found a piece of Lin's calligraphy:

悠悠萬事,唯此為大:克己復禮。
　　Among myriad things, this is the biggest issue: overcome oneself and return to ritual.⁴⁴

The group immediately identified that the last four characters were one of the most famous sayings from the *Analects*.⁴⁵ They further applied a reading from Yang Rongguo's report from two months previous: returning to ritual means going back to the Zhou dynasty's ritual, which is a slavery system. According to Yang, Confucius expressed his longing for restoration (*fubi* 復辟) of the slave-owning society. In parallel to Confucius, the group then accused Lin of longing for the restoration of capitalism. In the CCP language, "restoration" was a grievous accusation as it was in the opposition to the CCP's path. And it fit with Lin's attempted assassination of the leader of the CCP, Mao. Centered on the idea of restoration, the group compiled a collection of Lin's quotes from Confucius, *Lin Biao and the Way of Confucius and Mencius* (*Lin Biao yu Kong Meng zhi dao* 林彪與孔孟之道) in December of 1973. After Mao's approval of the collection, the movement of Criticizing Lin and Confucius became official.⁴⁶

In late 1973, Confucius became the most hated historical figure in CCP media. By the end of the year, the hatred was still concentrated on him, including the "Biography of Confucius" ("Kongzi zhuan" 孔子傳, October 16, 1973), "Right Leaning Opportunism and Confucian Thought" (November 22, 1973), and the eminent philosopher Feng Youlan's 馮友蘭 (1895–1990) two articles: "Criticism on Confucius and Self-Criticism on my Confucian Worship in the Past" (December 3, 1973) as well as "Restoration of the Past and Anti-Restoration of the Past Is the Struggles of Two Path" (December 4, 1973). Confucius found his contemporary worshipper in Lin Biao: "Confucius Wanted to 'Return to Ritual; Lin Biao Wanted to Restore'" (January 28, 1974), the news report version of "Lin Biao and the Way of Confucius and Mencius" (February 7, 1974), and "Both Confucius and Lin Biao Are Political Frauds" (March 11, 1974).⁴⁷

Jiang assumed the central role in the Criticizing Lin and Confucius movement. From the first meeting with the CCP leaders in January 1974, she was committed to making this into a nation-wide movement. Using Lin Biao, she and her allies smeared current leaders by associating them with Confucius; according to them, the CCP always had reincarnations of Confucius in their ranks who secretively sabotaged its progressive agenda.⁴⁸ A few months later, Jiang raised the alarm that these reincarnations were back among them:

> There is a problem in these essays: rarely do they mention the contemporary Confucians. Currently in the Criticizing Lin and Confucius, no contemporary Confucian is mentioned except for Lin [Biao] and Chen [Boda] … The struggle between Confucians and Legalists has gone through Chinese history: there must be Confucians in the past, later, and now. Otherwise, why do we criticize Lin and Confucius?⁴⁹

If "in the past" and "later" refer to Confucius and Lin, respectively, "now" refers to the disguised ones in the CCP. Jiang and her allies ordered the Liangxiao writing group to dog whistle Zhou Enlai and the then vice CCP Chairman Li Desheng 李德生 (1916–2011) in their essays.[50] She needed Confucius' thought to be alive so that she could knock down the party leaders.

Villain as the Hero

By "movement," Jiang meant a social movement that included every single part of society, especially the media. Comic books, or more literally, the "Linked Pictures" (*lianhuanhua* 連環畫) were channeled to spread the propaganda. Since Republican China, comic books were a popular media for storytelling and political satire. Due to their popularity, they were especially favored by the CCP as a vehicle to spread their mission. After the founding of the PRC, they served a political agenda as well as artistic expression and entertainment. But since the dawn of the Cultural Revolution in 1966, the comic book as an art form was accused of bourgeoisie taste, and many of its creators were sidelined. In 1971 with Zhou Enlai's approval, a few new comic books were published to "solve the problem of the spiritual nutrition of the next generation" (*jiejue xiayidai de jingshen shiliang wenti* 解決下一代的精神食糧問題).[51] Thus the creation of comic books was resurrected, but even more heavily sanctioned and politicized.

When the Criticism of Confucius and Lin Biao started, comic books had to join. This is not only because the art form had long been used to convey political messages to especially the youth, it was also because they were sidelined during the Cultural Revolution, and the comic book artists needed to redeem themselves from their bourgeoisie sin. Therefore, around a dozen comic books on Confucius and Lin were published from 1974 to 1976. In this section, we will focus on one particular book the *Sinful Life of Kong the Second* (*Kong lao'er zui'e de yisheng* 孔老二罪惡的一生) to see how the creators walked a fine line between artistic expression and politics.

The right way to draw

By 1974, comic books in China had an established stylistic convention. Instead of several images per page as in American comic books or Japanese manga, comic books in China had one image per page, ranging from thirty up to 200 per book. The images were printed on 5.4" × 3.9" paper, with landscape binding, rendering a landscape view. Under the images were the captions that introduced the relevant plot as well as the dialogue of the characters, without any dialogue bubbles inside the images. Each caption contained two to four lines in a language that was comprehensible to teenagers with some schooling, with occasional denotations of words and explanations of expressions.[52] In many ways, the format resembles a well-made storyboard of a movie.

At the time, the contents of the comic books were as formulaic. Under heavy sanction, only a few themes could be published: the eight model operas (*yangban xi* 樣板戲) initiated by Jiang Qing; lives of representative red guards, sent-down youth, factory workers, and soldiers; stories of heroes who contributed to the cause of progressive revolution, both historical and contemporary, Chinese and foreign; and traditional Chinese stories, such as parts from the *Romance of the Three Kingdoms* and *Journey to the West*.[53] In the production process, these stories were first approved by the party committee secretary of the press and assigned to specific authors as a working group. Members of the working group, especially the text editor, then would create a script that had to faithfully follow the original stories, not only in terms of the politics, but also the storyline. Centered on the script, the artists then created the characters, their actions, and scenes that could best illustrate the plot. In the 1970s, the group members also include laymen from the good classes (e.g., farmer or worker family), or young farmers and factory workers who did not have much experiences in the trade. The involvement of the party, artists, and the youth from the good classes, or the Unity of Three (*san jiehe* 三結合) was a common practice in the arts then to maintain the ideological correctness of a work.[54]

The images of the comic books also had guidelines to follow. First, in any visual representation, the good characters need to be emphasized; among the good characters, heroes need to be further emphasized; among the heroes, the central ones need to be further emphasized. This visual hierarchy, or Three Prominent (*san tuchu* 三突出) makes central roles always be in the visual center. Second, and artistically speaking, the main characters need to appear to be strong and healthy, or "flushed" (*hong* 紅); rendered in realistic but neat style, or "smooth" (*guang* 光); and in light shading, or "bright" (*liang* 亮). Third, the main characters need to be portrayed as tall (*gao* 高), big (*da* 大), and with all the good virtues (*quan* 全).[55]

Imagine an art work under these mantras. The main characters have to be in the center of the stage all the time with most of the lighting. Their heights need to be arranged hierarchically from the center to the side, always looking strong and healthy. The other characters, especially the villains, share the peripherial and darker side of the stage. Worst of all, because the main heroes need to be comprehensively virtuous, they have to look confident and positive, fully aware of their enemies' plots from the very beginning. This omnipotent setup of the heroes not only leaves little room for their character growth, but also deprives the drama of conflicts, where the villains shrink into an inconvenient obstacle at the dark corner of the stage. The mantras thus pivoted the story-telling toward a mass production of formulaic heroes.

Villain as the hero?

When the comic book authors and artists were told to join the Criticizing Lin and Confucius movement, they were faced with a dilemma: how to portray a villain as the main character of a comic book. They would undoubtedly be accused of being anti-revolutionary if they treated Confucius as the main hero of the comic book, or even just visually focused on him. But if not, the book would not really be about him either. Breaking the current rules and creating new ones was extremely dicey because artistic styles were politicized, and any deviation from the norm could lead to trouble. Avoiding the topic would also not be an option; it would be seen as a refusal to participate in this movement, adding to the already perilous status of the authors as cultural workers.

Dancing with shackles, the comic artists came up with a few strategies to solve the dilemma. The most aesthetically fitting way of the time was to write a comic book where Confucius was the primary villain. In this strategy, the most challenging part was finding a politically correct hero, as most of the notable historical figures around Confucius were from his social class too. Luckily, one figure passed layers of sanction: the legendary robber Liuxia Zhi 柳下跖, who, according to the stories in *Zhuangzi*, had a debate with Confucius.[56] Under the reframing of the *People's Daily*, he became a rebel leader of the people, capable of shaming Confucius. Thus, a few comic titles were created, centering on the theme of the robber "stoutly scolding" (*tongchi* 痛斥 or *tongma* 痛罵) Confucius.[57] A similar strategy was to focused on the people who were against anything Confucian. This was the most convenient one because any peasant movements in imperial China could be conceived as some type of working people rebelling against a Confucian institution. As a result, the "Battles against Confucius" (*fanKong douzheng* 反孔鬥爭) was the most prolific series as the party media continued perpetuating the theme.[58] Although this strategy could not fully focus on Confucius, it could carry out the anti-Confucius sentiment and his teleological reincarnation Lin Biao.

A riskier strategy is to directly focus on the life of Confucius, but this is also a more rewarding one. One advantage is that it fully matched the reading habits of the comic book readers of the time, who were used to following one particular hero's journey. And Confucius' life was much richer than the scarce mentioning of Liuxia Zhi to flesh out the pages. Since for the CCP, the purpose of comic books was to educate the masses, directly revealing the evil deeds of Confucius could be more instructive. A less obvious, but important, advantage for the time was that focusing on one single historical figure could avoid unnecessarily mentioning other names, historical or contemporary. Since the beginning of the Cultural Revolution, commenting on any figure could be seen as innuendoes toward the ones in power. Therefore, the more to the point the better.[59]

The comic artists Gu Bingxin 顧炳鑫 (1923–2001) and He Youzhi 賀友直 (1922–2016) chose this route. By 1974, their accomplishments certainly made them comfortable enough to take on the challenge. From the 1950s onwards, Gu was one of the most eminent comic book artists, creating the comic version of the most popular and ideologically correct works like *Red Crag* (*Hongyan* 紅岩), *The Red Guards on Honghu Lake* (*Honghu chiweidui* 洪湖赤衛隊) and *Lenin in 1918* (*Liening zai yijiuyiba* 列寧在一九一八). He was the winner of the first comic book award (1963) in the PRC. The winning work was the comic version of the monumental *Great Changes of the Mountainous Village* (*Shanxiang jubian* 山鄉巨變), a novel that vividly depicted how the party members established the socialist commune and encountered local pushback in a small village. He also created the comic version of other officially promoted titles such as *Li Shuangshuang* 李雙雙 and the *Wedding of Xiao'erhei* (*Xiao'erhei jiehun* 小二黑結婚).[60] Both artists were experienced in the industry and possessed political sensitivity.

Gu and He's first challenge was the creation of the text, which needed to be both artistically engaging and politically sanctioned. This was not easy because it was too dangerous for them to create a text just based on Confucius' life as drawn from traditional Chinese texts. Meanwhile, most of the articles criticizing Confucius such as Yang Rongguo's report were more focused on Confucius' thought instead of his life, which was less suitable for creating a plot. Fortunately, an article outside Beijing emerged as a good candidate in October 1973. Titled the "Biography of Confucius" ("Kongzi zhuan"), this article was published in the Shanghai-based *Study and Criticism* (*Xuexi yu pipan* 學習與批判), a newly established journal supported by Jiang Qing's ally Zhang Chunqiao 張春橋 (1917–2005). The establishment of the journal was very much aimed to initiate Jiang and Zhang's visions of political movements in the central government, especially Mao's criticism of Confucius.[61] Politically, the article was safe.

Telling a bad story of Confucius

Gu and He then turned "Biography of Confucius" into a comic script with the seasoned word editor Gan Liyue 甘禮樂 (1923–?). In line with the article, a core conflict dictates the storyline of the comic: Confucius was born to restore the slavery of the Zhou dynasty, but despite his strong will, he kept failing until his death. Accordingly, Confucius' story starts with young Confucius' longing to learn the rituals of the Zhou and wanting to join the noble class of his time, especially in his native state, the State of Lu. After being frequently rejected, he finally caught a break after the age of fifty, becoming a prime minister (*zaixiang* 宰相) of the State of Lu. As a restorationist would do, he suppressed all the progressions, including slaughtering the reformer Shaozheng Mao. Offending the progressive nobles, Confucius and his disciples were forced to bound from state to state, constantly rejected by the ruling class and humiliated by the working people. After returning to the state of Lu at the age of 68, he realized that his political career had ended, so he focused on teaching and writing the reactionary work *Spring and Autumn* (*Chunqiu* 春秋). On a sunny day in spring of 479 BCE, he died in disgrace with his "marbly stubborn head."[62]

This fatalist portrait fully took advantage of the same image of Confucius in the *Records of the Grand Historian*. In Chapter 1, we have already seen that the Han dynasty literati had conceded that Confucius had not achieved success in his life. But seeing him as a sage, they needed to explain away his failure. Gu and He reenforced such a theme in the framework of the party line. They included the moment of Confucius being called a "homeless dog" in the *Records of the Grand Historian*.[63] Following the original narrative of the text, they emphasized the moment of his wandering life with his disciples. They further picked up the connotation of "dog" (*gou* 狗) as a curse word in Mandarin and turned the name into working people's contempt and disparagement of Confucius, as if they had all seen through him as a failure. The comic book authors clarified in the caption, as admitted by Confucius himself, he "is like a homeless dog, which nobody cares about."[64]

Following contemporary propaganda, Gu and He went beyond the scope of the *Records of the Grand Historian*, both textually and ideologically. For example, they included a story where Confucius disapproved of the State of Jin making a tripod with their penal codes on it. They further illustrated the reason with Confucius' own words: "Punishments do not go up to the gentlemen, and rites do not go down to the ordinary people. Now as the State of Jin is molding the tripod, will this not this blur the boundary between the noble and the petty?"[65]

Focusing on the defense of the nobles, Gu and He adopted the slavery society narrative that was absent in the source of this story, the *Zuo Commentary on the Spring and Autumn Annals* (*Chunqiu Zuozhuan* 春秋左傳) from approximately the third century BCE.⁶⁶ Like the Shaozheng Mao story from *Xunzi*, the comic book authors stuck to an assortment of the well-recognized classical texts from early China, but retold the stories from a Maoist perspective.

To avoid accidentally creating a hero with a tragic fate, the comic book gets personal to cast Confucius as sinister and deceptive. Piecing together different scenes in the *Analects* and the *Records*, it tells us that once the young Confucius was once denied entrance to the noble family of Ji by their subject Yanghu 陽虎. Holding a grudge, he refused to meet with Yanghu later in his life. However, he accepted Yanghu's gift and chose a time to visit Yanghu when he was not home. In retelling this encounter, the comic book portrays him not only as greedy, but also hypocritical: he pretended to play nice with Yanghu because of the latter's gift. If Confucius consistently applied his "reactionary" vision, people could still respect or even admire his persistence. But the addition of hypocrisy further tarnished Confucius and muddled up his moral position in general: he was not who he claimed to be.

If one still did not get the message from all of the above, a euphemism for penis would help. The most obviously disparaging wording in the comic book is the reference to Confucius in the tile: Kong, the Second (Kong lao'er). In the *Analects*, Confucius was referred to as "master" (*zi* 子), an honorific term for teachers and the elderly in Classical Chinese. Since then, the term Master Kong (Kongzi 孔子, or Kongfuzi 孔夫子) has been the most common reference to Confucius until this very day. He was referred to by his first name Qiu 丘 or full name Kong Qiu when criticized, because it was considered offensive to refer to someone by their first name in traditional China.⁶⁷ As early as 1919, some republican scholars started referring to him by the sibling lineup as Kong the Second (Kong'er 孔二), further stripping his individuality.⁶⁸ The adaptation from *er* to *lao'er* since the beginning of the PRC added not only a sense of up-to-date colloquialism.⁶⁹ The word *lao'er* in northern Chinese dialects was also a euphemism for "penis." The comic book adoption of the name very much dog-whistled this pejorative sentiment to its readers.

How to visualize the villain Confucius

After finalizing the text, Gu and He were faced with the challenge of visually depicting Confucius. They needed to put Confucius on most of the pages to make a comic about him, but they could not present him in any way that was even remotely positive. In fact, Gu and He had never done such task. But as experienced artists, they developed a system to do so, some of which came from other artistic genres.

On the composition level, Gu and He cut part of Confucius' body out of the frame. Especially in a talking scene, they placed Confucius at the boundary of the frame, so that only part of his body could be in the frame. They intentionally left out either the top of the head, or from half of the chest down. Because like most audiences, the readers of the comic books were used to close-ups or bust portraits, these cuts could create an unnatural and interruptive feeling. They then left a large blank space in the center of the frame. In this way, Confucius would not appear in the center of the frame, as the Cultural Revolution aesthetics demanded, but could still be the focus of the readers, since nothing else was in the frame.[70]

A comic book certainly cannot afford to have too much blank space; Gu and He designed specific body gestures when they had to put Confucius in the center. In the book, Confucius is commonly in a bowing position, when he participates in rituals or interacts with the feudal lords. This body gesture suggests his submission to the reactionary tradition of his time.[71] When he teaches his students or advises the lords, he usually is in a seated position. Gu and He often added furniture to block part of his body or have a zoomed-out view to avoid fully recognizing Confucius' body.[72] When Confucius is traveling or interacting with the working people, Confucius is mostly in a crawling position, signaling that he is always fleeing (Fig. 3a).[73] The only occasion of a fully upright pose is from the back, showing that Confucius is being rejected or chased after.[74] In other words, not a single frame shows Confucius' full, frontal, upright look in the comic book, which was only reserved for the positive characters, such as the working people.

Gu and He's approach to Confucius as a villain was well-attested in other forms of art during the time. The actor of revolutionary operas Zhuge Ming 諸葛明 generalized a mantra for playing villains: conceding (*rang* 讓), hiding (*duo* 躲), receiving (*ying* 迎), shortening (*ai* 矮), and turning back (*bei* 背). That is to say, the villains on stage needs to concede the center of the stage to the protagonists, and they need to further hide their body. They would only come to the front to receive an action from the protagonists. Figure-wise, they also need to stand shorter than the main characters and turn their back to the audience.[75] Very much in line with this mantra, Gu and He's Confucius always hides from the center of focus and never stands straight.

Figure 3 Portraits of Kong Lao'er 孔老二 (a. bodily gesture, b. facial details, c. fingernail details, d. facial hair details). Redrawn by Sarah E. Brooker.

Gu and He also took advantage from the different perspectives that paintings could take. For example, in showing the pettiness of Confucius, the comic book takes a distant top view on Confucius and his disciple, so that the two figures look almost like two unrecognizable dots.[76] When Confucius encounters the working-class people, the book switches to an upward view from Confucius' perspective. In this way, the working-class people become much larger than Confucius.[77] Through the change of perspectives, Confucius is always shorter and smaller than the working-class people, even though he was allegedly taller than the majority of his contemporaries based on the *Records of the Grand Historian*.[78]

When it comes to character design, Gu and He stuck to a sense of deterioration for Confucius, symbolizing his social class. Signifying Confucius' literati origin, they dressed him with a Han dynasty style robe with long, broad sleeves, which was a conventional attire design in Chinese-history-themed comic books. Nevertheless, they made the robe too big for Confucius' figure. Therefore, with his crawling position, a bloated looking Confucius is lost in a sea of cloth, covering his whole body.[79] This differs from the positive literati figure such as Shaozheng Mao, whose robe fits his figure. It is especially in contrast with the working-class people's attire, which has short sleeves and tied pants. Confucius' attire not only hints that he could not practically engage in any physical labor, but also tells the readers that he could not put himself together.

The sense of deterioration goes to Confucius' finger nails and beard as well. Paintings from imperial China had already captured the literati's visibly long finger nails. When the missionaries and journalists from Europe and the United States saw it, long finger nails also became part of the exotic and oriental image of the Qing Chinese. Subsequentially, both the GMD government and later the PRC further promoted short finger nails as part of modern hygiene.[80] Confucius' longer finger nails then reminded their readers of China's imperial and backward past. Following this tradition, Gu and He gave Confucius a mustache and beard, common to traditional Chinese men, literati or not. But they depicted them as untrimmed together with his loosely tied hair (Fig. 3c, 3d).[81] In this way, Confucius looks dirty, as if his life is too rough to put himself together.

Confucius' dirty, disorganized appearance is very much in contrast with the working-class people in the comic books. In line with the Cultural Revolution aesthetics, most of the working-class people are free from facial hair, giving a neat and young look. They also univocally have short finger nails with visible muscles showing from short sleeves and vests.[82] These features demonstrate their engagement in physical labor. Meanwhile, the attire of the working-class people is never torn or covered with spots of mud. In this way, Gu and He presented the working-class people as clean and healthy as opposed to the dirty, crooked Confucius.

Gu and He further used prompts to create a sense of bad hygiene for Confucius. They often depicted him sitting on a mat with edges torn.[83] In a scene where Confucius is gifted with a carp from a feudal lord, they depicted the fish with flies around it, signifying its rottenness.[84] To further indicate Confucius' poverty, they added a spiderweb half the size of the frame in a scene where Confucius taught his student.[85] The spiderweb reminds the readers how much his living space is unclean and scarce of visitors. Such design was particularly in line with Gu's preference to use "small prompts" (*xiao daoju* 小道具) to create a particular mood.[86] Here the torn mat, smelly fish, and spiderweb all contribute to a sense of deterioration and filth.

Besides an atmosphere of decay, Gu and He also assigned different emotional tones to Confucius and his enemy. They adopted a "八" shaped eyebrow for Confucius, which often signals sadness and pathos in comics in general (Fig. 3b). In this way, Confucius gains a sad and defeated undertone throughout the book. The combination of the eyebrow shape with smile in turns creates a sinister joy. Gu and He particularly deployed this combination when Confucius felt satisfied or was plotting against others.[87] In contrast, the reformers, revolutionaries, and working-class people have the upside down "八" shaped eyebrows, representing the emotion of anger. In the comic book, these people certainly have reasons to be angry; they are oppressed by the very system that Confucius represents. By pairing these emotions, the two authors told their audience what to feel about Confucius.[88]

Through Gu and He's design, Confucius as a reactionary looks decisively different from the working-class people and reformers. He is physically weak, short, dirty, and always hiding in the dark alone with his sinister schemes. The working-class people are physically tall and strong, often appearing outraged in a group. They are the angry masses. On the one hand, Gu and He adopted the style from the PRC propaganda posters in 1960s and 1970s, where the revolutionaries always appeared to be healthy and robust.[89] On the other hand, the two artists still tried to maintain a realistic style through the story line without too much caricaturing. And in the main body of the comic book, there is no revolutionary-poster style interruption like other comic books, such as giant soldiers stepping on Confucius or pens from the sky stabbing his back.[90]

Concluding Remarks

Was it worth it to propagate such a sinister image of Confucius? Or more specifically, how did the creation of this image achieve the goals of certain individuals or groups? We can focus on the following: 1. Mao as the initiator; 2. Jiang Qing and her alliance as the propagator; 3. Yang Rongguo as an apparatus; 4. Gu and He as the comic book artists; and 5. the trickiest, the reception of the comic book and of the feudal Confucius.

As the initiator of the movement, Mao achieved his goal, if his goal was to gravely stigmatize Lin Biao. Since Lin's death in 1971, the party leaders categorized his behaviors as anti-revolutionary, a capital crime for CCP members. But it was not until the end of August in 1973 that the national newspapers started publicizing his crimes. The almost two-year pause provided a buffer for the public to emotionally distance themselves from the once close friend of the Great Leader. Then by linking Lin with this sinisterness of Confucius, no one seemed to question Mao's judgment in putting Lin into such a high position in the first place. After Mao's death, Lin was continuously being criticized and became a main scapegoat for the problems of the Cultural Revolution.[91]

Jiang Qing and her alliance barely accomplished their goal of overthrowing their enemies. Since the beginning of the Criticizing Lin and Confucius movement, Jiang was more than eager to make it a full-scale political movement, targeting senior CCP leaders, especially Zhou Enlai in 1974 and Deng Xiaoping in 1975. Zhou did receive pressure and was forced to make public self-criticism, but nothing worse. In fact, Mao put Jiang on a rather short leash and became upset with her usurping his authority during this movement.[92] Therefore, Jiang did create pressure to the senior officials through the movement, but she could not expand her power in the political center.

As a dedicated Marxist historian, Yang made his views well-known nationwide in 1974. After the *People's Daily* report, he turned from a beaten-down intellectual to a hot-shot theorist: he was frequently invited to give lectures by provincial officials and started working together with Jiang's Liangxiao group. After the arrest of Jiang and her allies in 1976, Yang was sidelined again, suspected of collaborating with Jiang and her closest allies, vilified after Mao's death as the "Gang of Four" (*Siren bang* 四人幫). Moreover, his national fame then turned into national disgrace; provincial newspapers criticized him as a watch dog of the Gang of Four, and when he was ill, he was denied hospitalization because he was accused of being anti-Zhou Enlai, an early communist hero who came to represent CCP purity following his death in 1976. Even when these accusations were officially dismissed, most people still cut ties with him. He died in 1978 with only his eldest daughter at his side.[93]

Gu and He fairly achieved their goal, if their goal was trying to ride out the political tides. By submitting the comic book, they did their duty for the movement. With the help of the editor, the contents of the book were almost completely focused on Confucius, without mentioning any contemporary political figures, including even Lin Biao. The sheer focus on history saved them from further political retribution when the Gang of Four fell. Meanwhile, the comic book could not represent the best quality of their works, even though 2.5 million copies were printed. Both authors shunned their usual style in order to stick to the Cultural Revolution standards; in comparison with their previous works, *Confucius the Second* looks especially rushed, lacking details in the characters and backgrounds. Later in both authors' memoirs and other written works, this work is never mentioned other than on their publication list. After serving its political goal, the two authors seemed to want this work to slip into obscurity.

Last, how did the public receive this feudal Confucius? It ironically rekindled people's interest in his teaching, negatively or positively. Up to the 1970s, the public was no longer familiar with Confucius and the literati training in imperial China as a long-term result from the new school system since Republican

China. The Socialist reforms further threw Confucius, together with traditional Chinese culture, into obscurity. Thus, it is particularly ironic that, the Criticizing Lin and Confucius movement informed the public on the teaching of Confucius and charged it with strong emotions.[94] Through the movement, Confucius returned to a paramount position in the eyes of the public, even though this time as the prince of crime. After the Cultural Revolution, many mainland Chinese and even the state felt the need to reconcile the role Confucius played both in the Chinese past and present. This charged attention kept him alive and thriving in the twenty-first century, the topic of the next chapter.

6

Confucius as Cute

On January 24, 2017, I was greeted by two Confuciuses in front of the Confucius Temple in Taipei. More precisely, they were two Hobbit-sized statues of Confucius, but I was rather certain that they were greeting me, as one of them had its right arm up waving at me, and the other was winking at me. It was unconventional, to say the least, to have Confucius greet visitors outside the Temple; usually he stayed in the main hall, waiting to be greeted with a bow. The unconventional feeling also came from the size and proportion of the statues: they were around one meter tall, and their heads made up more than one third of their body. On their bulbous heads were simply dots and lines to indicate eyes. "Kawaii," I thought.

I found more of the statues as I walked into the Confucius Temple. Some of them lined up to greet and guide the visitors; others popped up here and there like garden gnomes. They attracted much attention from the visitors because their perky white and blue colors contrasted with the more solemn crimson pillars, orange tiles, and brownish clay pathways of the temple. The cartoonish style seemed to clash with the classical aesthetic; for a moment, it was hard to tell whether the visitors or these toy models were more intrusive. I could not help but think the contrast was weird.

This sense of weirdness did not come from the unexpected contrasting aesthetics alone. Instead, the contrast highlighted another counterintuitive factor: cute is weird. Physically speaking, cuteness is often associated with infantile traits, such as small size, large eyes, a small nose, big forehead, and stubby limbs.[1] If we consider weirdness as a deviation from a norm, cuteness is, by definition, weird, because it emerges from deviations from an adult's physical body, a normative comparison point for most of human history. The Confucius Temple and its larger-than-life stone statues of Confucius primed me to expect a specific norm, which then highlighted the weirdness of these garden-gnome-like, kawaii Confuciuses.

In this chapter, we will make sense of this cute presentation of Confucius, or Hello Kongzi, as it was formally named by its designer, Broad Link Cultural & Creative. To better capture the outlandish feeling sparked by Hello Kongzi, we start with his origin story and his creator's inspirations. Next, we dig into contemporary theories of cuteness to contextualize the design. Then, we survey Broad Link Cultural & Creative's campaigns with Hello Kongzi from 2014 to 2017 to understand how they used this image in practice to achieve their goals. Lastly, contextualizing the campaigns in twenty-first-century consumerism and social media, we will discuss the intended and unintended implications and consequences of this rendering. As Broad Link would discover, their uncanny, cute Confucius would have to choose between being a forever impish rebel or an affable, yet forgettable, uncle.

Making Confucius Cute

On May 15, 2015, a Shenzhen-based company called Broad Link Group launched a campaign to promote traditional Chinese culture.[2] Dubbing the campaign "Cultural rebuild" (*wenhua zaizao* 文化再造), the company sought to promote traditional Chinese culture in a way that could attract children and young people. Meanwhile, they also hoped that the promotion could go beyond China to reach the rest of the world, bringing traditional Chinese culture to a broader world stage. During the launch banquet, the company also pledged to donate 25.66 million RMB to the Shenzhen Charity Federation (Shenzhenshi Cishan Hui 深圳市慈善會), where the number "2566" symbolized the 2,566th birthday of Confucius in 2014.[3] With the donation, Broad Link Group unambivalently presented the campaign as an education and charity program.

In 2014, it was not an odd move for a company to invest in education, nor even for one to invest specifically in traditional Chinese learning. Since the 1990s, many private education companies had emerged and thrived thanks to changes in national education policies.[4] Entering the 2000s, traditional Chinese learning experienced the converse of its suppression during the Cultural Revolution: not only did the public become increasingly receptive to it as part of education, private and public education programs also provided courses, certificates, and even majors on the topic. Occasionally, even the government flirted with traditional Chinese culture, particularly as represented by Confucius.[5] This fever for traditional Chinese learning was attractive to Broad Link Group as a consumer trend, not only because of the potential profit to be made, but also the cultural prestige to be held.

Nevertheless, Broad Link Group's approach was odd, or innovative. They created a new image of Confucius distinct from all previous ones: a Confucius with the height and body proportions of a child. Dubbed "Hello Kongzi," this Confucius' head is oval in shape, wider than his shoulders, and occupying one-third of his overall height. On his bulbous head, a black dot or a curve impressionistically symbolizes an open eye or a wink. Above and below the eyes are white, cloud-shaped convex eyebrows and a mustache, respectively. Right under the mustache continues a similarly white and curved beard, extending to the feet and covering almost the whole front of the body. Above the eyebrows is a shock of white hair tied in a bun with a writing brush stuck through it. On either side of the head, there are two semicircle-shaped ears, but a nose and mouth are absent from Hello Kongzi's face. The rest of the body is covered in a blue robe with broad sleeves with only the hands left visible. And the hands do not have fingers, only fist-like balls poke out of the sleeves.[6] Indeed, curves build this Confucius.

Why would Confucius be depicted as a handless garden gnome with an American football for a head? The answer is that it is intuitively pleasing, or more precisely, the specific proportions of Hello Kongzi do not remind us so much of fantastical creatures with missing appendages as they do small children or animals. In 1943, the zoologist Konrad Lorenz suggested that the physical features of small children, especially the "relatively large head," "bulging cheek region," "large and low-lying eyes," "short and thick extremities" provoke our affective feelings of parental care.[7] Hello Kongzi's oval face, disproportionally large head, and short limbs match Lorenz's description of "baby schema" (*kindchenschema*), which now we refer to as "cute."[8]

Many features of Hello Kongzi do find precedents in traditional portraits of Confucius. Since the seventh century CE, Confucius has been depicted with long eyebrows, Fu Manchu mustache, a full beard, or a soul patch. In most portraits, he also appeared with a widow's peak, with his hair tied and covered by a cloth cap. The lush facial hair implied seniority and thus wisdom. Meanwhile, as a widow's peak is most common among teenagers and men in their twenties, it rendered him robust. Hello Kongzi adopts this hair imagery and amplifies it to the extent that hair covers his mouth and half of his face. Hello Kongzi also draws on traditional portraits of Confucius, where he almost aways had a wide face, a bulging forehead, and large ears with ample earlobes. In fact, the portrait attributed to Ma Yuan 馬遠 (1160–1225) portrays a forehead so bulbous that his head resembles an up-side-down gourd.[9] Hello Kongzi further blows up the proportion of the head and ears to resemble an infant.

In concocting this design, Broad Link Group followed a tried-and-true trajectory for children's pop culture characters, in which they go through infantile metamorphoses to be more relatable. For example, in the past seventy years, the cartoon character Mickey Mouse's head, cranium, and eye size have substantially increased, making him look more and more juvenile. Teddy bears have gone through a similar shift in the twentieth century.[10] With this "progressive juvenilization," the two characters reached higher and more global popularity.[11] We can see Hello Kongzi as part of the same process in the context of more traditional portraits, especially when in the second decade of the twenty-first century, most Chinese people were well aware of some traditional portraits of Confucius or contemporary imitations.[12]

Riding this trend of "cutification," Hello Kongzi also omits certain features common in traditional portraits of Confucius. Visually speaking, a humanoid character appears more juvenile and androgynous with fewer details on its face. For example, a subject like Confucius appears more aged and masculine when the artist renders the facial organs, especially his nose, wrinkles, and facial shadows in a more detailed way. Following this principle, Hello Kongzi minimizes the details of his eyes. Where traditional portraits, especially in late imperial China, depicted buggy eyes with long, canted eyelids, Hello Kongzi only possesses two large black dots. More interestingly, Hello Kongzi completely loses his nose, which in the traditional portraits is wide and prominent. Similarly, a defining feature in the traditional portraits is Confucius' buck teeth; a few portraits render two of his front teeth sticking out of his mouth. However, they disappear from Hello Kongzi altogether along with his mouth, supposedly all buried in his mustache.[13]

Related, the thickness of a subject's neck can also signal to the audience their age and gender. The thicker it becomes, the more masculine and senior the subject appears. This is the case for the traditional portraits of Confucius, where he has a short and thick neck, matching his broad shoulders. Even though most of his neck is covered by the collar of his robe, it still creates a sense of bulky masculinity and seniority.[14] In contrast, Hello Kongzi's neck completely disappears; his shoulders directly touch his cheeks and chin, once again recalling the proportions of chubby-cheeked infants. This tactic has been adopted in Mickey Mouse since 1928 and has become a norm for many cute characters, such as teddy bears and Winnie-the-Pooh.

Hello Kongzi receives significant inspiration from two fictional characters from Japan: Hello Kitty and Doraemon. Created in 1974 by Sanrio, Hello Kitty is a female cat depicted in humanoid postures and considered representative of the *kawaii* (cuteness) culture in Japan. The cat features are on her head: she has cat ears in triangular shapes and three lines on each side of the cheeks as whiskers. But the rest of the body resembles a human and, like Hello Kongzi, she possesses black dot eyes and a large head that is almost half of her body. On the side of her left ear, Hello Kitty wears a pink bow tie (sometimes a pink flower), anthropomorphizing her femininity. Hello Kongzi mimics this style with a bun secured with a blue hair tie and stabbed with an ink brush for good measure. These small items not only suggest a gender, but also make him more personable.

In relating to the customers, Hello Kongzi resembles Hello Kitty in a crucial way: neither of them has a mouth. This is intentional for Hello Kitty, as the designer Yamaguchi Yūko 山口裕子 explains:

> It's so that people who look at her can project their own feelings onto her face, because she has an expressionless face. Kitty looks happy when people are happy. She looks sad when they are sad. For this psychological reason, we thought she shouldn't be tied to any emotion—and that's why she doesn't have a mouth."[15]

In other words, Hello Kitty can synchronize with her owner's emotions better without a mouth. This supports her parent company's intent to make Hello Kitty a companion for their customers.[16] Broad Link, on the other hand, uses a mustache and beard to completely cover Hello Kongzi's mouth. In that way, they could achieve the same effect without announcing he has no a mouth, which would be ironic, considering the *Analects* is literally a collection of his words. Perhaps more ironically, as we will see later in this chapter, more analogous to Hello Kitty than the historical Confucius, Hello Kongzi rarely talks.[17]

Like Hello Kitty, Hello Kongzi also winks. Besides the absence of a mouth, another identifying feature of Hello Kitty is her wink, which is symbolized by replacing one eye dot either with a curved line or "<". If mouthlessness creates a more neutral space for the audience to project their emotions, the wink actively invites or even lures the audience to interact with her. In general, winking has rich connotations, ranging from an innocent greeting or a manifestation of solidarity, to sexual innuendo.[18] Thus without the mouth, the wink creates an ideal combination where it decisively invites the audience to interact, but does not specify for what purpose. Hello Kongzi adopts the curved line wink, but perhaps to constrain its meaning, it always accompanies a hand waving gesture to indicate a friendly greeting. Indeed, all these features are aimed at inviting interaction with the audience; after all, both of these characters have "Hello" in their name.

Less obviously, Hello Kongzi also resembles another popular Japanese manga character, Doraemon. First appearing to manga readers in 1970, Doraemon is a blue robot cat that does not look like a cat: he walks like a human, talks like a human, and, does not have cat ears, because a mouse ate them. Only the whiskers and the bell around his neck remotely remind the readers of his felinity. Similar to Hello Kitty, his head is wider than his body, taking up half of his height. Going along with his curved silhouette, Doraemon does not have fingers, but only bun-shaped hands. While still functional, his hands do cause him to lose almost all rock, paper, scissors games. The shape of the hands and the backstory of this harmless clumsiness add to the cuteness of the character. And we can see that Hello Kongzi similarly has the blue color scheme, and more importantly the bun-shaped hands.

Doraemon also has a rich story that can help contextualize Hello Kongzi. Unlike Hello Kitty, a more free-floating character, Doraemon is very much rooted in the original, 1970–96 manga series. In the manga, he comes back in time from the twenty-second century to help a ten-year-old Japanese boy, Nobi Nobita 野比のび太, who receives poor grades at school and is bullied by the neighboring kids. Doraemon lives with Nobi's family and helps him by bringing out gadgets from the future to solve his problems, ranging from the Anywhere Door that can lead to any location, to the Take-copter that one can fly by putting on one's head. Set in a "ordinary life gag manga" style, each episode is a self-contained story in the following structure: Nobi runs into an everyday trouble and complains (often crying) to Doraemon; the latter brings out a gadget from his four-dimensional pocket and wipes out the initial trouble; nevertheless, the gadget creates certain unexpected effects, and Nobi has to solve them with Doraemon, in many cases together with his friends and family.[19] Through each of these mini-adventures, Doraemon provides advanced technology and guidance like a mentor. Meanwhile, he also accompanies Nobi through the emotional ups-and-downs like a friend.[20] This mentor-friend role could be instrumental for the rebranding of Confucius as Hello Kongzi.

From the point of view of Broad Link, this rebranding is needed. As one of the spokespeople of the company mentioned, "Confucius as one of the cultural symbols of China more often looks like a caricature (*keban xingxiang* 刻板形象) from a textbook."[21] Indeed, Confucius has been depicted as a venerable teacher and ancient wise man in Chinese textbooks since the eighties. For example, a seventh-grade Chinese (*yuwen* 語文) textbook provides one of the first chances for mainland Chinese children to learn about Confucius, and the first sentence from the *Analects* awaits them: "Is it not a pleasure to learn and practice it in a timely manner? ..." The lesson continues with a few more quotes on learning and self-reflection, together with exercises like "what are Confucius' and his disciples' views on attitudes toward and methods of learning."[22] Depicting him as a great teacher, the textbook draws a clear boundary between Confucius and his modern audience who fill the role of the reincarnations of his disciples.

Besides his advice about study, Confucius' wisdom does not seem to be relevant in school. In a middle school history textbook, Confucius appears as one of the first thinkers from Pre-Qin China, earning two pages elaborating on his moral ethics and contributions to education. The book deems him the founder of Confucianism (*rujia xuepai de chuangshi ren* 儒家學派的創始人) and acknowledges that his moral principles had profound impacts on the development of the subsequent societies.[23] However, due to its Marxist historiography, the textbook does not consider his teaching, or for that matter, any traditional Chinese figure, relevant to contemporary society. This legacy from the Cultural Revolution has remained in history textbooks since the 1980s, wherein Confucius and other historical figures are described as limited by their time, let it be feudal society or a less stereotypical term. Therefore, the story goes, their tenets of thought or their deeds might be progressive or even enlightened for their time, but they are not comparable to, and thus not useful to the most progressive time of the present.[24] As a result, it is natural for students from mainland China to see Confucius as an unapproachable master who only belongs to an irretrievable past.

For Broad Link, the essence of anime characters can bridge the present to the Confucius of the past. As the Chairman Lin Youwu 林友武 mentioned, a "cartoon" (*katong* 卡通) image of Confucius is more approachable, especially for children.[25] Indeed, Hello Kitty and Doraemon represent this approachability of anime characters in the first decades of the 2000s. In 2013 alone, Hello Kitty reportedly made US$8 billion in retail globally.[26] Yet more illustrative than this number alone is Hello Kitty's invasion of pop culture. Hello Kitty has become a fashion icon and focus of controversy, inspiring a whole sub-culture and a variety of artworks, such as the inclusion of Hello Kitty into the underground feminist punk movement Riot Grrrl and Leslie Holt's *Hello Dali*.[27] While not as popular in the North American market, Doraemon was arguably the most well-known anime character in East Asia in the 1990s and 2000s, where its manga and TV show were translated into several East Asian languages including Mandarin, Korean, Vietnamese, and Malay.[28] In 2008, it was appointed as

Japan's first "animation ambassador" by the foreign minister Kōmura Masahiko 高村正彦.[29] Both of the characters are masters of approachability.

The Many Meanings of Cute

Behind Hello Kitty and Doraemon there is a larger force at play: cuteness. This mesmerizing aesthetic has contributed to the success of animated characters like Hello Kitty and Doraemon, including the ever-ubiquitous Mickey Mouse. For the same reason, it is been accused of manipulative aesthetics, which is a manifestation of insidiously pervasive consumerism. Meanwhile, cuteness has also been celebrated as a way to rebel against the established social order. In this section, we will untangle the multiple implications of cuteness as a concept together with the terms connected to it. These implications can help us better understand how consumers "read" the design of Hello Kongzi even beyond the intent of his parent company.

Since Konrad Lorenz (1903–1989) discovered the phenomenon of the baby schema, his theory has become the go-to starting point for discussions of cuteness. The contention point is particularly on the nature of the human reaction to cuteness and its social and cultural implications. From Lorenz's perspective of evolutionary biology, this reaction is a parental one; the baby schema mechanically triggers humans to "release" parental care. That is to say, we are innately built to have a reaction, and hence he referred to it as the "innate releasing mechanism" (*angeborener Auslösemechanismus*). Lorenz mentioned that this initially parental mechanism can be used to arouse feelings towards other objects instead of human babies, such as small animals and dolls, which we then deem "lovable or 'cuddly."[30] This implies that the mechanism is somehow uncontrollable in humans and thus could be misused out of its original evolutionary context.

This implication of uncontrollability is impactful and casts a negative light on cuteness. In his 2000 book, Daniel Harries launches a systematic criticism of cuteness in the context of consumerism. He treats cuteness as a manipulative aesthetic that lures us to consume. Seeing the features of cuteness as linked to the grotesque and the malformed, he believes that it "arouses our sympathies by creating anatomical pariahs." He emphasizes that cuteness is our subjective projection on children, one that "aestheticizes unhappiness, helplessness, and deformity." In other words, Harries perceives cuteness as an aesthetic of belittling with sadistic undertones. How would the companies exploit this aesthetics?

According to him, they use cuteness to construct an idealized childhood replete with vulnerability and innocence, and then guilt parents into feeling inadequate in providing their children with this ideal.[31] To Harries, to be cute is not just to be little, but to be belittled.

Sianne Ngai further piles on cute as a consumerist aesthetic in her 2012 book *Our Aesthetic Categories: Zany, Cute, Interesting*.[32] She situates cute in the global production and consumption of art, putting it into the weak or trivial aesthetic categories. Following Harries, Ngai further emphasizes cuteness both as an objective style and a subjective, feelings-based judgment. Looking into the English literary history of cuteness from the nineteenth to the twentieth century, she reconstructs the development of the word "cute" and its connotations: it derives from, or more specifically, truncates the word "acute," meaning "coming to a sharp edge or point." She takes this truncation as a symbolic example of rendering a word "cuter" in order to reverse the meaning of the word to the opposite. Similarly, she follows Harries to argue that making something cute disempowers the object, taking all of its agency away, including its capacity for speech and even consciousness. Ngai adds that this cuteness provokes an urge of aggression, i.e., "cute aggression" or even violence toward the object. Hence, a cute thing is "the most objectified of objects or even an 'object' par excellence."[33] Based on her theory, Hello Kongzi would be an extremely objectified figure, especially given his lack of a mouth, inviting hugging, cuddling, and even more intense physical interactions.

Predictably, Lorenz's original theory together with Harris and Ngai's negative views met with pushback. Starting with the exclusively parental reaction, Gary Sherman and Jonathan Haidt in 2011 argue that the cute does provoke affective reactions, but toward various social relationships, including "(a) high-quality potential mates, (b) trustworthy exchange partners, and (c) genetically related individuals, especially one's own children." They further theorize the common mechanism behind these potential relationships: cuteness helps people perceive the object as an agent possessing a mind, i.e., it helps them mentalize the object. As a result, the object would become more human-like. Seeing it as one of us, we tend to create a social connection with it. In other words, cuteness humanizes an object and urges social bonding that is not exclusive to parental relationship.[34] In other words, within Sherman and Haidt's framework, Hello Kongzi is potentially a trustworthy companion version of Confucius.

If Sherman and Haidt critique the evolutionary biological side of negative theorizations of cuteness, Joshua Paul Dale together with his colleagues focus on the aesthetics side, disputing the negative connotations presented by Ngai. In a 2017 edited volume, Dale follows Sherman and Haidt's model of multiplicity and argues that cuteness is a potential human response to a definable set of stimuli, instead of something instinctive and reflexive. He further emphasizes that cuteness is not necessarily a result of helplessness, but an appeal to others to create companionship and cooperation. Since cuteness itself can lead to multiple reactions, Dale disputes cuteness's inevitable connection to aggression; he argues that a catharsis is in the response to cute, preventing the subject from harming the cute object. According to his reasoning, the result is playful growling, squeezing, biting, and pinching.[35]

In the same volume, Megan Arkenberg ingeniously proves that there is a boundary of violence in cuteness. She focuses on two videogames *Portal* (2007) and *Portal 2* (2011), where in certain missions the protagonist needs to annihilate cute enemies. These enemies not only have typical cute physical shapes, but also have behaviors showing their helplessness, uttering lines with a childish voice such as "Nap time!," "Ouch, it burns," "Please stop." as well as "I don't hate you" before they die.[36] This game mechanism can only work if the players are torn between their intention to eliminate the enemies and the enemies' cuteness that prevents the elimination. In this way, Arkenberg admits that cute does provoke a physical reaction, but there is still a catharsis that restrains the subjects from harming the cute objects. Indeed, we might want to cuddle or even squeeze a Hello Kongzi stuffed toy, but few of us really want to dismember it.

Viewing it positive or negatively, most scholars do agree that cuteness constitutes a set of definable physical features, and it provokes affective reactions leading to certain types of social interactions. They also acknowledge the ubiquitous use of it in consumer culture since the beginning of the twentieth century. In the USA, cuteness emerged as a defining feature for children at the turn of the twentieth century as middle-class parents started viewing their children as priceless instead of just economic assets. "Children" then became an independent social identity that was defined by innocence and naïveté, and cuteness was a manifestation of this identity. Parents thus purchased cute toys, especially dolls, for their children, hoping to realize and maintain their children's "childishness" through material means. As consumers themselves, children reciprocally desired products that could build this image of innocence.[37]

For the rest of the twentieth century, the market saw cute and innocent fantasy characters gradually dominating children's lives. Expanding their sales, toy companies used radios and televisions to perpetuate a narrative of their products. Together with other media forms, such as comics, cartoons, and TV shows, they created fantasy worlds that were exclusive to children. As long as these worlds were wholesome, parents tolerated and sometimes even celebrated them, because they needed these worlds to entertain, educate, and babysit their children. A good example is Mickey Mouse from Disney, who was initially an impish movie character. Soon his image was licensed to toy companies to make Mickey dolls and other novelties. Finding success in the marriage between content and material products, Disney featured him in full-length cartoons and TV shows, adding more characters such as Donald Duck. Accordingly, Mickey and others have become cuter and more wholesome as sanctioned by the parents' standard of innocence. At the same time, these characters together with the physical products became the children's fantasy-world companions invading every single part of their daily life.[38]

Employing cuteness is not exclusive to North American markets; the culture of cuteness, or *kawaii* has taken over Japan since the 1970s. The Japanese word *kawaii* is derived from the early twentieth-century word *kawayushi*, meaning "pathetic," "vulnerable," "darling," "loveable," and "small." Retaining the meaning of "loveable" and "small," *kawaii* was used to describe the childish handwriting styles that were trendy among Japanese teenage girls in the 1970s. Meanwhile, this child-like trend influenced clothes, food, and idol culture, where dressing up like a child or eating sugary milky desserts became increasingly popular among young women. By the nineties, *kawaii* had been established as the general term to refer to this culture of cuteness in Japan, and it invoked meanings like "childlike," "innocence," "naïve," and "warm emotional contact."[39] This was exactly the ground where Hello Kitty and Doraemon grew.

Kawaii culture in Japan reveals specific functions of cuteness that are less obvious in North America. At the time of writing, *kawaii* culture is not only still going strong in Japan, it also has become globally visible, as we can see from the many anime and video game characters like Doraemon and Super Mario on display during the 2021 Tokyo Olympics.[40] *Kawaii* might be a fantasy of childishness, but certainly not a fantasy just for children. Adults' indulgence in manga, video games, and cute products in general is ubiquitous in Japan. Perhaps even more so than children, this indulgence in the fantasyland could help adults keep their innocence and naivety. And it could be seen as a refusal of or even a rebellion against the existing social order, as an anime cosplayer with blue hair would stand out among the suited-up white-collar workers of Shibuya, Tokyo. In other words, in *kawaii* culture, people not only perceive cuteness, but also intend to be cute.[41]

As *kawaii* culture provides a channel for the expression of individuality, it also benefits institutions. Many authoritative institutions, such as police forces and banks, adopt fluffy animals or juvenile anime figures as mascots. As noted above, these cute characters can soften the intimidation of the authorities and make these institutions more acceptable and accessible to the public. A celebrated example is the mascot of Kumamoto Prefecture of Japan, Kumamon (くまモン), which is an anthropomorphized black bear with the facial expression of surprised laugh. It has not only increased people's awareness of Kumamoto Prefecture, but has also generated around US$90 million through its licensed products.[42] A more sinister example is the doe-eyed anime characters painted onto anti-tank attack helicopters as part of the Japanese armed forces' strategy of recruitment.[43]

If we put these uses together, cuteness ultimately creates a sense of uncertainty. As Simon May observes, cuteness can project weakness, but also manipulation; it can provoke physical aggression but also prevents its excess; it sends out both innocent and impish signals; it can personify as well as objectify; it can even blur the boundary between masculinity and femininity. He reasons that this is because we perceive cuteness across a spectrum, with one side occupied by pure sweetness, the other, by menace and alienation. More than seventy years ago, Lorenz already pointed out that a certain amount of exaggeration of physical features can create sweetness, but exceeding the limit produces eeriness. May turns this observation on its head and argues that it is this particular ambivalent edge between sweet and eerie that makes cute mesmerizing, like E.T. Because of this ambivalence, it can be used to oppress as well as to rebel.[44]

Traditional China also had its own tradition of cuteness. As early as the fifth century CE, features of children were celebrated and referred to as "lovable" (*ke'ai* 可愛). At the same time, the word was also linked to being "gentle and weak" (*wenruo* 文弱), as opposed to assertiveness.[45] It can also refer to inanimate objects that were soft (*ruan* 軟), round (*yuan* 圓), and in bright colors (*xianming* 鮮明).[46] Clay miniatures in the shape of children (*ni'er* 泥兒) were a popular toy in medieval and late imperial China, which inspired affection in young girls who hoped to have children as lovable as the miniatures. Curved features can also be found in popular toys such as the swallow-shaped kite, with its round head, and stuffed tigers with a pillow-shaped body and big eyes.[47]

Meanwhile, the Chinese "loveable" has a wider range than the concept of cute. The Classical Chinese word could include anything or anyone who was lovable, as opposed to despicable. This connotation dictated the use of the word in the first decades of the PRC. It first came from a 1951 piece of investigative journalism called "Who is the Most Lovable Person" (Shui shi zui ke'ai de ren

誰是最可愛的人). Written by Wei Wei 魏巍 (1920–2008), the piece reports on the People's Liberation Army (PLA) soldiers during the Korean War (1950–53). It celebrates their dedication to China with vividly grotesque descriptions of their sacrifices, such as how, in one battle, a fire burned their bodies into various poses, including one soldier whose mouth still contained half an enemy's ear. Aware of the odd use of the word, the essay starts with the rhetorical question of how these common, faceless soldiers could be called "lovable," and it spends the rest of its pages linking the word with the soldiers' patriotism and a sense of sacrifice.[48] As a propaganda piece, this essay redefined the word "lovable," marginalizing the connotation of cuteness. This conformed with the aesthetics of the first thirty years of the PRC, in which positive figures needed to be rendered in a realistic, non-comic way.

Amidst "reform and opening-up," cute reemerged in the 1980s with the import of American and Japanese animation. In 1984, Shanghai Animation Film Studio released a few animations, including the *Little Fox* (*Xiao huli* 小狐狸) and the famous *Black Cat Detective* (*Heimao Jingzhang* 黑貓警長), wherein a humanoid black cat solves crimes.[49] In the same year, the CEO of Disney, Michael Eisner, visited Beijing, and the year after, a cartoon of Mickey Mouse appeared on the nationwide channel China Central Television (CCTV). In 1987, People's Fine Arts Publishing House (Renmin Meishu Chubanshe 人民美術出版社) published eleven volumes of *Doraemon* in Chinese, giving it a more straightforward title for mainland readers: Robot Cat (Jiqi mao 機器貓).[50] With its wide popularity among children, Doraemon appeared on CCTV in 1991. By then, children in mainland China were increasingly exposed to the same cuteness as their North American and Japanese counterparts.

By the time Hello Kongzi was born in 2014, China had seen cute culture prosper thanks to the animation industry boom and the era of social media. A group of round, cuddly goats and a big-eyed wolf from *Pleasant Goat and Big Big Wolf* (*Xiyangyang yu Huitailang* 喜羊羊與灰太狼) had dominated children's channels and the toy market for almost a decade.[51] Characters like Shrek, Buzz Lightyear, and the minions from *Despicable Me* became popular icons. And the newest Japanese anime and manga like *One Piece* and *Case Closed* can be found on Chinese streaming websites like AcFun and Bilibili. Undoubtedly, cuteness sat in the very center of the animation market, which produced US$13 billion in 2013 alone.[52]

The Chinese government has also employed cuteness in its international and domestic communications. Its panda policy has been perhaps the most effective diplomatic campaign using cuteness. Since 1941, the Chinese government has gifted or leased panda bears to other countries as a token of friendship.[53] The pandas' black and white color, their peculiar diet of bamboo, and clumsy demeanor were internationally celebrated as cute. Exclusively associated with China, pandas have now entered the realm of cats and dogs as a representative of cuteness.[54] Domestically, like other East Asian countries, China has adopted cartoons or other cute renderings to represent their governmental agencies. This is especially the case for the police force; on Weibo 微博, a Twitter-like app, police accounts very often use a cartoon drawing of a police officer with a disproportionately large head. Sometimes these cartoon police officers become the face of police announcements and promotional videos.[55] They aim to use cuteness to disarm both the criminals and the public. As of 2022, cuteness is ubiquitously employed by all levels of Chinese government agencies.

As cuteness expands in both the private and public sectors, the language of cuteness has expanded in China. The time-honored "lovable" now mainly refers to cute animals, babies, and anime characters. Since the 1990s, a new expression, "cute version" (*Q ban* Q版) emerged in colloquial and advertising language. Likely derived from the English word "cute," it referred to a smaller and hence cuter version of people, animals, or objects. As a soymilk advertisement in 1996 claimed, their cute-version package of soymilk was small and delicate, which children would welcome. Since cartoons rendered cute characters, the Chinese word for "cartoon" (*katong* 卡通) also gained the meaning of cute, especially when it was used as an adjective to describe a person or object. In the early 2000s, the Japanese word *moe* 萌 became popular in China and has since entered the Mandarin lexicon. The word originally referred to a strong affective feeling toward characters in anime, manga, and video games (ACG), wherein the characters did not always possess the physical features of cuteness. Nevertheless, in Mandarin, it has become the newest word to refer to small animals, cartoon characters, especially their clumsy, sometimes-impish behaviors.[56] As of 2022, there are several Mandarin words used to say "cute," depending on one's age, gender, and social status.

As a result, cuteness could grant Confucius several advantages in the 2010s. Most directly, it could make Confucius more effective as a companion and soften his authoritativeness. The sense of companionable cuteness neutralizes a fundamental attribute of most state-sponsored and mainstream images of Confucius: his status as a master teacher. This attribute suggests that his audiences are his disciples, and, in 2010, this meant that Confucius and his thought might hold prestige in the classroom, but they were also confined to the classroom. When portrayed as a master teacher, he is not responsible for others' emotions or providing companionship. The softening effect of companionable cuteness applies to another mainstream attribute of Confucius: he is revered for his wisdom. This reverence-derived authority creates distance between Confucius and his audience. Thus, a cute image of him has a similarly disarming effect as a cartoon police officer. Meanwhile, the ambivalence of cuteness allows creative leeway for reinventing Confucius; he could be a sweet advisor or a trickster friend, for example. More importantly, by 2014, all these features of cuteness had been widely adopted and commercialized in mainland China throughout the 2000s. In other words, the market was ready for Hello Kongzi.

Managing the Cute Confucius

In the previous two sections, we have seen the power of cute in the consumer culture of the twenty-first century and its application to Confucius in the making of Hello Kongzi. In this section, we will trace how its parent company Broad Link sold the character to their targeted audience in practice. We will focus on two tours of Hello Kongzi: the Taiwan tour from the end of 2014 to the beginning of 2015, and the North America tour, particularly the New York stop in February, 2016. These two tours demonstrate how the rich spectrum of cute could paint Hello Kongzi in different lights, from sweet to cool. At the same time, we will see to what extent the campaigns of Hello Kongzi accomplished the company's stated goal, that is, promoting traditional Chinese culture through a more accessible image of Confucius.

The Sweet Trail: The Taiwan Tour

On December 23, 2014, Hello Kongzi World Tour kicked off at the Confucius Temple in Taipei, Taiwan. Here, it took the format of an exhibition, where the Confucius Temple was divided into six exhibition areas. Each area introduced different life stages of Confucius together with his moral teachings. In keeping with Hello Kongzi's color scheme, both cartoon posters and physical statues of Hello Kongzi were displayed against a blue background. This gave the exhibition a vibrant, cartoonish tone. The tour lasted until January 31, 2015, covering seven locations, including the Taipei National Palace Museum, Taipei City Hall Square, Eslite Bookstore, and the Buddhist site Fo Guang Mountain in Kaohsiung.[57] These locations commonly attract both local residents and tourists who seek traditional Chinese heritage and knowledge.

During an interview to promote the tour, the Chairman of Broad Link Lin Youwu expressed his passion for promoting traditional Chinese culture through this "cartoonish" Confucius. He first blamed the current education system for making children unreflective, fragile, and struggling to find purpose. He then pointed to a solution that could enrich children's lives and help them identify life goals: increasing exposure to traditional Chinese learning. Since the classic works of traditional China were too "hard" (*shengying* 生硬) for children to absorb, he decided to launch this "cute, amiable cartoon image of Confucius" (*ke'ai de, he'aikeqin de Kongzi xingxiang* 可愛的、和藹可親的孔子形象), so that children could more easily learn from the wisdom of Confucius' words. To make his story more compelling, Lin further revealed that the death of his father made him realize the importance of filial piety, and he and his company were thus committed to promoting traditional Chinese virtues.[58] Clearly to Lin, the Hello Kongzi campaign was a teaching opportunity, and cuteness was the study aid.

Per Lin's wishes, making Confucius amiable shaped the publicity team's campaign strategy. On the official poster, the slogan in the biggest font reads "Johnny 踹貢!" Here "Johnny" is the English name given to Hello Kongzi, after the pronunciation of Confucius' style name Zhongni 仲尼. In other words, the poster wants readers to refer to Hello Kongzi by a common English first name, just as younger Taiwanese people refer to their friends. Meanwhile, the poster does not use more established words to address Confucius, such as "Confucius" or even the Chinese characters 孔子, but the less conventional alphabetization such as the Pinyin "Kongzi" or "Johnny."[59] The campaign was determined to forge a new identity without the burden of the "master."

Chuaigong 踹貢 tapped into the Min dialect and Internet slang. The Mandarin pronunciation of the two characters, *chuaigong*, sound similar to the Min dialect phrase, *chhòai kóng*, meaning "come out and speak up." No doubt this expression was chosen because Min dialect was one of the most commonly spoken languages in Taiwan, but the expression also became particularly trendy on Taiwanese Internet forums in 2010, when a netizen mixed it in a Mandarin sentence to defend his school: "What's wrong with Chung Hua University? If you don't like it, **speak up**!" (中華大學又怎樣啦, 不爽踹共啦).[60] The provocative tone and the trans-lingual style struck a chord among the younger netizens, since on that platform, word choice was influenced more strongly by the shared knowledge of a particular community than by the urge to stay within linguistic boundaries. The slogan, "Johnny 踹貢," drew on this trend to create a more personable version of Confucius, literally calling, "Confucius, come out and speak up!" The Broad Link Group thus played the role of a mediator, taunting Confucius into talking to his audience.

With the taunt staged, the Broad Link team further designed Hello Kongzi's response to the provocation. At the exhibition, the visitors could scan QR code through their smart phone, and they would receive a phone call from "Hello Kongzi," who spoke to them in Mandarin about life advice. The technology of the QR code has been ubiquitously implemented in public and private sectors, especially in East Asia, where QR codes serve as a point-to-point encrypted way to transfer information, including registering personal information and transferring money. Museums and temples have also adopted this practice. For example, they might produce a QR under certain exhibited items, and, after scanning it, the audience receives information about the item that is more detailed and digitalized than the traditional item tags. Temples have also integrated QR codes into temple oracles and fortune telling, where a single scan of the code could send the fortune of the user to their phone. With the help of QR codes, one does not need to search through the *Analects* and decipher a Classical Chinese sentence; the Master actively finds you and provides the most relevant guidance possible.

Like the choice of the poster, the theme song of the tour also emphasized Hello Kongzi's accessibility to the public, especially to younger people. The song, titled "Hallo Confucius" ("Halou, Kongzi" 哈囉, 孔子), was written and performed by the then 28-year-old Taiwanese pop singer Lu Guangzhong 盧廣仲 (Crowd Lu). Lu gained popularity in Taiwan through his lighthearted lyrics that depicted the daily life of students and youth. The song followed his common style, but the lyrics, as commissioned by the Broad Link Group featured what the tour wanted the audience to know and feel about Confucius. The lyrics depicts Confucius as a sneaker-wearing traveler who comes to the neighborhood of the singer and has a casual conversation over a coffee. The lyrics are indeed based on the life and teaching of a more mainstream Confucius who travelled to different states and promoted his teachings on humanity and filial piety.[61] "The mission is heavy and there is still a long way to go" is a direct quote from the *Analects* and is already part of the Mandarin lexicon.[62]

Going beyond the mainstream image of Confucius, the lyrics also embrace companionship. In the song, he does not go to meet with kings and officials, but comes to the singer's neighborhood. Not in awe of his visit, the singer visits him with coffee, a beverage of casual meetups. Similarly, Hello Kongzi meets him wearing sneakers and asks him to sit next to him, further emphasizing casualness. Trendy among younger Taiwanese people, Hello

Kongzi's sneakers are a signpost showing that Hello Kongzi is not only willing to reach out to the young people, but also capable of adopting part of their life style. No wonder the singer exclaims in the climax of the song that Confucius accompanies the singer "like a friend."[63] Unmistakably, Hello Kongzi here is a friend who provides companionship instead of moral teaching to young people in their daily life.

The music video of the song aims to appeal to young adults as well as children. Besides the singer Lu Guangzhong and a CG Hello Kongzi, it also features a then six-year-old twin duo, Zony and Yony, who had become popular a few months before by imitating the K Pop song Bar Bar Bar. Inundated with bright, perky colors of blue, orange, green, and pink, the video starts with the twins in traditional Chinese broad-sleeved robes writing their English names with brush pens. Lu then wakes up from bed wearing sneakers and a Chinese tunic suit, and begins singing along to the song with a guitar. During the video, they do several juvenile things such as taking the arms out of a clock and using them to break balloons. Gradually the video gets to its point; Zony and Yony open a book entitled the *"Analects"* and Hello Kongzi flies out from it through CG effects. The background then starts flashing *"Analects* Rock" (論語 Rock) in different colors.[64] From small children to college students, the Broad Link Group made sure there was something for everyone.

As in mainland China, Confucius and the *Analects* are part of the middle school curriculum in Taiwan, and many Taiwanese people recognize Confucius as part of their cultural heritage.[65] Therefore, the tour's aim was not so much to inform the audience about his teachings as to create a more affectionate bond with him. At the very least, the Taipei audience recognized Hello Kongzi as cute. Some of the audience, for example, referred to Hello Kongzi as "the miniature Confucius" (*Kongzi gongzai* 孔子公仔) and used the adjectives like *ke'ai* or *meng* to describe it. According to a news report, elementary school children were eager to take pictures with the miniatures, and one of them exclaimed: "Confucius turned cute!" (*Kongzi bian ke'ai le* 孔子變可愛了!) While it was hard to measure how much the cuteness eventually translated into children's willingness to learn Confucius' teachings through this forty-day tour, the tour did draw a big crowd.[66]

Toward a cool Confucius

Compared with the Taiwan tour, the North America tour in February 2016 was aimed to connect with the younger people by combining cuteness with coolness.

The tour, formally named "Global Culture Exhibition" made three stops: Los Angeles from February 7 to 14, New York from February 16 to 18, and Montreal from February 18 to March 3. Like the Taiwan tour, it employed formations of Hello Kongzi statues at tourist spots, such as Times Square. In addition, the North American tour dove even more into social media such as YouTube, Twitter, Facebook, and Instagram to promote Hello Kongzi as a character. As the General Manager of Broad Link Ye Yizhou 葉益洲 explained, the mission of the tour also shifted subtly: nowadays, children and young people around the world grow up familiar with Japanese and Korean pop culture, but in fact there is great "cultural IP" (Intellectual Property) in China like Confucius that is worth knowing for the rest of the world. Turning Confucius into a trademarked product, Ye in fact revealed the ambition to use Hello Kongzi as a token to enter the global competition with Hello Kitty and Mickey Mouse, instead of just as a revitalized symbol of cultural heritage for Chinese audiences.[67]

With this different goal in mind, the design of the tour also changed. From January 22 to March 3, the design team released a series of promotional videos to cultivate the personalities of Hello Kongzi. Among them, "Taxi!" was a good continuation of the cute image that was cultivated through the Taiwan tour. In the video, Hello Kongzi is played by a person wearing a full-body, mascot-style costume. Given the character design, the headpiece is disproportionately large. In addition to this clumsy look, he is also mute like most mascots. The video starts with Hello Kongzi trying to get a taxi after a snowy day in New York without success: his first taxi is stolen by a white female, shouting at him: "Ladies first!"; and second one by a white male, shouting: "I am meeting Donald Trump; get out of my way!" What's worse, the pile of snow around the street corner also trips him. He then hides away, and when a black male is about to get a taxi, Hello Kongzi jumps out and bows. Confused and annoyed, the black male bows back. But when he straightens his body, he sees Hello Kongzi is trying to steal his taxi, but his head is too big to fit. The skit ends with Hello Kongzi enjoying the ride with his large head sticking out of the taxi window.[68]

This video plays with the well-established cute-impish pairing. Throughout the story, Hello Kongzi is mute and can only express his intentions through body language. His big head, blue robe, and white mittens add to the clumsiness. Furthermore, the two taxi stealers make the audience sympathetic and thus connected with Hello Kongzi. However, he does not get a taxi out of sympathy, but by tricking others. As part of traditional Chinese etiquette, bowing is often stereotypically perceived to signal Chineseness or respect for Chinese culture. But here Hello Kongzi uses it playfully; he takes advantage of the stereotype of bowing and uses it as a ploy to steal the third stranger's taxi. Eventually, his success in getting a taxi is not due to his moral high ground or profound wisdom, but this instance of trickery. This amoral impishness was often found in portraits of children in the first decades of the twentieth century, and here it is used to show that Hello Kongzi is not here to teach, but to entertain.[69]

In line with this impish image, two more videos depict Hello Kongzi as daring and cool. The kickoff video of the North America tour from January 22, 2016 features Hello Kongzi bungee jumping off the Bridge to Nowhere in the San Gabriel Mountains, California. The video has no plot or dialogue, only hard rock background music with different shots of Hello Kongzi bungee jumping. At the end of the shots, a graffiti style caption reads: "Hello Kongzi in New York!" Almost two weeks later on February 3, 2016, a second video, "Hello Kongzi + Skateboard" was released. It features Hello Kongzi skateboarding through New York's graffitied neighborhoods. Then he arrives at a skateboard park and makes several slick moves despite the inconvenience of his large head and Ugg-like boots. Both videos move away from depicting him as helpless or trickster-like, but instead, as an expert on daring, countercultural activities. Here he became slick or cool.[70]

This coolness defined the main exhibition that took place in Grand Central Station, New York. Hiring a local media team, it featured a 360° projection mapping of Hello Kongzi, where different costumes, looks, and animations were projected onto a larger-than-life sculpture of Hello Kongzi in the center of the exhibition. Unlike simply projecting images onto a flat surface, the 360-degree projection mapped the complete topography of the sculpture, turning the whole physical body into a customized screen. Therefore, when the projections changed, it was as if Hello Kongzi changed his costume. The media team projected animated "costumes" such as beads pouring in, water filling up, and laser rays dividing the body of Hello Kongzi. With the dim lighting, the projection created a futuristic atmosphere.[71]

Interaction lay at the heart of the New York Exhibition, and technology was the highlight of the show. The activity "Dance with Kongzi" used motion capture to synchronize the movements of the audience with Hello Kongzi on the screen; "Everyone can be Kongzi" was a face tracking device that took pictures of the audience and put Hello Kongzi's hair and beard onto their face; Hello Kongzi Interactive VR provided a Hello Kongzi head piece with a VR goggle on it, which played a chariot-riding scene in a 3D model of a Spring-and-Autumn-period city. Using the format of the *Analects* and "Confucius says," there was even a PLINKO machine, a randomized word generator that could produce

"Confucius'" sayings on audience demand.[72] Through these technological integrations, the exhibition showed that Confucius could dance and talk with the audience, who, in turn, could experience the life of Confucius.

How approachable could Hello Kongzi get? The North America tour strove to associate Hello Kongzi with the local counterculture. For example, the video "Hiphop Dance" uploaded on March 3rd, 2016 features Hello Kongzi in a dance battle with a group of young people. In the video, Hello Kongzi performs pop and lock to hip hop music.[73] Another video, "Rap Battle" is one of the only occasions that Hello Kongzi talks, because in it he engages in a friendly rap battle with a few people in an underground tunnel with graffiti on the wall. With English-Mandarin bilingual subtitle, he raps about his fame and several cultural cues of China, such as the Yellow River and the Great Wall.[74] In both videos, the crowd acts very impressed.

Two issues stand in his way of becoming a counterculture icon in these two videos. The first issue is technical or superficial. In the "Hiphop Dance" video, Hello Kongzi is supposed to transition from one smooth move to another as the aesthetic of pop and lock dictates, but his head piece and robe are too big and loose to synchronize with his body. This renders the dance moves clumsy. Similarly, in the "Rap Battle" video, Hello Kongzi has to be able to talk, but he is designed not to have a mouth, and previously he did not speak except for on the phone. Instead, he always used clumsy yet efficient body language to communicate. Therefore, when he starts talking, it is hard to identify whether it comes from him or a voiceover. Furthermore, the generic rap lyrics with stereotypical symbols of China and Chineseness, such as the "Great Wall" and "Yellow River" add more awkwardness to the videos.

While these technical issues could have been addressed, the second and more fundamental issue is the intrinsic tension between cute and cool in merchandized characters. Impishness could add to the cuteness of a character, but there is a limit to what degree of impish tomfoolery a broad audience will tolerate; the more mainstream a character is, the more restrictive the limit appears to be. For example, as Mickey Mouse gained popularity globally, he became more wholesome, and thus better tolerated by protective parents.[75] This is even more so for Hello Kongzi, not only because he is based on the historical Confucius, but also because Broad Link intends to use him as an emblem of traditional Chinese culture. Therefore, the lyrics we have seen are tame in nature: they share the common hip hop tropes of the celebration of one's own identity and self-aggrandization, but miss the social criticism and gritty portrayals of human life that make hip hop a counterculture in the first place. The resulting videos are juvenile and cringe-worthy. On the other hand, making Hello Kongzi edgier would risk his approachability, and even damage the reputation of the traditional Chinese culture that he is supposed to promote. It is simply hard to mingle cultural authority and countercultural authority in one body.

It is also questionable how much Hello Kongzi could educate his North American audience about traditional Chinese culture. Fueled by Broad Link's strategic deployment of a cute, companionable Hello Kongzi, the character and his accompanying interactive media activities were warmly received. But to what extent did Hello Kongzi's message amount to the teaching of the historical Confucius, not to mention the nebulous "traditional Chinese culture" that Broad Link was so eager to revive? Does the cross-cultural education lie in the audience trying their best to pronounce the Mandarin word "Kongzi" or in learning about bowing, which is not practiced in mainland China, Taiwan, Singapore, or any places with substantial Chinese populations in the twenty-first century? Does it lie in the exhibition of key moral terms from the *Analects* like "humanity" and "righteousness" printed in big font on posters and projected on walls? If so, then we seem to have arrived back at the same pedagogical approach we see employed in Chinese history textbooks, only with more entertaining in-classroom activities.

Since 2016, the campaign of Hello Kongzi has been narrowed to focus on pre-school children. The tours have completely stopped, and the few visible developments are the Hello Kongzi kindergarten and a short cartoon series of Hello Kongzi teaching Chinese characters. While this appears to be a retreat by Broad Link, this might be a good business choice, since educational products for all other age groups of children have more competition and are more heavily regulated by the state. Regardless, Hello Kongzi might not have achieved the educational goal that Broad Link set out to achieve. But it did become an image of Confucius that is reflective of its era, where attention is currency, where cuteness sells, and where tradition is not necessarily obsolete, but fading away, and struggling to stay "cool."

Conclusion

Could Confucius be a half-human, half-divine prophet? Or a demon hunter? Or a sinister trickster? The answer in this book is yes. To some communities and individuals, these images are even more important or relevant than who Confucius really was historically. For others, these images of Confucius might appear outlandish, blasphomous, inconsistent, and historically inaccurate. Nevertheless, from the ruler's anxiety to the fear of the unseen world, from the justification of exclusionism to a means of making profit, these images provided comfort, guidance, and strategies to those in need. This book thus shifts our perspective from who Confucius was to what people wanted from Confucius.

With this new perspective, we see that Confucius could be anything. For example, could he be a teenage girl? Or a muscular old man? Or a supporter of same-sex marriage? The answer is still yes. A "cute" translation (*moe-yaku* 萌訳) of the *Analects* in Japan portrays Confucius as a teenage girl, with green hair and eyes, as well as big glasses and an ample bosom. This gender-bender *rori* style is a popular fetishism in Japanese animation, giving us an anime, female Confucius that appeals to a teenage audience. Meanwhile, a web-comic biography of Confucius renders him as a bulky, muscular but balding old man, labeling him as the "strongest muscly teacher" (*zuiqiang jirounan laoshi* 最強肌肉男老師). As the author Zhenshuo 朕說 makes clear, the biography is not intended to make Confucius unreasonably masculine, but to bust the myth that Confucius was physically weak. Moving outside of the world of comics, in an essay called "Would Confucius Condone Same-sex Marriage," the journalist Alex Lo suggests the possibility that Confucius and Confucianism could support any type of marriage, given their emphasis on families.[1]

One might find these images weird, at least initially. Old man vs. teenage girl, aging teacher vs. bulky muscles, traditional wisdom vs. modern identities, some of these images are even intentionally provoking, demanding the reader's attention because of how weird they seem. This sense of weirdness comes from violating our idea of who Confucius was and should be. They replace or break the most common traits we assign to Confucius. Sometimes this violation is a depature from historical accuracy, perceived or not. But in other cases, the violation serves to revive the real Confucius. For example, Zhenshuo's webcomic is aimed to correct the common misunderstanding that Confucius was short and physically weak. This misunderstanding stems from two common images of Confucius: Confucius is (somehow) always an old man and he prefered civil to military means, making him thin and weak. After all, in practice, one's authentic Confucius could be perceived by others as weird, erroneous, and even blasphamous.

Weird or not, new images of Confucius will continue to be generated one way or another. The pursuit of authenticity will continue to be one direction and standard of creating new images of him, which we can see in several books published starting in the early twenty-first century, such as *Authentic Confucius* and *Real Confucius*. The evaluation and elaboration of his legacy is another direction, especially when integrating his thought with contemporary political discourse.[2] In this book, our direction has been instrumentality, allowing us to explore the images of Confucius that have deviated, intentionally or otherwise, from our idea of the historical Confucius. Nevertheless, we have barely touched on the full spectrum of images, and more directions await us.

After all, the appeal of Confucius lies in the generative power behind him, in the charisma that we give him. Mainstream or weird, images of Confucius are fluid because the needs of the people are constantly changing. Today, we might still picture him as an old man with a beard, but with the rise of youth consumerism, a more juvenile look might become the mainstream.[3] With the rising discussion of LGBTQ issues, Confucius' theme color might switch from blue to rainbow. The more we come back to him, reinterpret him, and reimagine him, the more vibrant, resilient, and relevant he will become. His images represent our desires, emotions, and visions of the world. What can Confucius do for you?

Notes

Introduction

1. In fact, there are ready made objections to some of the depictions. See, for example, Bao Pengshan 鮑鵬山, *Kongzi yuanlai: Bei wujie de Kongzi* 孔子原來:被誤解的孔子 (Beijing: Zhongguo qingnian, 2019), 159–69; 258–72; 397–408.
2. For an insightful survey of the changing images of Confucius, see Michael Nylan and Thomas Wilson, *Lives of Confucius: Civilization's Greatest Sage through the Ages* (New York: Doubleday, 2010).
3. For the iconography of Confucius, see Julia K. Murray, "Visual Representations of Confucius," in *A Concise Companion to Confucius*, ed. Paul R. Goldin (Hoboken: Wiley, 2017), 92–129; "Confucian Iconography," in *Modern Chinese Religion I: Song-Liao-Jin-Yuan (960-1368 AD)*, ed. Pierre Marsone and John Lagerway (Leiden: Brill, 2015), 801–43; "Miraculous Portraits of Confucius: Images and Auspicious Presences," *Ars Orientalis* 50 (2021): 78–105; "Illustrations of the Life of Confucius: Their Evolution, Functions, and Significance in Late Ming China," *Artibus Asiae* 57, no. 1/2 (1997): 73–134.

    For seeing him as an essential philosopher in human history, see, for example, Karl Jaspers, *The Great Philosophers*, trans. Ralph Manheim, 4 vols. (New York: Harcourt, Brace & World, Inc., 1962–1995); Karen Armstrong, *The Great Transformation: The Beginning of Our Religious Traditions* (New York: Knopf, 2006). For a comprehensive survey of portraits and evaluations of Confucius in Europe and America, see Kevin Michael DeLapp ed., *Portraits of Confucius: The Reception of Confucianism from 1560 to 1960* (London and New York: Bloomsbury Academic, 2022).
4. Sima Qian 司馬遷, *Shiji* 史記 (Beijing: Zhonghua, 1963), 47: 1909.
5. Li Ling 李零, *Sangjia gou: Wo du Lunyu* 喪家狗:我讀《論語》 (Taiyuan: Shanxi renmin, 2007). For two critiques particularly spurred by the title, see Zhang Peiyuan 張培元, "Kongzi shi sangjia gou, ni shi shenme 孔子是喪家狗,你是什麼," Henan shangbao, May 18, 2007, https://news.sina.com.cn/c/pl/2007-05-18/050113015692.shtml (accessed October 24, 2023); Zhang Yongjun 張永軍, "Xueshi guiqiu jingren ju, xuewen shenzuo jingren yu: Li Ling jiaoshou *Sangjia gou: Wo du* Lunyu duhou 學詩貴求驚人句,學問慎作驚人語——李零教授《喪家狗:我讀<論語>》讀後," *Shehui kexue luntan*, no. 8 (2008): 131–2.
6. For the secularization of the modern world and scientism, see Pippa Norris and Ronald Inglehart, *Sacred and Secular: Religion and Politics Worldwide*

(Cambridge: Cambridge University Press, 2011), 3–32, esp. 24-5; D. W. Y. Kwok, *Scientism in Chinese Thought, 1900–1950* (New Haven: Yale University Press, 1965). For the creation of a "modern mentality" as a justification to dismiss practices like divination, see Brian Epstein, "The Diviner and the Scientist: Revisiting the Question of Alternative Standards of Rationality," *Journal of the American Academy of Religion* 78, no. 4 (2010): 1048–86; Zhao Lu, "Introduction to Thought and Mantic Arts," in *Handbook of Divination and Prognostication in China*, ed. Michael Lackner and Zhao Lu (Leiden: Brill, 2022), 50–4.

7   Lionel M. Jensen, *Manufacturing Confucianism: Chinese Traditions & Universal Civilization* (Durham: Duke University Press, 1997), esp. 81; Nylan and Wilson, *Lives of Confucius*; Michael Hunter, *Confucius beyond the Analects* (Leiden: Brill, 2017).

8   Randall Collins, *Interaction Ritual Chains* (Princeton: Princeton University Press, 2004), 10; *The Sociology of Philosophies: A Global Theory of Intellectual Change* (Cambridge, MA: Belknap Press of Harvard University Press, 1998), 21–56.

9   By "Confucian," I refer to Confucius' immediate and self-identified followers who were devoted to Confucius' teachings and texts associated to him, especially the *Analects* and the Five Classics. I thus refer to the thought and practice of Confucius and his followers as "Confucianism." Given the rather big range of time and space, I only use these two terms heuristically to point out to the individuals, tenets of thought, and practices related to Confucius. Other scholars have given more rigorous definitions of the terms for more specific occasions. See, for example, Paul R. Goldin's definition of Confucianism in dealing with early Confucian thought in his *Confucianism* (Berkeley: University of California Press, 2011), 5.

10 Sima, *Shiji*, 1905–18.

11 Ibid., 1919–45.

12 See the commentary in the beginning of the biography, ibid., 1905.

13 Ibid., 47; 1907: 21, 35–8, 43–4, 47.

14 Wang Aihe, *Cosmology and Political Culture in Early China* (Cambridge: Cambridge University Press, 2000), 59–60.

15 Sima, *Shiji*, 1919: 21, 33, 42; *Lunyu jizhu* 論語集注, Zhu Xi 朱熹 ed., *Sishu zhangju jizhu* 四書章句集注 (Beijing: Zhonghua, 1983), 5, 110–11.

16 Sima, *Shiji*, 1945–6; Thomas A. Wilson, "Ritualizing Confucius/Kongzi: The Family and State Cults of the Sage of Culture in Imperial China," in *On Sacred Grounds: Culture, Society, Politics, and the Formation of the Cult of Confucius*, ed. Thomas A. Wilson (Cambridge, MA: Harvard University Asia Center, 2002), 43–94; Joseph S. C. Lam, "Musical Confucianism: The Case of 'Jikong yuewu,'" in *On Sacred Grounds: Culture, Society, Politics, and the Formation of the Cult of Confucius*, ed. Thomas A. Wilson (Cambridge: Harvard University Asia Center, 2002), 141. For a chronology of Confucius temples from 478 BCE to 2004 CE, see James A. Flath, *Traces of*

the Sage: Monument, Materiality, and the First Temple of Confucius (Honolulu: University of Hawai'i Press, 2016), 205–11.

17　See, for example, Benjamin A. Elman, *A Cultural History of Civil Examinations in Late Imperial China* (Berkeley: University of California Press, 2000), 5–61.

18　See Chapter 4.

19　Thierry Meynard, *The Jesuit Reading of Confucius: The First Complete Translation of the Lunyu (1687) Published in the West* (Leiden: Brill, 2015), 59; Jensen, *Manufacturing Confucianism*, 70–5.

20　See, for example, Bryan W. Van Norden, *Taking Back Philosophy: A Multicultural Manifesto* (New York: Columbia University Press, 2017), 19–29, 159.

21　Hu Shi 胡適, *Zhongguo zhexueshi dagang* 中國哲學史大綱, vol. 1 (Shanghai: Shangwu, 1947), 1–10, 69–122; Jiaoyubu 教育部 ed., *Yuwen: Qinian ji, shangce* 語文:七年級上冊, Yiwu jiaoyu jiaokeshu (Beijing: Renmin jiaoyu, 2016).

22　John Blake, "This World-class Athlete Talks like Aristotle and Acts like Confucius. We Can All Learn from Him," *CNN*, May 27, 2022, https://edition.cnn.com/2022/05/27/world/rafael-nadal-philosophy-blake-cec/index.html (accessed October 25, 2023).

23　Randy Kluver, "Chinese Culture in a Global Context: The Confucius Institute as a Geo-Cultural Force," in *China's Global Enagagement: Cooperation, Competition, and Influence in the 21st Century*, ed. Jacques Delisle and Avery Goldstein (Washington: Brookings Institution Press, 2017), 389–416.

24　For more reflections on strangeness especially in the context of the traditional Chinese categories, see Robert Campany, *Strange Writing: Anomaly Accounts in Early Medieval China* (Albany: State University of New York Press, 1996), 28.

Chapter 1

1　The statement reads: "The Master [Confucius] did not talk about the strange, strength, disorder, and wonders." (*Zi bu yu guai li luan shen* 子不語怪力亂神). *Lunyu*, 4: 98.

2　So far the most comprehensive study on the generic name of apocryphal texts is Chen Pan 陳槃, *Gu Chenwei yantao ji qi shulu jieti* 古讖緯研討及其書錄解題 (Shanghai: Guji, 2009), 148–71. In the study, Chen Pan convincingly points out that the many names, such as *chen*, *wei*, *tuchen* 圖讖, *tuwei* 圖緯 are largely interchangeable during the Eastern Han dynasty.

3　Chen Pan, *Gu Chenwei yantao*, 141–8.

4　See, e.g., *Chunqiu wei* 春秋緯, in Yasui Kōzan 安居香山 and Nakamura Shōhachi 中村璋八 eds., *Weishu jicheng* 緯書集成 (Shijiazhuang: Hebei renmin, 1994), 912–42.

5　This translation convention likely started from Tjoe Som Tjan, *Po Hu T'ung: The Comprehensive Discussion in the White Tiger Hall* (Leiden: Brill, 1949–52), 100; Jack

L. Dull, "A Historical Introduction to the Apocryphal (Ch'an-wei) Texts of the Han Dynasty" (University of Washington, 1966), 5–6. For the term "apocrypha," see Hans van Ess, "The Apocryphal Texts of the Han Dynasty and the Old Text/New Text Controversy," *T'oung Pao* 85, no. 1 (1999): 31–6.

6 Michael Loewe, "The Former Han Dynasty," in *The Cambridge History of China. Vol. 1, The Ch'in and Han Empires, 221 B.C.–A.D. 220*, ed. Denis Twitchett and Michael Loewe (Cambridge: Cambridge University Press, 1985), 179–97. For more political events that reflect this transition, see Michael Loewe, *Crisis and Conflict in Han China, 104 BC to AD 9* (London: George Allen & Unwin, 1974), 139–43.

7 Ban Gu 班固, *Hanshu* 漢書 (Beijing: Zhonghua, 1962), 36: 1950.

8 See Michael Loewe, *The Men Who Governed Han China: Companion to* A Biographical Dictionary of Qin, Former Han, and Xin Periods (Leiden: Brill, 2011), 421–56. For the role of Heaven in early China, see Luo Xinhui 羅新慧, "Zhoudai tianming guannian de fazhan yu shanbian 周代天命觀念的發展與嬗變," *Lishi yanjiu*, no. 5 (2002): 4–18; Herrlee G. Creel, *The Origins of Statecraft in China* (Chicago and London: University of Chicago Press, 1970), 81–100.

9 For this feeling of *fin de siècle*, see Loewe, "The Former Han Dynasty," 221–2; Tanaka Masami 田中麻紗巳, *Ryōkan shisō no kenkyu* 両漢思想の研究 (Tokyo: Kenbun Shuppan, 1986), 77–9.

10 Loewe, *Crisis and Conflict in Han China,* 142–3.

11 Hans Bielenstein, "Wang Mang, The Restoration of the Han Dynasty, and Later Han," in *The Cambridge History of China. Vol. 1, The Ch'in and Han Empires, 221 B.C.–A.D. 220*, ed. Denis Twitchett and Michael Loewe (Cambridge: Cambridge University Press, 1987), 224–39.

12 Bielenstein, "Wang Mang, The Restoration of the Han Dynasty," 240–50.

13 Yasui Kōzan 安居香山 and Nakamura Shōhachi 中村璋八, *Isho no kisoteki kenkyū* 緯書の基礎的研究 (Tokyo: Kokusho Kankōkai, 1976), 261–3.

14 *Mengzi jizhu* 孟子集注, Zhu Xi 朱熹 ed., *Sishu zhangju jizhu* 四書章句集注 (Beijing: Zhonghua, 1983), 14: 376.

15 *Mengzi jizhu*, 3: 234.

16 Sima, *Shiji*, 47: 1947.

17 This has been insightfully pointed out in Michael J. Puett, "Following the Commands of Heaven: The Notion of Ming in Early China," in *The Magnitude of Ming: Command, Allotment, and Fate in Chinese Culture*, ed. Christopher Lupke (Honolulu: University of Hawai'i press, 2005), 49–69, esp. 67.

18 *Mengzi jizhu*, 6: 272.

19 Adapted from James Legge, *The Chinese Classics with a Translation, Critical and Exegetical Notes, Prolegomena, and Copious Indexes. Vol. 1: Confucian Analects, The Great Learning, and the Doctrine of the Mean* (London: Trübner, 1961), 281–2.

20 Liu An 劉安, *Huainanzi jishi* 淮南子集釋 (Beijing: Zhonghua, 1998), 9: 697.

21 Adapted from Roger Ames, *The Art of Rulership: A Study of Ancient Chinese Political Thought* (Albany: SUNY, 1994), 205.
22 Chen Guying 陳鼓應 ed., *Zhuangzi jinzhu jinyi* 莊子今注今譯 (Beijing: Zhonghua, 1983), 337.
23 Liu Xiang 劉向, *Shuiyuan jiaozheng* 說苑校證 (Beijing: Zhonghua, 1987), 5: 95.
24 Many Western Han scholars believed that the *qilin* was an omen sent by Heaven. See, for example, Ban, *Hanshu*, 75: 3156.
25 Ban, *Hanshu*, 36: 1968; 81: 3343.
26 Yang Xiong 揚雄, *Fayan yishu* 法言義疏 (Beijing: Zhonghua, 1987), 8: 254.
27 *Mengzi*, 14: 376–7.
28 The role Heaven played, especially in granting its mandate, had been complex for many early Chinese thinkers, such as Confucius and Mencius. See Puett, "Following the Commands of Heaven," 53–68.
29 *Chunqiu yan kong tu*, Yasui and Nakamura, *Weishu jicheng*, 580. The fragment is preserved in the commentary in *Liji zhengyi* 禮記正義, ed. Ruan Yuan 阮元, *Shisanjing zhushu* 十三經注疏 (Beijing: Zhonghua, 1980), 1628.
30 *Lunyu jizhu*, 2, 68.
31 For a summary of the use of the Five Phases and the evolution of this theory during the Han dynasty, See Loewe, *The Men Who Governed Han China*, 457–521; Loewe, *Divination, Mythology and Monarchy in Han China* (Cambridge: Cambridge University Press, 1995), 55–60.
32 *Chunqiu yan kong tu* in Yasui and Nakamura, *Weishu jicheng*, 576. The fragment is preserved in the commentary on *Hou Han shu*, 40b: 1377.
33 Chen, *Zhuangzi*, 337.
34 There are two examples where Eastern Han scholars referred to Confucius as such, and they are from at earliest the Eastern Han. See, for example, Fan Ye 范曄, *Houhan shu* 後漢書 (Beijing: Zhonghua, 1965), 40b, 1376.
35 *Xiao jing gou ming jue* 孝經鉤命決 (The tally of the key to the mandate in the *Classic of Filial Piety*), Yasui and Nakamura, *Weishu jicheng*, 1011. Yasui Kōzan punctuates the sentence as 邱為制法之, 主黑綠不代蒼黃 to correspond to another similar sentence: 邱為制法, 主黑綠不代蒼黃. However, if we parse *zhu* 主 as the verb of the second clause in the former sentence, then it is difficult to understand the function of *zhi* in the first clause. If we assume that *zhi* is not redundant or caused by any textual corruption, it is better to parse *zhu* to the first part of the sentence as a noun. Also see *Weishu jicheng*, 988. The fragment is preserved in the commentary in *Liji*, 1257.
36 *Chunqiu yan kong tu*, Yasui and Nakamura, *Weishu jicheng*, 579. The fragment is preserved in the commentary in *Chunqiu Gongyang zhuan zhushu* 春秋公羊傳注疏, ed. Ruan Yuan 阮元, *Shisanjing zhushu* 十三經注疏 (Beijing: Zhonghua, 1980), 2195.

37 *Chunqiu yan kong tu*, Yasui and Nakamura, *Weishu jicheng*, 579.
38 *Chunqiu yan kong tu*, Yasui and Nakamura, *Weishu jicheng*. The fragment is preserved in the commentary in *Chunqiu Gongyang zhuan*, 2195.
39 Chunqiu *shuo tici* 春秋說題辭,Yasui and Nakamura, *Weishu jicheng*, 855.
40 *Chunqiu yan Kong tu* 春秋演孔圖, Yasui and Nakamura, *Weishu jicheng.*, 578. The passage is preserved in *Chunqiu Gongyang zhuan*, 2354.
41 *Chunqiu Gongyang zhuan*, 2353–4.
42 See Xu Yan's 徐彥 sub-commentary on this apocryphal passage, in ibid., 2354.
43 *Chunqiu yankong tu*, Yasui and Nakamura, *Weishu jicheng*, 578. The passage is preserved in *Chunqiu Gongyang zhuan*, 2354.
44 *Chunqiu shuo tici*, Yasui and Nakamura, *Weishu jicheng*, 854. The passage is preserved in *Chunqiu Gongyang zhuan*, 2195.
45 This attribute of sagehood is not just exclusive to Confucius; as Ning Chen points out, *sheng* 聖 was cognate to 聲 *sheng*. The connotation of *sheng* 聖 in Shang dynasty oracle bones to Zhou dynasty bronze inscriptions thus contains "sound," "news," "acute hearing ability" and by extension, "wise." See Ning Chen, "The Etymology of sheng (Sage) and its Confucian Conception in Early China," *Journal of Chinese Philosophy* 27, no. 4 (2000): 412–15. Considering in pre-imperial China, knowledge was transmitted most often through oral avenues, acute auditory sense is also linked with "knowledgeable." In examining literati texts around the second century BCE, Miranda Brown and Uffe Bergeton also add superb perceptiveness, ability to penetrate subtlety, and capability in evading disruptions to the list of a sage's characteristics. See Miranda Brown and Uffe Bergeton, "'Seeing' like a Sage: Three Takes on Identity and Perception in Early China," *Journal of Chinese Philosophy,* Journal of Chinaese J 35, no. 4 (2008): 641–62.
46 Sima, *Shiji*, 47: 1912–13. The exclamation can also be interpreted as "Indeed sage!", which means Confucius was truly a sage.
47 Sima, *Shiji*, 47: 1912. I use "odd creature" to render the term *guai* 怪, which literally means "odd" or "oddness." In this context, it indicates creatures that are uncommon in those environments.
48 Confucius' prediction *Kong sheng mo, Zhou shi wang* (孔聖沒, 周室亡) is almost identical to *Kong sheng mo, Zhou Ji wang* (孔聖沒, 周姬亡), the variation of which might be due to textual transmission. But obviously, the blood writing is a much longer prophecy than what Confucius predicted.
49 Zhao Lu, *In Pursuit of the Great Peace: Han Dynasty Classicism and the Making of Early Medieval Literati Culture* (Albany: SUNY, 2019), 3–12.
50 Sima, *Shiji*, 47 (1963): 1905.
51 Commentators of this passage read *ye he* 野合 as "illicit copulation." See Sima, *Shiji*, 47 (1963): 1906. However, in the other two occasions of this term in early Chinese texts, *ye he* either means musical instruments "harmonizing in the wild" or troops "encountering each other in the wild." Also, the following sentence mentions

praying to a mountain for pregnancy, suggesting the place where they had coitus. Therefore, I understand the term from its literal sense. See Lu Jia 陸賈, *Xinyu jiaozhu* 新語校注 (Beijing: Zhonghua, 1986), 78; Yang Bojun 楊伯峻 ed., *Chunqiu Zuozhuan zhu* 春秋左傳注 (Beijing: Zhonghua, 1990), 1578.

52 The logic is not obvious since concave surfaces are usually associated with a "basin" instead of a "mountain." If we trust commentators' definitions, one explanation could be that Sima Qian or others perceive this feature as that a circle of mountains creating a concave topography. Sima, *Shiji*, 47 (1963): 1906.

53 *Chunqiu yan Kong tu*, Yasui and Nakamura, *Weishu jicheng*, 576. The fragment is preserved in Li Fang 李昉 et al. ed., *Taiping yulan* 太平御覽 (Beijing: Zhonghua, 1960), 361: 1663.

54 Sima, *Shiji*, 8 (1963): 341; Ban Gu, *Hanshu*, 1: 1.

55 Sima, *Shiji*, 2 (1963): 94–6.

56 Lü Buwei 呂不韋, *Lüshi chunqiu zhushu* 呂氏春秋注疏 (Chengdu: Bashu, 2002), 22: 2780. *Kongsang* also appears as a place name in the *Classic of Mountains and Seas*. See Yuan Ke 袁珂 ed., *Shan hai jing jiaozhu* 山海經校注 (Chengdu: Bashu, 1996), 4:126.

57 For this type of birth, often referred to as "*gan sheng* 感生," see Yasui Kōzan 安居香山, "Kanseitei setsu no tenkai to Isho shisō 感生帝說の展開と緯書思想," *Nihon Chūgoku Gakkai hō*, no. 20 (1968): 63–78; Lin Sujuan 林素娟, "Handai gansheng shenhua suo chuanda de yuzhouguan jiqi zai zhengjiao shang de yiyi 漢代感生神話所傳達的宇宙觀及其在政教上的意義," *Cheng Da zhongwen xuebao* 4, no. 28 (2010): 35–82.

58 Sima, *Shiji*, 3 (1963): 91; 4: 111.

59 See the passage in *Shangshu diming yan*, Yasui and Nakamura, *Weishu jicheng*, 367. The fragment is preserved in Li Fang 李昉 et al., *Taiping yulan*, 533: 2418a.

60 *Shangshu diming yan* 尚書帝命驗, Yasui and Nakamura, *Weishu jicheng*, 369. The fragment is preserved in Li Fang 李昉 et al., *Taiping yulan*, 82: 380b.

61 *Annals' Tallies of Corresponding to the Essence*, Yasui and Nakamura, *Weishu jicheng*, 741. The fragment is preserved in Li Fang et al. eds., *Taiping yulan*, 84: 396b.

62 *Chunqiu yuanming bao* 春秋元命包, ibid., 591. The fragment is preserved in Xiao Ji 蕭吉, Nakamura Shōhachi 中村璋八 ed., *Wuxing dayi* 五行大義 (Tokyo: Kyūko shoin, 1984), 5: 454.

63 *Chunqiu Han han zi* 春秋漢含孳, Yasui and Nakamura, *Weishu jicheng*, 815.

64 *The Annals' Diagrams of Elaborating Confucius*, *Weishu jicheng*, 576. The fragment is preserved in Li Fang 李昉 et al., *Taiping yulan*, 377: 1740a.

65 During the Han dynasty, one *chi* was theoretically equal to 23.1 cm. See the measurements shown on excavated measuring sticks and related discussions in Qiu Guangming 丘光明, Qiu Long 邱隆, and Yang Ping 楊平, *Zhongguo kexue jishu shi: Du liang heng juan* 中國科學技術史: 度量衡卷 (Beijing: Kexue, 2001), 198–211.

66 *Wei* 圍 is an approximate unit for measuring the perimeter of objects. One *wei* can either stand for the perimeter of the circle made by the length from one's thumb to the index finger of the same hand or one's arm span. Here it is very likely that nine *wei* is measured the former way.
67 *Chunqiu yan Kong tu*, Yasui and Nakamura, *Weishu jicheng*, 577.
68 Wang Tianhai 王天海 ed., *Xunzi jiaoshi* 荀子校釋 (Shanghai: Shanghai guji, 2005), 162; note 13 on page 67.
69 Ibid., 159.
70 Sima, *Shiji*, 47: 1909. In the original context, Confucius' height was "九尺有六寸," or "9.6 *chi*." I understand 1 *chi* as 0.23 meter, which was the measurement of 1 *chi* in Sima Qian's time. It is unclear whether *chi* should be understood as such or to what extent the information was accurate.
71 Sima, *Shiji*, 47: 1921.
72 Rune Svarverud, "Body and Character: Physiognomic Descriptions in Han Dynasty Literature," in *Minds and Mentalities in Traditional Chinese Literature*, ed. Halvor Eifring (Beijing: Culture and Art Publishing House, 1999), 120–46.
73 *Chunqiu Yan Kong tu*, Yasui and Nakamura, *Weishu jicheng*, 574.
74 *The Annals' Inclusion of the Primary Mandate*, *Weishu jicheng*, 590. The fragment is preserved in Li Fang 李昉 et al., *Taiping yulan*, 79: 368b.
75 Taiwei is located at β (Vir), containing 10 stars. See the commentary attached to this apocryphal passage in Yasui and Nakamura, *Weishu jicheng*, 590; Sun Xiaochun and Jacob Kistemaker, *The Chinese Sky During the Han: Constellating Stars and Society* (Leiden: E.J. Brill, 1997), 152.
76 *Chunqiu yan Kong tu*, *Weishu jicheng*, 574.
77 Zhao Lu, "To Become Confucius," *Asia Major* 28, no. 1 (2015): 115–44.
78 Ban Gu 班固, *Baihu tong shuzheng* 白虎通疏證 (Beijing: Zhonghua, 1994), 7: 334–40.
79 *Xuan* 玄 was changed to *zhi* 至 due to a taboo in 1012 CE. The father of the founder of the Song dynasty had a style name Xuanlang 玄朗. See Li Tao 李燾, *Xu Zizhi tongjian changbian* 續資治通鑑長編 (Beijing: Zhonghua, 1979), 70: 1574; Li You 李攸 ed., *Songchao shi shi* 宋朝事實 vol. 11, Songdai Biji Xiaoshuo 宋代筆記小說 (Shijiazhuang: Hebei jiaoyu, 1995), 7: 300.
80 Kang Youwei 康有為, *Kongzi gaizhi kao* 孔子改制考, ed. Jiang Yihua 姜義華 and Zhang Ronghua 張榮華, vol. 3, Kang Youwei quanji 康有為全集 (Beijing: Zhongguo Renmin Daxue, 2007), 3.

Chapter 2

1 For considering records of the strange as a genre and their characteristics, I follow Campany, *Strange Writing*, 21–32. For the term *zhiguai* and its history of referring to recording supernatural stories, see Li Jianguo 李建國, *Tang qian zhiguai*

xiaoshuo shi 唐前志怪小說史 (Tianjin: Jiaoyu), 11–12. For more discussions on the genre, see Robert Campany, *Signs from the Unseen Realm: Buddhist Miracle Tales from Early Medieval China* (Honolulu: University of Hawai'i Press, 2012), 1–62; Zhou Ciji 周次吉, *Liuchao zhiguai xiaoshuo yanjiu* 六朝志怪小說研究 (Taipei: Wenjin, 1990)., 1–62; Wang Guoliang 王國良, *Wei Jin Nanbeichao zhiguai xiaoshuo yanjiu* 魏晉南北朝志怪小說研究 (Taipei: Wenshizhe, 1984); Donald E. Gjertson, "The Early Chinese Buddhist Miracle Tale: A Preliminary Survey," *Journal of the American Oriental Society* 101 (1981): 287–301.

2. The first approach is partly represented by Zhenjun Zhang, *Buddhism and Tales of the Supernatural in Early Medieval China: A Study of Liu Yiqing's (403–444) Youming lu* (Leiden: Brill, 2014). The second approach is represented by Lu Xun 魯迅, *Zhongguo xiaoshuo shilue* 中國小說史略 (Beijing: Renmin wenxue 1973). The third approach is represented by Campany, *Signs from the Unseen Realm*, 38; Campany, "On the Very Idea of Religions (in the Modern West and in Early Medieval China)," *History of Religions* 42 (2003): 287–319.

3. Buddhist and Daoist elements are the most frequently mentioned subjects in the studies of the *zhiguai* literature. The image of Confucius and his disciples as well as the learning of the Five Classics, which were very common to early medieval Chinese literati, has not been studied. When they are mentioned, they often function as a setup for the normal and worldly society, which contrast with the *zhiguai* literature. See the works from the previous note and for example, Liu Yuanru 劉苑如, "Xingxian yu mingbao: Liuchao zhiguai zhong guiguai xushu de fengyu—yi ge 'daoyi wei chang' moshi de kaocha 形見與冥報：六朝志怪中鬼怪敘述的諷喻———一個'導異為常'模式的考察," *Zhongyang yanjiuyuan zhongguo wenzhe yanjiu jikan* 29 (2006): 1, 17.

4. See Campany, *Signs from the Unseen Realm*, 17–27; Zhang, *Buddhism and Tales of the Supernatural*, 20–60.

5. We can see this narrative most obviously online, such as "Kongzi duidai guishen de taidu shi zenyang de 孔子對待鬼神的態度是怎樣的," Douban, https://www.zhihu.com/question/25408139; Guoxue yuan 國學園, "Kongzi weishenme bu yuanyi tanlun guishen 孔子為什麼不願意談論鬼神," Wangyi, March 5, 2020, https://www.163.com/dy/article/F6VO4UN805431K92.html (accessed October 25, 2023). The philosopher Li Zehou 李澤厚 calls Confucius' view on deities in the *Analects* "pragmatic rationality" (*shiyong lixing* 實用理性). See Li Zehou, *Lunyu jindu* 論語今讀 (Hefei: Anhui wenyi, 1998), 160.

6. See Chapter I.

7. Sima, *Shiji*, 47: 1912–3.

8. Wang Jia 王嘉, *Shiyi ji* 拾遺記 (Changchun: Jilin Daxue, 1992), 3: 5a–b.

9. This story was included in several official commentaries on the Confucian classics during the Tang dynasty (618–907 CE), as well as a Northern Song dynasty (960–1127 CE) imperial encyclopedia. Yasui and Nakamura, *Weishu jicheng*, 576.

10 As far as I am aware, the earliest mentioning of Zhengzai is in the "Tangong" 檀弓 chapter of *Liji*, 1313.
11 Consider, Houji's 后稷 birth, the legendary ancestor of the Zhou people. Because Houji was born fatherless, he was considered inauspicious. Sima, *Shiji*, 4: 111.
12 "Zhi guai" 志怪, Xiao Yi 蕭繹, Xu Yimin 許逸民 ed., *Jinlouzi jiaojian* 金樓子校箋 (Beijing: Zhonghua, 2011), 5: 1185.
13 "Zhi guai" 志怪, 5: 1131–218.
14 *Xiao shuo* 小說, in Lu Xun 魯迅 ed., *Gu xiaoshuo gouchen* 古小說鉤沈 (Beijing: Renmin wenxue, 1973), 213.
15 For example, see his conversation with his disciple Zilu about ghosts and deities, and life and death. *Lunyu jizhu*, 6: 125.
16 Sima, *Shiji*, 47: 1944.
17 See Li Jianfeng 李劍鋒, "Wei Jin Nanchao zhiguai xiaoshuo zhong de Kongzi xingxiang 魏晉南朝志怪小說中的孔子形象," *Kongzi yanjiu*, no. 1 (2008): 102–8; Shi Yan 史燕, "Liuchao xiaoshuo zhong de Kongzi xingxiang 六朝小說中的孔子形象" (Master Thesis: Zhengzhou Daxue, 2012).
18 Yasui and Nakamura, *Weishu jicheng*, 578; 854.
19 Yasui and Nakumura, *Weishu jicheng*, 579.
20 *Xiao shuo*, in Lu Xun 魯迅, *Gu xiaoshuo*, 212.
21 In the passage, it is not clear whether Confucius or Yan Yuan answers the other disciples' question. I take it as Confucius because in stories about Confucius and his disciples, Confucius often acts as the authoritative mediator and explainer of his disciples' disagreements.
22 *Lunyu jizhu*, 4: 97. It is not completely clear whether the word *yi* 易 here indicates any specific forms of the *Book of Changes*. It could even simply mean "change" or "difference," two meanings well testified in early Chinese sources. In this way, what Confucius wanted to learn was simply changes or differences. However, the exegesis of this passage historically took *yi* as the *Book of Changes*. This reading was further strengthened by Sima Qian's records of Confucius, where Confucius read the *Changes* so many times, it caused the leather bindings to break three times. See Sima, *Shiji*, 47: 1937.
23 *Shiji*, 47: 1937.
24 See, for example, *Lunyu jizhu*, 3: 76, 5: 77, 6: 123, 27.
25 This story is not in the received version of *Han Shi waizhuan*, but quoted as *Han Shi waizhuan* in the Tang dynasty encyclopedia compiled by Yu Shinan 虞世南. See Yu Shinan 虞世南 ed., *Beitang shuchao* 北堂書鈔 (Beijing: Zhongguo Shudian, 1989), 137: 565a.
26 Gan Bao 干寶, *Sou shen ji* 搜神記 (Beijing: Zhonghua, 1979), 19: 234.
27 I take it as *shishou* 失手, meaning "out of control" or "by accident."
28 *Lunyu jizhu*, 8: 161.

29 Liu, *Shuiyuan*, 18: 465.
30 Liu, *Shuiyuan*, 18: 465.
31 *Xiao shuo*, in Lu Xun, *Gu xiaoshuo*, 212.
32 *Lunyu jizhu*, 5: 116; 7: 49.
33 See Zhang, *Buddhism and Tales of the Supernatural*, 89–91.
34 Kristofer Schipper and Franciscus Verellen eds., *The Taoist Canon: A Historical Companion to the Daozang*, vol. 3 (Chicago: University of Chicago Press, 2004), 269–72.
35 For the idea of "strangeness" as an anxiety of the literati reflected in the *zhiguai* literature, see Chen Shiyun 陳世昀, "Weijin Nanbeichao zhiguai xiaoshuo 'yi' de xushu 魏晉南北朝志怪小說「異」的敘述," *Changgeng renwen shehui xuebao* 12, no. 2 (2019): 235–70.
36 See Robert Campany, "The Earliest Tales of the Bodhisattva Guanshiyin," in *Religions of China in Practice*, ed. Donald S. Lopez Jr. (Princeton: Princeton University Press, 1996), 82–96; Campany, "The Real Presence," *History of Religions* 32 (1993): 233–72.
37 This is not only common among modern scholars, but it is also built into the primary sources from early medieval China. For example, see how Daoism and Buddhism were put into opposition, while Confucianism became irrelevant in the late sixth-century Buddhist polemical text *Xiao dao lun* 笑道論. For an English translation of the text, see Zhen Luan 甄鸞, *Laughing at the Tao: Debates among Buddhists and Taoists in Medieval China*, trans. Livia Kohn (Princeton: Princeton University Press, 1995).
38 For a trenchant study on the practice of reading from early China to early medieval China, see Jack Chen, "On the Act and Representation of Reading in Medieval China," *Journal of the American Oriental Society* 129, no. 1 (2009): 57–71. K.E. Brashier also has an informative survey of chanting practice in early China. See Brashier, *Public Memory in Early China* (Cambridge, MA: Harvard University Asia Center, 2014), 9–57.
39 *Xunzi jiaoshi*, 22–3; *Mengzi jizhu*, 12: 339; *Lunyu jizhu*, 9: 115.
40 Lü, *Lüshi chunqiu* 7: 66.
41 Liu An, *Huainanzi*, 20: 1375. Wang Chong 王充 from the first century CE also criticized this view at length, which indirectly testified the popularity of this view in the late first century CE. See his chapter "Gan xu" 感虛 in Wang Chong 王充, *Lunheng jiaoshi* 論衡校釋 (Beijing: Zhonghua, 1990), 5: 227–60.
42 Ying Shao 應劭, *Fengsu tongyi* 風俗通義 (Beijing: Zhonghua, 2010), 9: 423.
43 For the historiography on Emperor Wu of the Han dynasty, see Xin Deyong 辛德勇, *Zhizao Hanwudi* 制造漢武帝 (Beijing: Sanlian, 2015).
44 Fan, *Houhan shu*, 82b: 2730.

45 For social changes in early medieval China, see for example Mark Edward Lewis, *China Between Empires: The Northern and Southern Dynasties* (Cambridge, MA: Belknap Press of Harvard University Press, 2009), 86–143; Charles Holcombe, *In the Shadow of the Han: Literati Thought and Society at the Beginning of the Southern Dynasties* (Honolulu: University of Hawai'i Press, 1994), 34–72. For the importance of mountains socially and religiously, see Wei Bin 魏斌, "*Shanzhong*" de Liuchao shi "山中"的六朝史 (Beijing: Zhonghua, 2019). For how rumors and legends feed on the anxieties of their transmitters, see Beverly Crane, "The Structure of Value in 'The Roommate's Death': A Methodology for Interpretive Analysis of Folk Legends," *Journal of the Folklore Institute* 14 (1977): 133–41; Timothy R. Tangherlini, "'It Happened Not Too Far from Here…': A Survey of Legend Theory and Characterization," *Western Folklore* 49 (1990): 381.

46 Gan, *Sou shen ji* 18: 224. This passage seems to be rather corrupted and obscure. My reading is based on comparing the *Sou shen ji* version with the version from *Fengsu tongyi* and other ones. Wang Liqi's commentaries on the *Fengsu tongyi* version of the story are also very helpful for understanding the story. See Ying, *Fengsu tongyi*, 427–32.

47 "*Yi ben*" seems to refer to a chapter from *Da dai liji* 大戴禮記, "*Yi ben ming*" 易本命. It is unclear what *Liu Jia* refers to as a text.

48 See Keith Knapp, *Selfless Offspring: Filial Children and Social Order in Medieval China* (Honolulu: University of Hawai'i Press, 2005), 82–112.

49 They also drew a *jiu gong* 九宮, a square divided equally into nine blocks, on a copy of the chapter of the *Filial Piety* which they recited on that day. In other words, chanting was part of the exorcist ritual. See Liu Zhen 劉珍 et al., Wu Shuping 吳樹平 ed., *Dongguan Han ji* 東觀漢記 (Beijing: Zhonghua, 2008), 17: 757. Also see Wang Liqi's commentary on the story, Ying Shao 應劭, *Fengsu tongyi*, 429–30.

50 Fan, *Houhan shu*, 81: 2694.

51 *Shu sheng* 書生 literally means student of the books. In imperial Chinese texts, it mostly indicates students of the classics. For early medieval China, see the examples in Yan Zhitui 顏之推, *Yanshi jiaxun jijie* 顏氏家訓集解 (Shanghai Guji, 1980), 5: 316; Ge Hong 葛洪, *Shenxian zhuan jiaoshi* 神仙傳校釋 (Beijing: Zhonghua, 2010), 5: 190. *Shenxian zhuan* especially makes a good case: 天師張道陵, 字輔漢, 沛國豐縣人也。本太學書生, 博采五經。(The celestial master Zhang Dongling's style name was Fuhan, and he was from county Feng of the state of Pei. He was originally a *shusheng* of the national university, who was erudite in the five classics).

52 Gan, *Sou shen ji* 18: 229.

53 For the heavenly bureaucracy in Daoism, see Peter S. Nickerson, "Taoism, Death, and Bureaucracy in Early Medieval China" (Ph.D. dissertation: University of California, Berkeley, 1996).

Chapter 3

1. For good surveys of the Dunhuang region in history, see Valerie Hansen, *The Silk Road: A New History* (Oxford: Oxford University Press, 2012); Rong Xinjiang 榮新江, *Eighteen Lectures on Dunhuang*, trans. Imre Galambos (Leiden: Brill, 2013).
2. For the role Dunhuang played, as well as a reflection on the term Silk Road, see Hansen, *The Silk Road*, 9, 167–97.
3. Hansen, *The Silk Road*, 6–7.
4. The five Liang dynasties are the Former Liang (301–376 CE), Later Liang (386–403 CE), Northern Liang (407–439 CE), Southern Liang (397–414 CE), and Western Liang (400–421 CE).
5. Rong, *Eighteen Lectures*, 56.
6. Rong, *Eighteen Lectures*, 62–70.
7. Rong, *Eighteen Lectures*, 62–70.
8. Rong, *Eighteen Lectures*, 70–6.
9. Moreover, local people gradually adopted Tibetan-sounding names, the Tibetan alphabet, and Tibetan languages in drafting government documents. See Takata Tokio 高田時雄, "Multilingualism in Tun-huang," *Acta Asiatica* 78 (2000): 49–70.
10. See Hansen, *The Silk Road*, 184–7. For the flourishing of Buddhist art during this period, see Lilla Russell-Smith, *Uygur Patronage in Dunhuang: Regional Art Centres on the Northern Silk Road in the Tenth and Eleventh Centuries* (Leiden: Brill, 2005), 22.
11. For this period, see the surveys by Rong, *Eighteen Lectures*, 73–7, and Hansen, *The Silk Road*, 187–97. For more information about the history of the Guiyi Circuit, see Rong Xinjiang 榮新江, *Guiyijun shi yanjiu: Tang Song shidai Dunhuang lishi kaosuo* 歸義軍史研究: 唐宋時代敦煌歷史考索 (Shanghai: Guji, 1996). Also see Russell-Smith, *Uygur Patronage,*, 31–76. For the wealth of Buddhist monasteries, see Rong Xinjiang 榮新江, "Khotanese Felt and Sogdian Silver: Foreign Gifts to Buddhist Monasteries in Ninth and Tenth-Century Dunhuang," *Asia Major* 17, no. 1 (2004): 15–34.
12. Rong Xinjiang, "The Relationship of Dunhuang with the Uighur Kingdom in Turfan in the Tenth Century," in *De Dunhuang à Istanbul: Hommage à James Russell Hamilton*, ed. Louis Bazin and Peter Zieme (Turnhout: Brepols, 2001), 275–98.
13. Rong, *Eighteen Lectures*, 76–7.
14. For how the texts in the grotto were discovered and taken away, see Rong's recount in *Eighteen Lectures*, 79–108.
15. For detailed information about the construction of grottoes no.16 and 17, see Yan Wenru 閻文儒, "Mogao ku de chuangjian yu Cangjing dong de kaizao jiqi fengbi 莫高窟的創建與藏經洞的開鑿及其封閉," *Wenwu*, no. 6 (1980): 59–62.

16 There has been debate on when the grotto was sealed and for what reason. I follow Rong Xinjiang's speculation. For a summary of different speculations and Rong's assessment, see Rong, *Eighteen Lectures*, 109–36. For more detailed summaries of the speculations, see Liu Jinbao 劉進寶, "20 shiji Dunhuang cangjing dong fengbi shijian ji qi yuanyin yanjiu de huigu 20世紀敦煌藏經洞封閉時間及其原因研究的回顧" *Dunhuang yanjiu*, no. 2 (2000): 29–35.

17 Rong Xinjiang 榮新江, "The Nature of the Dunhuang Library Cave and the Reasons for its Sealing," *Cahiers d'Extrême-Asie* 11 (1999): 251; 64–6.

18 405 and 1002 are the earliest and latest dates found in the colophons of the texts, respectively. See Hansen, *The Silk Road*, 179 and footnote 30 on the page.

19 Wu Qiyu 吳其昱 has calculated the percentages of various kinds of texts in the four largest collections: British Library, Bibliothèque Nationale de France, St. Petersburg Branch of the Institute of Oriental Studies, Russian Academy of Science, with some from the Chinese National Library (Zhongguo Guojia Tushuguan 中國國家圖書館) as well. Among the four collections, the Buddhist texts take 84.07 percent, 57.81 percent, 85.17 percent, and 99.35 percent, respectively. In general, according to Ikeda, religious texts take 88.27 percent, 68.99 percent, 86.63 percent, and 99.37 percent, respectively. See Wu Qiyu 吳其昱, "Tonkō Kanbun shahon Gaikan 敦煌漢文写本概観," in *Tonkō Kanbun bunken* 敦煌漢文文獻, ed. Ikeda On 池田溫 (Tokyo: Daitō Shuppansha, 1992), 29–43.

20 For education and Buddhism in medieval China, see Victor H. Mair, "Lay Students and the Making of Written Vernacular Narrative: an Inventory of Tun-huang Manuscripts," *Journal of Chinese Oral and Performing Literature* 10, no. 1 (1981): 5–96; Erik Zürcher, "Buddhism and Education in T'ang Times," in *Neo-Confucian Education: The Formative Stage*, ed. Wm. Theodore de Bary and John W. Chaffee (Berkeley: University of California Press, 1989), 19–56; Naha Toshisada 那波利貞, "Tōshōhon zatsushō kō: Tōdai shomin kyōiku kenkyū no ichi shiryō 唐鈔本雜抄考——唐代庶民教育研究の一資料" *Shinagaku kenkyū* 10 (1942): 1–91; Yan Gengwang 嚴耕望, "Tangren dushu shanlin siyuan zhi fengshang: Jianlun shuyuan zhidu zhi qiyuan 唐人讀書山林寺院之風尚——兼論書院制度之起源," *Zhangyang Yanjiuyuan Lishi Yuyan Yanjiusuo jikan* 30 (1959): 689–728; Dai Jun 戴軍, "Tangdai siyuan jiaoyu yu wenxue 唐代寺院教育與文學" (Zhongguo Shehui Kexueyuan, 2003). For a survey of education in Dunhuang, see Qu Zhimin 屈直敏, *Dunhuang wenxian yu zhonggu jiaoyu* 敦煌文獻與中古教育 (Lanzhou: Gansu jiaoyu, 2011); Gao Mingshi 高明士, *Zhongguo zhonggu de jiaoyu yu xueli* 中國中古的教育與學禮 (Taipei: Taida, 2005).

21 For the use of the term, see for example, Ban, *Hanshu*, 30: 1763–75. For the discussion of the term *shushu*, see Marc Kalinowski, "Typology and Classification of the Mantic Arts in China," in *Handbook of Divination and Prognostication in China*, ed. Michael Lackner and Zhao Lu (Leiden: Brill, 2022), 203–7.

22 *Lunyu jizhu*, 4: 98.

23 The second-century CE literatus Wang Chong 王充 even quoted Confucius' words to criticize some of the contemporary beliefs of divination. See Wang Chong 王充, *Lunheng*, 998–1007, esp. 1001. As Liao Hsien-huei points out, the literati in medieval China often had a complex relationship with divination, where they were suspicious of it but socially engaged in the activity. See Hsien-huei Liao, "Critique and Recognition: Mantic Arts and Their Practitioners in the Writings of Song Literati," in *Handbook of Divination and Prognostication in China*, ed. Michael Lackner and Zhao Lu (Leiden: Brill, 2022), 304–44.

24 Divinatory texts have been well researched, especially bibliographically since 2000. In western languages, the standard work on Dunhuang divination texts is Marc Kalinowski, *Divination et société dans la Chine médiévale: Étude des manuscrits de Dunhuang de la Bibliothèque nationale de France et de la British Library* (Paris: Bibliothèque Nationale de France, 2003). In Chinese, the most recent and exhaustive work is Wang Jingbo 王晶波, *Dunhuang zhanbu wenxian yu shehui shenghuo* 敦煌占卜文獻與社會生活 (Lanzhou: Gansu jiaoyu, 2011). In addition, see Sugawara Shinkan 菅原信海, "Senzei sho 占筮書," in *Tonkō Kanbun bunken* 敦煌漢文文獻, ed. Ikeda On 池田溫 (Tokyo: Daitō Shuppansha, 1992), 187–214; Marc Kalinowski, "Dunhuang shuzhan xiaokao 敦煌數占小考," *Faguo Hanxue*, no. 5 (2000): 187–214; Huang Zhengjian 黃正建, *Dunhuang zhanbu wenshu yu Tang Wudai zhanbu yanjiu* 敦煌占卜文書與唐五代占卜研究 (Beijing: Xueyuan, 2001); Wang Aihe 王愛和, "Dunhuang zhanbu wenshu yanjiu 敦煌占卜文書研究" (Lanzhou University, 2003).

25 The numbers follow Wu Qiyu's statistics based on the catalogue of the St. Petersburg Branch of the Institute of Oriental Studies collection. The statistics of other collections may vary. See Wu Qiyu, "Tonkō Kanbun shahon Gaikan," 40–1.

26 Some of the attendees who left behind their copies of certain techniques went on to further succeed in officialdom more broadly. For example, Zhang Daqing 張大慶 (ca. 920 CE) became an advisor for the Guiyi Circuit and wrote the *Records of Topography in the Sha and Yi Provinces* (*Shazhou Yizhou dizhi* 沙州伊州地志). More famously, the student Zhai Zaiwen 翟再溫 (883—ca. 959 CE) later on became an Erudite (Boshi 博士) in the provincial school. He also compiled several calendars and hand-copied a version of the *Ullambana Sutra*. For the divination text copied by students, see P. 3322, P. 2859, BX (北新). 836. *Shazhou Yizhou dizhi* is also a Dunhuang text labelled S.367. Zhai's calendars can be found in P. 3247, P. 2765, and P. 2623. For more information, see Gao Mingshi, *Zhongguo zhonggu*, 317–56, 45–7.

27 *Lunyu jizhu*, 4: 97; Sima, *Shiji*, 47: 1937.

28 For example, the *Records* account mentions Confucius wrote several moral and cosmological elaborations on the core text of the *Changes* as we can see from the received version of the text. See Sima, *Shiji*, 47: 1937.

29 For the name of the text, see Zhang Zhiqing 張志清 and Lin Shitian 林世田, "S.6349 yu P.4924 Yi sanbei xiejuan zhuihe zhengli yanjiu S.6349與P.4924易三備寫卷綴合整理研究," *Wenxian*, no. 1 (2006): 50. There are three Dunhuang copies of the text: S.6349A+P.4924; S.6015; and P.5031/11. Of these, S.6015 can be dated to the Tang dynasty. For general introductions and textual issues on this, see Wang Jingbo, *Dunhuang zhanbu*, 11–22; Huang Zhengjian, *Dunhuang zhanbu wenshu*, 11–5; Kalinowski, "Dunhuang shuzhan," 193; *Divination et société*, 306–59. Zhang Zhiqing and Lin Shitian have meticulously edited and arranged the originally disorganized manuscripts. See Zhang Zhiqing 張志清 and Lin Shitian 林世田, "S.6015 Yi sanbei zhuihe yu jiaolu: Dunhuang ben Yi sanbei yanjiu zhi yi S.6015 <易三備>綴合與校錄——敦煌本 <易三備>研究之一," *Dunhuang Tulufan yanjiu* 9 (2006): 389–401; "S.6349 yu P.4924," 47–54.

30 S.6349/2.

31 "Generation" is a term based on a particular way of generating and arranging the hexagrams, called the Eight Palace Hexagrams (*ba gong gua* 八宮卦). If we start with one of the trigrams and duplicate the image vertically, we would have a hexagram with identical upper and lower parts. In the Eight Place Hexagrams system, this would be a "hexagram master" (*gua zhu* 卦主) of a hexagram family. Accordingly, seven more hexagrams can be generated from the master. The first-generation hexagram would be the one that the bottom line, or line 1 is changed to the opposite of the master hexagram. For example, the first-generation hexagram derived from Qian is Gou. The second-generation hexagram would have both line 1 and 2 opposite the master hexagram. Similarly, the fifth-generation hexagram has lines 1 to 5 opposite to the master hexagram, and hence the Bo is the fifth generation of Qian in this case. However, in one hexagram family, besides the first five hexagrams, the remaining two are generated in a more complex way. For a more detailed explanation, see Bent Nielsen, *A Companion to Yi Jing Numerology and Cosmology: Chinese Studies of Images and Numbers from Han* 漢 *(202 BCE–220 CE) to Song* 宋 *(960–1279 CE)* (London: RoutledgeCurzon, 2003), 1–5.

32 The generation line is the one that marks the change of a generation hexagram from the hexagram master, in this case, the fifth line. Similarly, the first to fourth generation hexagrams' generation lines would be lines 1 to 4, respectively.

33 By seeing a hexagram as two trigrams vertically posited, a corresponding line is the one that in the same position as the generation line, but in the other trigram. That is to say, if the generation line is the fifth line of a hexagram (the middle line of the upper trigram), its corresponding line would be the second line (the middle line of the lower trigram). The same is true for the sixth vs. third, fourth vs. first, and vice versa.

34 The *Three Completions of the Changes* manuscripts do not specify the divinatory method.

35 Nielsen, *A Companion*, 1.
36 S.6349/2.
37 See for example, Wei Shou 魏收, *Wei shu* 魏書 (Beijing: Zhonghua, 1974), 57: 1264–5.
38 S.6349/1.
39 *Yi* 易 or *Changes* does not show up here, but the colophon in S.6349 names the relevant parts as *Zhouyi xiabei zhan zangri ji dixia shi* 周易下備占葬日及地下事 (The Lower Completion of the *Changes of Zhou*: divining the burial day and places) and *Yi zhongbei juan dier* 易中備卷第二 (The Second Chapter: The Middle Completion of the *Changes*). Therefore, the *Changes* is assumed in the title. See Zhang Zhiqing and Lin Shitian, "S.6349 yu P.4924," 50.
40 The "classic" refers to the *Three Completions* itself.
41 Zhang Zhiqing and Lin Shitian, "S.6349 yu P.4924," 51–2.
42 For the meaning of the title, see Kristofer Schipper, "*Laozi zhongjing* chutan 《老子中经》初探" *Daojia wenhua yanjiu* 16 (1999): 206. For more textual information about this text, see Schipper and Verellen, *The Taoist Canon*, 92–4.
43 Sima, *Shiji*, 63: 2141.
44 In contrast, the title *Inner Scripture of Laozi* gives a sense that it is "inner," and hence reveals something more essential. This is based on the dichotomy between inner (*nei* 內) and outer (*wai* 外) which was common in medieval China. In certain contexts especially, "inner" is considered to be closer to the core teaching, such as the *Inner Classic of the Yellow Emperor* (*Huangdi neijing* 黃帝內經) and *The Inner Chapters of Baopuzi* (*Baopuzi neipian* 抱樸子內篇).
45 Sima, *Shiji*, 47: 1937.
46 Ban Gu, *Hanshu*, 30: 1704.
47 Lu Deming 陸德明, *Jingdian shiwen* 經典釋文 (Beijing: Zhonghua, 1983), 1:11.
48 For a thorough study of the authorship of *Zixia's Commentary*, see Chen Hung-sen 陳鴻森, "*Zixia Yi zhuan* kaobian 子夏易傳考辨," *Zhongyang Yanjiuyuan Lishi Yuyan Yanjiusuo jikan* 56, no. 2 (1985): 359–404, esp. 363.
49 Wei Zheng 魏徵 and Linghu Defen 令狐德棻, *Suishu* 隋書 (Beijing: Zhonghua, 1973), 32: 909.
50 See the inventory of divinatory manuals on location choosing from Dunhuang in Wang Jingbo, *Dunhuang zhanbu*, 339–93.
51 Yan Yuan already took a special place in the Confucius Temple in the late second century CE. See Huang Chin-shing 黃進興, "Xueshu yu Xinyang: Lun Kong Miao congsi zhi yu Rujia daotong yishi 學術與信仰：論孔廟從祀制與儒家道統意識" *Xin shixue* 5, no. 2 (1994): 9–12.
52 There are four Dunhuang copies: P.3782+S.557 (792 or 912 CE), P.4048 (late Tang or later), P.4984V (after Tang), and S.9766+9766V. Among these copies, only P.3782 mentions its title. For more textual information, see Wang Jingbo, *Dunhuang*

zhanbu, 65–74; Huang Zhengjian, *Dunhuang zhanbu wenshu*, 19–22; Kalinowski, "Dunhuang shuzhan," 194–5. The received version of the text is called *Lingqi benzhang zhengjing* 靈棋本章正經 (the *Classic of the Sublime Tokens*). For general information about the received *Lingqi jing* (HY 1035), see Schipper and Verellen, *The Taoist Canon*, 82–4.

53 On the issue of the authorship and who the commentator "Yan" was, see Yu Jiaxi 余嘉錫, *Siku tiyao bianzheng* 四庫提要辨正 (Beijing: Zhonghua, 1980), 738–41.

54 The method differs from text to text in terms of the tools and procedures. See, for example, P.4048.

55 The format of the results varies in different versions. While P.3782+S.557 uses the characters, P.4048 uses horizontal lines on top, vertical lines in the middle, and horizontal lines again in the bottom to symbolize the results.

56 See for example, Werner Banck, *Das chinesische Tempelorakel* (Taipei: Guting Book Store, 1976). For research on temple oracles especially in Chinese Buddhism, see Michel Strickmann, Bernard Faure ed., *Chinese Poetry and Prophecy: The Written Oracle in East Asia* (Stanford: Stanford University Press, 2005), 76–97.

57 In the received version of the poem in the *Book of Poetry*, the line is *xian fu cheng cheng* 賢夫成城 instead of *ren* in the second character. *Maoshi zhengyi* 毛詩正義, ed. Ruan Yuan 阮元, *Shisanjing zhushu* 十三經注疏 (Beijing: Zhonghua, 1980), 18: 577.

58 The sentence in the received version is 哲王又不寤, and my translation follows the received version.

59 P.3782. The same entry in the received version is significantly different from this Dunhuang version. Cf. *Lingqi benzhang zheng jing* 靈棋本章正經 (HY 1035, 2:11b–12a), *Zhengtong daozang* 正統道藏 (Beijing: Wenwu; Shanghai: Shudian, Guji, 1988), vol. 23, 471.

60 *Kou xia shi gao* 叩下史告 is unclear to me. Here I read *shi* as a borrowing for *li* 吏, meaning officials. While this *shi/li* borrowing is common, this reading breaks the rhythm from the previous sentences. An alternative reading is "when one inquires the people below, they will start talking." The downside of this reading is that *shi* is read as *shi* 始, meaning "start to." The *shi/shi* borrowing or merging is less common because their initials were similar but still distinctive in Middle Chinese.

61 *Maoshi*, 18: 577–8. For the most recent study of "Li sao" and Wang Yi's commentary, see Gopal Sukhu, *The Shaman and the Heresiarch: A New Interpretation of the* Li sao (Albany: SUNY, 2012).

62 Schipper and Verellen, *The Taoist Canon*, 82.; *Lingqi benzhang zheng jing* (HY 1035, 1:1a–5a), *Zhengtong daozang*, vol. 23, 455–6.

63 Besides the specification of "Yan Yuan," the contents of the several Dunhuang copies also differ. For example, from time to time, the "Yan Yuan" commentary gives elaborations on the *yin yang* principles that are absent in the other copies. See Wang Jingbo, *Dunhuang zhanbu*, 70.

64　Of course, we should not assume that when readers of the other copies encountered the name "Yan", they would necessarily assume that Yan indicated Yan Youming. They could still think that it indicated Yan Yuan.
65　See Chapter 2.
66　Yu Shinan 虞世南, *Beitang shuchao*, 137: 565a. Ouyang Xun 歐陽詢, *Songben yiwen leiju* 宋本藝文類聚 (Shanghai: Guji, 2013), 71: 1847; Li Fang et al., *Taiping yulan*, 728: 3229.
67　In 1981, Li Zhizhong already pointed out this characteristic. See Li Zhizhong 李志忠, "Gushu xuanfeng zhuang kao bian 古書旋風裝考辨," *Wenwu*, no. 2 (1981): 75–8.
68　This concern also led to the rise of the codex in European late antiquity in the third century CE. See Anthony Grafton and Megan Williams, *Christianity and the Transformation of the Book: Origen, Eusebius, and the Library of Caesarea* (Cambridge, MA: Belknap Press, 2006), 10–12, 103.
69　Scholars have pointed out that this binding is a rather transitional one because the binding methods varied from case to case. At the same time, many issues are still up to debate, such as whether the above page should be shorter than the one below, or even which manuscript should be considered as using a whirlwind binding. On the length of the papers, compare Colin Chinnery's introduction with Wang Chuanlong 王傳龍, ""Xuanfeng zhuang" banben huikao '旋風裝'版本匯考" *Daxue tushuguan xuebao*, no. 3 (2009): 78–84. Wang also tries to clarify which manuscripts use whirlwind binding and which had been mistakenly taken as one.
70　The title comes from S.2578. There are four Dunhuang copies of this divinatory manual: S.813C; S.9501V+S.9502+S.11419+S.13002V; S.1339; and S.2578. Bibliographically, this text can be traced back to the Sui dynasty. For more information about the textual and bibliographical issues, see Wang Jingbo, *Dunhuang zhanbu*, 100–11; Huang Zhengjian, *Dunhuang zhanbu wenshu*, 25–7; Kalinowski, "Dunhuang shuzhan," 199.
71　S.2578.
72　S.9501V.
73　S.9501V.
74　S.9501V.
75　For a summary of common divinatory methods as well as the symbols in the *Changes*, see Constance A. Cook and Zhao Lu, *Stalk Divination: A Newly Discovered Alternative to the I Ching* (Oxford: Oxford University Press, 2017), 7–23.
76　S.2578. See the editing of the text in Guan Changlong 關長龍 ed., *Dunhuang ben shushu wenxian jijiao* 敦煌本數術文獻輯校 (Beijing: Zhonghua, 2019), 448.
77　S.2578.
78　The two copies are S.2578b and S9501v+S9502V+S11419+S13002V+S1339. It is worth clarifying that the majority of topics in the two copies are still the same,

despite the different wording and orders. Also see Guan Changlong, *Dunhuang ben shushu wenxian*, 439–48.

79 Kalinowski, "Dunhuang shuzhan," 197–8.

80 Lin's works also include *Illustrations of the Qi Machines* (*Qi qi tu* 欹器圖), the *Classic of the Bronze Seismoscope* (*Didong tongyi jing* 地動銅儀經). See Wei Zheng and Linghu Defen, *Sui shu*, 78: 1778–9.

81 For Dunhuang manuscripts containing some version of this method, see: P.2574, P.2859C/P, BD14636, and S.5614C. The title only appears in the first manuscript, not the second and the third. The fourth one has a different title: *A Method of Divining Twelve Hours* (*Zhan shier shi fa* 占十二時法). For more textual and technical information about this text, see Wang Jingbo, *Dunhuang zhanbu*, 108–11; Huang Zhengjian, *Dunhuang zhanbu wenshu*, 30–1; Kalinowski, "Dunhuang shuzhan," 199.

82 P.2574.

83 For the *jianchu* 建除 system, popular from the late Warring States period to the Western Han dynasty, see Loewe, *Divination, Mythology and Monarchy*, 214–35; Kudō Motoo 工藤元男, *Suikochi Shinkan yori mita Shindai no kokka to shakai* 睡虎地秦簡よりみた秦代の國家と社會 (Tokyo: Sōbunsha, 1998), 131–40. In the recent decades, because of the accelerating discoveries of excavated early Chinese texts, many scholars have turned to studying the day books, starting from Liu Lexian 劉樂賢, *Shuihudi Qin jian rishu yanjiu* 睡虎地秦簡日書研究 (Taipei: Wenjin, 1994). Joachim Genz has discussed the technical aspects of day books in his "Elf Thesen zur Eigenart und Systematik früher chinesischer Chronomantik," *Oriens Extremus* 44 (2003/04): 101–10. For a selected translation of Shuihudi daybooks, see Lisa Raphals, *Divination and Prediction in Early China and Ancient Greece* (Cambridge: Cambridge University Press, 2013), 412–21. While many scholars concentrate on the Qin daybooks, Ethan R. Harkness analyses one of the daybooks from the Han dynasty in his "Cosmology and the Quotidian: Day books in Early China" (Ph.D. dissertation: University of Chicago, 2011), 97–160. Daniel Sou discusses the functions of daybooks among Qin dynasty local officials in his "In the government's service: A study of the role and practice of early China's officials based on excavated manuscripts" (PhD dissertation: University of Pennsylvania, 2013), 209–56.

84 P.2574.

85 *Qu* 取 here is read as *qu* 曲. See Guan Changlong, *Dunhuang ben shushu wenxian*, 1126.

86 For this image of the Duke of Zhou and his relationship with *Zhouli* in early and medieval China, see the many contributions in Benjamin A. Elman and Martin Kern eds., *Statecraft and Classical Learning: The Rituals of Zhou in East Asian History* (Leiden: Brill, 2010). In a primer from Dunhuang, the Duke of Zhou's

achievements, including achieving the Great Peace, were delineated. See P.2570 and Zheng A'cai 鄭阿財, "Dunhuang xieben 'Kongzi beiwen shu' chutan 敦煌寫本《孔子備問書》初探," *Dunhuang xue* 17 (1991): 111.

87 See the divinatory texts entitled with the Duke of Zhou, such as S.561, P.3908, P.3281VD, and S.612.

88 For example, the Duke of Zhou was portrayed as a powerful diviner in Ming and Qing dramas. See Vincent Durand-Dastès, "Divination and Fate Manipulation in a Popular Myth of Late Imperial China: *The Wedding of Zhougong and Peach Blossom Girl*," in *International Consortium for Research in the Humanities: Selected Lectures* (International Consortium for Research in the Humanities, November 11, 2010), 1–34.

89 For more technical details of this method and bibliographical information about the manuscripts, see Wang Jingbo, *Dunhuang zhanbu*, 75–89; Huang Zhengjian, *Dunhuang zhanbu wenshu*, 23–5; Kalinowski, "Dunhuang shuzhan," 194.

90 We can see this narrative in the *Book of Documents* and the *Records of the Grand Historian*: *Shangshu* 尚書, ed. Ruan Yuan 阮元, Shisan jing zhushu 十三經注疏 (Beijing: Zhonghua, 1980), 13:195–6; Sima, *Shiji*, 33: 1516–18.

91 Both S.3724V and S.3724+S.11415 have this title.

92 S.3724V.

93 For the authorship of the *Dao de jing*, see William G. Boltz, "*Lao tzu Tao te ching* 老子道德經," in *Early Chinese Texts: A Bibliographical Guide*, ed. Michael Loewe (Berkeley: University of California Press, 1993), 269–71. For Confucius visiting Laozi and its textual and visual rendering during the Han dynasty, see Sima Qian 司馬遷, *Shiji*, 63: 2140; Xing Yitian 邢義田, *Huawai zhi yi: Handai Kongzi jian Laozi huaxiang yanjiu* 畫外之意: 漢代孔子見老子畫像研究 (Beijing: Sanlian, 2020). For Laozi as a fictitious figure, see A. C. Graham, "The Origins of the Legend of Lao Tan," in *Lao-tzu and the Tao-te-ching: Studies in Ethics, Law, and the Human Ideal*, ed. Livia Kohn and Michael LaFargue (Albany: SUNY, 1998), 23–40; Livia Kohn, "The Lao-tzu Myth," in *Lao-tzu and the Tao-te-ching: Studies in Ethics, Law, and the Human Ideal,* ed. Livia Kohn and Michael LaFargue (Albany: SUNY, 1998), 41–62.

94 Such as the Scripture of the Names and Images of Laozi in Ten Directions (Laozi shifang xiangming jing 老子十方像名經), One Hundred and Eighty Rules of Lord Lao (Laojun shuo yibaibashi jie 老君說一百八十戒), the Scripture of the Transformation of Laozi (Laozi bianhua jing 老子變化經). For the many Daoist scriptures named after Laozi, see Wang Ka 王卡, Dunhuang Daojiao wenxian yanjiu: Zongshu, Mulu, Suoyin 敦煌道教文獻研究——綜述·目錄·索引 (Beijing: Shehui kexue, 2004), 187–93.

95 Laozi is the most important figure in Daoism and has been well studied by generations of scholars. For a concise introduction to the image of Laozi in

Daoism, see Fabrizio Pregadio ed., *The Encyclopedia of Taoism* (London; New York: Routledge, 2004), 611–6.

96 Text Indian Office Library Manuscript, Stein (c): Fr. 55 (vol.68, fol. 115–6). The transliteration and translation come from F. W. Thomas, *Ancient Folk-Literature from North-Eastern Tibet* (Berlin: Akademie Verlag, 1957), 151. Also see the discussion by Shen-yu Lin, "The Tibetan Image of Confucius," *Revue d'Etudes Tibétaines* 12 (2007): 107.

97 For Confucius' image in apocrypha, see Chapter 1 of the book and Zhao Lu, "To Become Confucius," 115–44. During the Tang dynasty, Confucius was often referred to as the "dark sage" (*xuansheng* 玄聖) by the literati. See, for example, Ouyang Xun, *Yiwen leiju*, 38: 924. For the images of Confucius after the Tang, see the series of depictions on Confucius' life, "Kongzi shengji tu" 孔子聖跡圖 (Images of Confucius' sagely traces), which can be traced back to the Yuan dynasty. See Murray, "Miraculous Portraits of Confucius," 78–105; Ling Yuxuan 凌玉萱, "Jian'gou shenshengzhe chuanqi: Cong *Shishi Yuanliu* dao *Shengji tu* de chuanqi yunsheng tuxiang fazhan guocheng 建構神聖者傳奇——從《釋氏源流》到《聖蹟圖》的傳奇孕生圖像發展過程," *Yishu fenzi* no. 8 (2007): 15–42.

98 For the image of Confucius in Tibet, see Lin, "The Tibetan Image of Confucius," 105–29.

99 This is also the case for Confucius in certain Dunhuang texts. See "Kongzi beiwen shu" 孔子備問書 (A book of comprehensive questions towards Confucius) as edited by Zheng A'cai, "'Kongzi beiwen shu,'" 101–15.

100 In several Dunhuang texts, *xian* is used as a general term to include people both narrowly considered as sages, such as Confucius, and the ones narrowly considered as worthies, such as Wu Zixu 伍子胥. Here I also use the word "worthy" as a general term for these exemplary figures. For *xian* used as a general term, see the Dunhuang text *Gu xian ji* 古賢集, as annotated by Chen Qinghao 陳慶浩, "*Gu xian ji jiaozhu* 古賢集校注," *Dunhuang xue* 3 (1976): 63–102. For sages and worthies, see Michael J. Puett, "Sages, Creation, and the End of History in the *Huainanzi*," in *The Huainanzi and Textual Production in Early China* ed. Sarah A. Queen and Michael J. Puett (Leiden: Brill, 2014), 269–90; David Elstein, "Beyond the Five Relationships: Teachers and Worthies in Early Chinese Thought," *Philosophy East and West* 62, no. 3 (2012): 375–91.

101 "Han Peng fu" 韓朋賦, in Wang Chongmin 王重民 et al. eds., *Dunhuang bianwen ji* 敦煌變文集 (Beijing: Renmin, 1957), 137–9.

102 For more information about this text, its copies, bibliographical information, and especially who this heir might be, see Yang Mingzhang 楊明璋, "Dunhuang ben 'Qian Han Liu jia taizi zhuan' kaolun 敦煌本《前漢劉家太子傳》考論," *Dunhuang xue* 28 (2010): 91–110.

103 "Qian Han Liujia taizi zhuan" 前漢劉家太子傳, Wang Chongmin et al., *Dunhuang bianwen ji*, 161.

104 The *bianwen* texts stimulate many debates, including what the word *bian* means, what is the usual format of a *bianwen* text, what can be considered as a *bianwen* text, etc. For these issues, I follow Victor Mair's arguments in his *T'ang Transformation Texts: A Study of the Buddhist Contribution to the Rise of Vernacular Fiction and Drama in China* (Cambridge, MA: Harvard University Press, 1989), 27, 65, 134, and 39. Also see Eugene Eoyang, "Oral Narration in the *Pien* and *Pien-wen*," *Archiv orientální: Journal of the Czechoslovak Oriental Institute* 46 (1978): 232–52; Hiroshi Arami 荒見泰史, *Dunhuang bianwen xieben de yanjiu* 敦煌變文寫本的研究 (Beijing: Zhonghua, 2010); Li Xiaorong 李小榮, *Dunhuang bianwen* 敦煌變文 (Lanzhou: Gansu jiaoyu, 2013).

105 For the dating of this text, see Wang Weiqin 王偉琴, ""Li Ling bianwen" zuoshi zuozhe kaolun 《李陵變文》作時作者考論" *Yuwen zhishi* no. 2 (2012): 6–8.

106 "Li Ling bianwen" 李陵變文, in Wang Chongmin et al., *Dunhuang bianwen ji*, 86.

107 See Ban, *Hanshu*, 54: 2451–3. For the plot of the story as well as a more detailed analysis on the literary representations of Li Ling in the transformation texts and the *Book of Han*, see Yu Taolai 俞陶來, "'Li Ling bianwen' chu tan 《李陵變文》初探," *Dunhuang yanjiu* no. 4 (1988): 72–7.

108 Ban, *Hanshu*, 54: 2453.

109 This is why the Tang dynasty commentator of the *Book of Han*, Yan Shigu 顏師古 (581–645 CE) commented on the passage, saying that the morale was not boosted by drumming. Ban, *Hanshu*, 54: 2453.

110 For weather and cloud divination texts from Dunhuang, see especially S.3326 and DB (敦博).076V. Wang Jingbo has a comprehensive survey on the weather divination texts from Dunhuang in his *Dunhuang zhanbu*, 150–64. Zhu Lei 朱雷 points out the custom of not having women in a troop and the divinatory connotations related to it. See his Zhu Lei 朱雷, "'Li Ling bianwen,' 'Zhang Yichao bianwen,' 'Pomo bian' zhupian bianyi 《李陵變文》、《張義潮變文》、《破魔變》諸篇辨疑," *Wei Jin Nanbeichao Sui Tang shi ziliao* 13 (1994): 48–9.

111 David Johnson has thoroughly studied this text in his articles David Johnson, "The Wu Tzu-hsü Pien-wen and its Sources: Part I," *Harvard Journal of Asiatic Studies* 40, no. 1 (1980): 93–156; Johnson, "The Wu Tzu-hsü Pien-wen and Its Sources: Part II," *Harvard Journal of Asiatic Studies* 40, no. 2 (1980): 465–505.

112 "Wu Zixu bianwen" 伍子胥變文, in Wang Chongmin et al., *Dunhuang bianwen ji*, 8.

113 This core story can be traced back to texts like *Zuozhuan* 左傳 and *Guoyu* 國語. For more classical sources about Wu Zixu, see Johnson, "Part I," 119–28.

114 Stephen W. Durrant, *The Cloudy Mirror: Tension and Conflict in the Writings of Sima Qian* (Albany: SUNY, 1995), 75–97.

115 Chen Qinghao, "*Gu xian ji*," 79.

116 Johnson, "Part I," 146.

117 Wang Chong, *Lunheng*, 26: 1069.

118 See, for example, how Confucian classics and divinatory texts were copied together by various kinds of students in Dunhuang as reflected by the colophons. Li Zhengyu 李正宇 has collected them in his "Dunhuang xuelang tiji jizhu 敦煌學郎題記輯注" *Dunhuang xue jikan* no. 1 (1987): 28, 30, 34, 38.

119 For a good review and reflection on this issue, see Epstein, "The Diviner and the Scientist: Revisiting the Question of Alternative Standards of Rationality," 1048-86.

Chapter 4

1. For the history of Jesuits in China, see D. E. Mungello, *Curious Land: Jesuit Accommodation and the Origins of Sinology* (Honolulu: University of Hawai'i Press, 1985); Liam Matthew Brockey, *Journey to the East: The Jesuit Mission to China, 1579–1724* (Cambridge, MA: The Belknap Press of Harvard University Press, 2007).
2. For a detailed history of Civil Examination, see Elman, *A Cultural History of Civil Examinations in Late Imperial China*.
3. As Trude Dijkstra and Thijs Weststeijn have pointed out, this is not the first translation of the *Analects* in European languages. According to them, the first translation in a European language was in Dutch by Pieter van Hoorn in 1675. See Trude Dijkstra and Thijs Weststeijn, "Constructing Confucius in the Low Countries," *De Zeventiende Eeuw* 32 (2016): 137–64.
4. For a more comprehensive survey of the Jesuits' attempt to translate the *Analects* and the Four Books, see Meynard, *The Jesuit Reading of Confucius*, 2–15; Jensen, *Manufacturing Confucianism*, 31–75. For the accommodationist approach Acosta and Ricci employed, see Andrés I. Prieto, "The Perils of Accommodation: Jesuit Missionary Strategies in the Early Modern World," *Journal of Jesuit Studies* 4 (2017): 395–414.
5. Meynard, *The Jesuit Reading of Confucius*, 15–19.
6. For studies of Confucius' image in *Confucius, the Philosopher of China*, see ref; Meynard, *The Jesuit Reading of Confucius*, 57–78.
7. Meynard, *The Jesuit Reading of Confucius*, 36.
8. Mungello, *Curious Land*, 57–63.
9. For the official titles that Confucius received, see Thomas A. Wilson, "Culture, Society, Politics, and the Cult of Confucius," in *On Sacred Grounds: Culture, Society, Politics, and the Formation of the Cult of Confucius*, ed. Thomas A. Wilson (Cambridge, MA: Harvard University Asia Center, 2002), 3.
10. Of course, this does not mean that Confucius' thought cannot be categorized as philosophy in this definition or other conventional senses. See, for example, Van Norden, *Taking Back Philosophy*.
11. The translation is from Meynard, *The Jesuit Reading of Confucius*, 93.

12 Meynard, *The Jesuit Reading of Confucius*, 35–6, 65, 93; Jensen, *Manufacturing Confucianism*, 70--5. For the meaning of *ren* in Confucius' thought, see Goldin, *Confucianism*, 18–22.
13 Meynard, *The Jesuit Reading of Confucius*, 50, 76–8; 614.
14 For the Gold Rush and the Chinese immigrants' experiences, see Mary Roberts Coolidge, *Chinese Immigration* (New York: Henry Holt, 1909), 498–504; Mae M. Ngai, *The Chinese Question: The Gold Rushes and Global Politics* (New York: W. W. Norton & Company, Inc., 2021), 39–95. For railroad construction in the 1860s, see Alexander Saxton, *The Indispensable Enemy: Labor and the Anti-Chinese Movement in California* (Berkeley, CA: University of California Press, 1971), 60–7; Michael Bottoms, *An Aristocracy of Color: Race and Reconstruction in California and the West, 1850–1890* (Norman: University of Oklahoma Press, 2013), 137. For the violence that Chinese immigrants received, see Beth Lew-Williams, *The Chinese Must Go: Violence, Exclusion, and the Making of the Alien in America* (Cambridge, MA: Harvard University Press, 2018), 89–165.
15 Lew-Williams, *The Chinese Must Go*, 24–43.
16 "From the Morals of Confucius," *New-York Weekly Journal* January 24, 1737, 1–3; "The Continuation of the Morals of Confucius," *New-York Weekly Journal* February 13, 1737, 1–3; "Advertisement," *Boston Evening-Post* September 12, 1743, 2. For the readership of newspapers in colonial America, see Uriel Heyd, *Reading Newspapers: Press and Public in Eighteenth-century Britain and America* (Oxford: Voltaire Foundation, 2012), 18–22.
17 Thomas Paine, *The Age of Reason* (Toronto: W.B. Cooke & W.M. Scott, 1887), 31–2; 60–2. For an elaboration of Paine's thought, see Kerry S. Walters, *The American Deists: Voices of Reason and Dissent in the Early Republic* (Lawrence: University Press of Kansas, 1992), 209–39.
18 Rev. Supper's letter was written two years earlier on May 18, 1815. See J. C. Supper, "From the Rev. J. C. Supper, Secretary of the Java Auxiliary Bible Society, May 18, 1815," *Christian Messenger* January 22, 1817, 1.
19 "Confucius," *Christian Messenger* March 10, 1819, 4.
20 Kathryn Gin Lum, *Heathen: Religion and Race in American History* (Cambridge, MA: Harvard University Press, 2022), esp. 28, 68, 91.
21 Samuel Wells Williams, *Middle Kingdom; A Survey of the Geography, Government, Education, Social Life, Arts, Religion, &c., of the Chinese Empire and Its Inhabitants* (New York & London: Wiley & Putnam, 1849), 296–7, 334.
22 Joshua Paddison, *American Heathens: Religion, Race, and Reconstruction in California* (Berkeley: University of California Press, 2012), 21, 43. "Democratic Logic," *Elevator* August 30, 1867, 2; "Chinese in America," *American Missionary* October 1875, 229. For African American activists' view on Chinese in mid-nineteenth century, see Leigh Dana Johnsen, "Equal Rights and the 'Heathen

Chinee': Black Activism in San Francisco, 1865–1875," *Western Historical Quarterly* 11, no. 1 (1980): 57–68.
23. *People v. Hall*, 4 California (1854).
24. For the legal status of the Chinese immigrants and its comparison to African Americans, see Najia Aarim-Heriot, *Chinese Immigrants, African Americans, and Racial Anxiety in the United States* (Urbana: University of Illinois Press, 2006), 30–45.
25. For the connotations of "heathen" in nineteenth-century America, see Lum, *Heathen*, 151–74; Sylvester A. Johnson, *The Myth of Ham in Nineteenth-Century American Christianity: Race, Heathens, and the People of God* (New York: Palgrave Macmillan, 2004), 135; Jennifer C. Snow, *Protestant Missionaries, Asian Immigrants, and Ideologies of Race in America, 1850–1924* (New York: Routledge, 2007), 2–3. For the argument made for African Americans, see William Higby, *Privileges and Immunities of Citizenship* (Washington: Government Printing Office, 1866), 6–7; Paddison, *American Heathens*, 19–20.
26. Paddison, *American Heathens*, 23–4.
27. Paddison, *American Heathens*, 35–6; "Republican State Convention," *Sacramento Daily Record* June 29, 1871, 5; "The Chinese, Shall He Be Welcome?," *Elevator* March 8, 1873, 3.
28. Andrew Gyory, *Closing the Gate: Race, Politics, and the Chinese Exclusion Act* (Chapel Hill: The University of North Carolina Press, 1998), 245–55; Lew-Williams, *The Chinese Must Go*, 45–52. As Lew-Williams points out, in 1882 there was no national consensus supporting Chinese exclusion, and the act was focusing on restriction rather than exclusion.
29. Ronald Takaki, *Strangers from a Different Shore: A History of Asian Americans* (Boston, Toronto, and London: Little, Brown and Company, 1989), 111–12.
30. "The Chinese New Year," *Worcester Daily Spy* January 28, 1884, 1. For the most comprehensive documentation of Confucius in American newspapers since 1849, see Zhang Tao 張濤, *Kongzi zai Meiguo: 1849 nian yilai Kongzi zai Meiguo baozhi shang de xingxiang bianqian* 孔子在美國: 1849年以來孔子在美國報紙上的形象變遷 (Beijing: Beijng Daxue, 2011).
31. A.W. Loomis, *Confucius and the Chinese Classics; or Readings in Chinese Literature* (San Francisco: A. Roman & Company, 1867).
32. "A Modern Chinese Moralist," *Philadelphia Inquirer* February 14, 1884, 3.
33. "Street Scenes in Papeete, Tahiti," *Chicago Daily Tribune* May 27, 1876, 2.
34. "The Chinese," *Chicago Daily Tribune* December 26, 1879, 2.
35. "Table Gossip," *Boston Daily Globe* September 15, 1877, 4.
36. "From Our Exchanges," *Zion's Herald* November 29, 1877, 1.
37. "Ah Bak, the Christian. The Chinaman Who Embraced Modern Religion But Clung to His Opium Habit," *Boston Daily Globe* September 25, 1882, 1.

38 "A Chinese Gambling Hell," *New York Times* October 2, 1883, 8; "Celestial Chess," *Boston Daily Globe* August 25, 1889, 18.
39 "Editorial Article," *Boston Daily Globe* April 17, 1877, 4.
40 Stephen Powers, "Aborigines of California: An Indo-Chinese Study," *The Atlantic* (March, 1874): 316.
41 For "sons of Confucius," see, for example, "Enterprise of the Chinese," *The Daily Graphic* January 31, 1876, 7.
42 "The Chinese: Moon-eyed Knights of the Wash-Tub and Sad-Iron. How They Dress, Eat, Sleep and Earn Their Living. Their Peculiarities, Superstitions and Vices as a People," *Boston Daily Globe* August 19, 1878, 2.
43 James G. Blaine, *Life and Work of James G. Blaine* (New York: Western W. Wilson, 1893), 297.
44 Blaine, *Life and Work,* 300–1.
45 Blaine, *Life and Work,* 297, 302.
46 Blaine, *Life and Work,* 293–99.
47 Lew-Williams, *The Chinese Must Go,* 17–51. For the support of Chinese immigration, see Paddison, *American Heathens,* 38–56.
48 Paddison, *American Heathens,* 35.
49 Paddison, *American Heathens,* 37–44.
50 "Chinese Characteristics: Fifth Discourse in Rev. Dr. Newman's Series–'Confucius and Confucianism,'" *New York Herald* May 27, 1878, 11.
51 "Chinese Characteristics."
52 "Chinese Characteristics."
53 Certain commentary of *Liezi* already points out that the passage is set up to promote Buddhism. See Yang Bojun 楊伯峻 ed., *Liezi jishi* 列子集釋 (Beijing: Zhonghua, 1985), 4:121. For Emperor Ming's dream, the most frequently cited source is Fan, *Houhan shu,* 88: 2922. For a definitive study of Confucius' prophecy on Jesus in *Confucius, the Philosopher of China,* see Zhu Yanbing 朱雁冰, "*Zhongguo zheren Kongzi*" 14-5.
54 "Some Remarkable Giants," *San Francisco Bulletin* May 18, 1889, 6. For a more substantial study of Zhan's life, see Wang Zhenzhong 王振忠, "Cong 'Hongguan changren' dao 'Zhongguo juren': Wanqing Wuyuan Zhan Shichai shengping shiji kaozheng 從'虹關長人'到'中國巨人': 晚晴婺源詹世釵生平事跡考證," *Anhui Shifan Daxue xuebao* 45 (2017): 529–42.
55 "A Modern Chinese Moralist," *Philadelphia Enquirer,* February 14, 1884, 3.
56 "A Chinaman was Testifying in Richmond," *New York Tribune* May 17, 1878, 8.
57 Mark Twain, "John Chinaman in New York," in *Mark Twain's Sketches, New and Old,* ed. Mark Twain (Hartford: American Publishing, 1875), 231–32. For an illuminating study of this piece and Twain's view on Chinese in his works, see Hsin-yun Ou, "Mark Twain's Racial Ideologies and His Portrayal of the Chinese," *Concentric: Literary and Cultural Studies* 36, no. 2 (2010): 33–59, esp. 38–40.

58 For the life and political orientations of Thomas Nast, see Fiona Deans Halloran, *Thomas Nast: The Father of Modern Political Cartoons* (Chapel Hill: The University of North Carolina Press, 2012), esp. 257. For Nast's views on and depictions of Chinese as well as the creation of John Confucius, see Wenxian Zhang, "Standing up against Racial Discrimination: Progressive Americans and the Chinese Exclusion Act in the Late Nineteenth Century," *Phylon* 56, no. 1 (2019): 20–3; Michele Walfred, "Chinese Americans," https://thomasnastcartoons.com/the-chinese-cartoons/ (accessed October 25, 2023); John Kuo Wei Tchen, *New York Before Chinatown: Orientalism and the Shaping of American Culture 1776–1882* (Baltimore: The Johns Hopkins University Press, 1999), 202–3.

59 Thomas Nast, "Civilization of Blaine," *Harper's Weekly* XXIII (March 8, 1879): cover page. For a study of the background of this cartoon, see Michele Walfred, "'Civilization of Blaine' 1879," April 8, 2014, https://thomasnastcartoons.com/2014/04/08/civilization-of-blaine-8-march-1879/ (accessed October 25, 2023). David Bindman, "Am I Not a Man and a Brother? British Art and Slavery in the Eighteenth Century," *Anthropology and Aesthetics* 26 (1994): 79.

60 Thomas Nast, "A Matter of Taste," *Harper's Weekly* XXIV (March 15, 1879): 118; Michele Walfred, "'A Matter of Taste' 15 March 1879," April 1, 2014, https://thomasnastcartoons.com/2014/04/01/a-matter-of-taste-15-march-1879/ (accessed October 25, 2023).

61 For a survey of this stereotype in nineteenth-century America, see Yong Chen, *Chop Suey, USA: The Story of Chinese Food in America* (New York: Columbia University Press, 2014), 14–20; Andrew Coe, *Chop Suey: A Cultural History of Chinese Food in the United States* (Oxford: Oxford University Press, 2009), 58–63. For using the feeling of disgust to construct social groups, see Michael Owen Jones, "What's Disgusting, Why, and What Does It Matter?," *Journal of Folklore Research* 37, no. 1 (2000): 53–71.

62 "Ah Sin–Chin Shin Yin," *Pomeroys Democrat* August 17, 1878, 6.

63 For more of these reports, see Zhang Tao, *Kongzi zai Meiguo*, 97–204.

64 *Lunyu jizhu*, 9: 175.

65 Guillaume Zagury and Laurie Underwood, "How Pandemic Proves China's 'Digital Confucianism' is Superior to the West," *South China Morning Post* September 16, 2021.

Chapter 5

1 Ban, *Hanshu*, 1b: 76. For the imperial sacrifice to Confucius, see "Wilson, "Culture, Society, Politics, and the Cult of Confucius," 1–42.

2 For the history of civil examination, see Elman, *A Cultural History of Civil Examinations in Late Imperial China*.

3   John K. Fairbank and Kwang-Ching Liu eds., *Late Ch'ing, 1800–1911, Part 2, The Cambridge History of China* (Cambridge: Cambridge University Press, 1980), esp. 142–201.

4   See, for example, Yi Baisha 易白沙, "Kongzi pingyi shang 孔子平議 (上)," *Xin qingnian* 1, no. 6 (1916); "Kongzi pingyi xia 孔子平議 (下)," *Xin qingnian* 2, no. 1 (1916). Centered on the journal *New Youth* (*Xin qingnian* 新青年), the intellectuals like Chen Duxiu 陳獨秀 (1879–1942) told their readers that the imperial connotations of Confucius' teaching were necessarily at odds with contemporary life. See Zhu Hong 朱洪, "Cong chongji Kongjia dian dao faqi wenxue geming: Chen Duxiu 1916 nian zhubian *Xin qingnian* di'er juan sixiang pingxi 從衝擊孔家店到發起文學革命——陳獨秀1916年主編《新青年》第二卷思想評析," *Wenhua xuekan*, no. 1 (2018): 109–15.

5   Wu Yu 吳虞, "Chiren yu lijiao 吃人與禮教," *Xin qingnian* 6, no. 6 (1919).

6   For the sense of humiliation of Qing and Republican China, see Rana Mitter, *A Bitter Revolution: China's Struggle with the Modern World* (Oxford: Oxford University Press, 2004), 30–5.

7   For the diverse attitude toward westernization during Republican China, see Zhao Libin 趙立彬, "Wanqing zhi Minguo shiqi xihua sixiang de fasheng yu fazhan shulun 晚清至民國時期西化思想的發生與發展述論," *Zhongshan Daxue xuebao luncong*, no. 3 (2000): 139–49.

8   For the various intellectual paths and social movements, see Mitter, *A Bitter Revolution*, 102–49.

9   For Marxism and its impact on the revolutions in modern China, see Arif Dirlik, *Marxism in the Chinese Revolution* (Lanham: Rowman & Littlefield Publishers, Inc., 2005), 17–71; Adrian Chan, *Chinese Marxism* (London: Continuum, 2003), 29–46; Maurice Meisner, *Li Ta-Chao and the Origins of Chinese Marxism* (Cambridge, MA: Harvard University Press, 1967), 29–70.

10 For the establishment of the CCP and its early years, see Hans J. Van de Ven, *From Friend to Comrade: The Founding of the Chinese Communist Party, 1920–1927* (Berkeley: University of California Press1991), 9–54. For the intellectual debates of the twenties and thirties, see Timothy Cheek, *The Intellectual in Modern Chinese History* (Cambridge: Cambridge University Press, 2015), 70–108.

11 Arif Dirlik, "The Ideological Foundations of the New Life Movement: A Study in Counterrevolution," *The Journal of Asian Studies* 34, no. 4 (1975): 961–7.

12 GMD, for example, revived the sacrificial ritual to Confucius. See Li Junling 李俊領, "Kangzhan shiqi Guomindang yu Nanjing Guomin Zhengfu dui Kongzi de jisi dianli 抗戰時期國民黨與南京國民政府對孔子的祭祀典禮," *Shehui kexue pinglun*, no. 4 (2008): 45–62. For the GMD's leadership's view on Confucius and Confucianism, see Maggie Clinton, *Revolutionary Nativism: Fascism and Culture in China, 1925–1937* (Durham: Duke University Press, 2017), esp. 19, 32–33, 66–73.

13 Mao's attitude toward Confucius was generally positive. See Han Yanming 韓延明, "Mao Zedong tan Kongzi 毛澤東談孔子," *Dangshi wenhui*, no. 10 (2020): 37–41.
14 Deng Tuo 鄧拓, "Shui lingdao le Wusi yundong? 誰領導了五四運動," *People's Daily* April 29, 1950, 4.
15 For the slogan of "Beat down the Confucius shop" (*dadao Kongjia dian* 打倒孔家店) in Republican China, see Jennifer May, "Sources of Authority: Quotational Practice in Chinese Communist Propaganda" (University of Heidelberg, 2008), 96–124.
16 A representative of historiography is *An Outlined Compilation of Chinese History* (*Zhongguo tongshi jianbian* 中國通史簡編), first published in Yan'an in 1942. It served as a foundation for a high school history textbook in 1951. And in the beginning years of the PRC in general, this type of histography was intended to be taught in middle schools. See Fan Wenlan 范文瀾, *Zhongguo tongshi jianbian* 中國通史簡編, vol. 7-8, Fan Wenlan quanji 范文瀾全集 (Shijiazhuang: Hebei Jiaoyu, 2002), 1-30; Li Guangbi 李光璧, "Guanyu gao chuzhong benguoshi gudai bufen jiaocai jiaofa de yixie wenti 關於高初中本國史古代部分教材教法的一些問題," *Lishi jiaoxue*, no. 2 (1952): 18; Li Yu 李雨, "Jianguo chuqi (1949-1953) zhongxue lishi jiaokeshu jiazhi quxiang yanjiu 建國初期(1949–1953)中學歷史教科書價值取向研究" (Henan Shifan Daxue, 2016), 10–3, 15–20. For a salient critique of labeling the Zhou dynasty as "feudal," see Li Feng, "'Feudalism' and Western Zhou China: A Criticism," *Harvard Journal of Asiatic Studies* 63, no. 1 (2003): 115–44.
17 Sima, *Shiji*, 47: 1905; 44.
18 Fan, *Zhongguo tongshi jianbian*, 71.
19 For the meaning of humanity, or *ren* 仁, see Goldin, *Confucianism*, 18–9.
20 *Lunyu jizhu*, 3:91; Fan, *Zhongguo tongshi jianbian*, 72.
21 *Zhongguo tongshi jianbian*, 72–3.
22 *Zhongguo tongshi jianbian*, 73.
23 See, for example, Yan Jiayan 嚴家炎, "Ping 'Wusi,' 'Wenge,' yu chuantong wenhua de lunzheng 評'五四'、'文革'與傳統文化的論爭," *Zhongwai wenhua yu wenlun* (1999): 62–5.
24 See Roderick MacFarquhar, *Contradictions Among the People, 1956–1957, The Origins of the Cultural Revolution* (London: Oxford University Press, 1974), 15–25, 30.
25 For these two practices and a survey of the Great Leap Forward Movement in general, see *The Great Leap Forward, 1958–1960, The Origins of the Cultural Revolution* (New York: Columbia University Press, 1983), esp. 77–90, 113–16.
26 Officially this period is called the Three-Year Famine, or *sannian ziran zaihai* 三年自然災害 by the PRC. This arguably is a maneuver to distance the death rate from the Great Leap Forward. See Nancy Qian and Pierre Yared, "The Institutional Causes of China's Great Famine, 1959–1961," *Review of Economic Studies* 82, no. 4 (2015): 1568–611.

27 For the reason for the Cultural Revolution, see Roderick MacFarquhar, *The Coming of the Cataclysm, 1961–1966. The Origins of the Cultural Revolution* (Oxford and New York: Oxford University Press and Columbia University Press, 1997), 364–6, 75–7; Roderick MacFarquhar and Michael Schönhals, *Mao's Last Revolution* (Cambridge, MA: Harvard University Press, 2006), 3–9.

28 MacFarquhar and Schönhals, *Mao's Last Revolution*, 24, 39–44, 115–23, 85–90, 273–84.

29 MacFarquhar and Schönhals, *Mao's Last Revolution*, 354–7; 94; Alan P. L. Liu, "Mass Communication and Media in China's Cultural Revolution," *Journalism Quarterly* 42, no. 2 (1969): 314–9.

30 Chen jin 陳晉, "Mao Zedong yuedu shilüe wu 毛澤東閱讀史略(五)," *Zhonggong dangshi yanjiu*, no. 10 (2013): 19–20.

31 For an annotation of the poem, see Hu Weixiong 胡為雄 ed., *Mao Zedong shizhuan* 毛澤東詩傳 (Beijing: Zhongyang Dangxiao, 2014), 296–300.

32 For Guo's evaluation of Confucius and the First Emperor, see Guo Moruo 郭沫若, *Shi pipan shu* 十批判書 (Shanghai: Qunyi, 1945), 63–92; 382–94.

33 Mao mentioned his reasoning on December 17, 1972, July 4 and 17, 1973. See Zhonggong zhongyang wenxian yanjiushi 中共中央文獻研究室, *Mao Zedong nianpu: 1949–1976* 毛澤東年譜:1949–1976, 6 vols., vol. 6 (Beijing: Zhongyang wenxian, 2013), 458, 85, 88. For Mao's evaluation of the First Emperor, see Wang Zijin 王子今, "Mao Zedong lunxi Qin Shihuang 毛澤東論析秦始皇," *Bainian chao*, no. 10 (2003):38–43

34 Zhonggong zhongyang wenxian yanjiushi, *Mao Zedong nianpu 1949–1976*, 485. Mao Zedong 毛澤東, "*Mao Zedong sixiang wansui*: 1958–1960 毛澤東思想萬歲 1958–1960" (Gang'er si Wuhan Daxue zongbu 鋼二司武漢大學總部, 1969). For variants of this set of primary source, see Chen Biao 陳標, "*Mao Zedong sixiang wansui* zai haiwai de liyong 《毛澤東思想萬歲》在海外的利用," *Dangdai Zhongguo shi yanjiu* 16, no. 4 (2009): 114–19.

35 For a detailed account of the alleged assassination, see Wang Dongxing 汪東興, *Wang Dongxing huiyi: Mao Zedong yu Lin Biao fangeming jituan de douzheng* 汪東興回憶:毛澤東與林彪反革命集團的鬥爭 (Beijing: Dangdai Zhongguo, 1997), 182–212.

36 Yang Rongguo 楊榮國, "Kongzi: Wangu di weihu nulizhi de sixiangjia 孔子——頑固地維護奴隸制的思想家," *Renmin ribao* August 7, 1973, 2.

37 Rongguo 楊榮國, "Kongzi," *Renmin ribao* August 7, 1973, 2.

38 Rongguo 楊榮國, "Kongzi," *Renmin ribao* August 7, 1973, 2.

39 Yang Rongguo 楊榮國, *Kong Mo de sixiang* 孔墨的思想 (Hong Kong: Shenghuo shudian, 1943).

40 Zhonggong zhongyang wenxian yanjiushi, *Mao Zedong nianpu 1949–1976*, 458; *Mao Zedong nianpu: 1949–1976* 毛澤東年譜:1949–1976, vol. 5 (Beijing: Zhonguang wenxian, 2013), 568; honggong zhongyang wenxian yanjiushi, *Mao Zedong*

nianpu 1949–1976, 458; *Mao Zedong nianpu 1949–1976* 毛澤東年譜:1949–1976, 6 vols., vol. 5 (Beijing: Zhonguang wenxian,2013), 568; Chen Jin 陳晉, *Mao Zedong zhi hun* 毛澤東之魂 (Beijing: Zhongyang wenxian, 1997), 276.

41 Li Jinquan 李錦全, *Xiandai sixiang shijia Yang Rongguo* 現代思想史家楊榮國 (Guangzhou: Zhongshan Daxue Press, 2009), 124.

42 Fan Ge 凡歌, "Yang Rongguo: Yige lishi xuezhe de xuanze ti 楊榮國:一個歷史學者的選擇題," *Guojia lishi*, no. 2 (2010): 37.

43 For the history of this group especially from the perspective of the main members, see Fan Daren 范達人, "'Liangxiao' de chengli yu zhongjie '梁效'的成立與終結," *Yan Huang chunqiu*, no. 6 (2014): 17–25; Tang Yijie 湯一介, "Wo yu 'Liangxiao' 我與'梁效'," *Shiji*, no. 1 (2016): 25–8. It is worth pointing out that all the major decisions of this group were approved by Mao.

44 See a historical interpretation of this sentence from the *Analects* in Goldin, *Confucianism*, 19.

45 *Lunyu jizhu*, 12:131.

46 Fan Daren, "'Liangxiao' de chengli yu zhongjie," 17–18.

47 Liu Xiuming 劉修明, "Kongzi zhuan 孔子傳," *Xuexi yu pipan*, no.2 (1973): 83–91; Feng Youlan 馮友蘭, "Duiyu Kongzi de pipan he duiyu wo guoqu de zunkong sixiang de ziwo pipan 對於孔子的批判和對於我過去的尊孔思想的自我批判," *Guangming ribao* December 3, 1973, 3; "Fugu yu Fanfugu shi liangtiao luxian de douzheng 復古與反復古是兩條路線的鬥爭," *Guangming ribao* December 4, 1973, 3; Wang Jiyun 王際雲, "Kongzi yao 'fuli', Lin Biao yao fubi 孔子要'復禮',林彪要復辟," *Renmin ribao* January 28, 1974, 2; Beijing Daxue Qinghua Daxue da pipanzu 北京大學、清華大學大批判組, "Lin Biao yu Kong Meng zhi dao 林彪與孔孟之道," *Guangming ribao* February 7, 1974, 1–2; Kang Li 康立, "Kongzi he Lin Biao doushi zhengzhi pianzi 孔子和林彪都是政治騙子," *Renmin ribao* March 11, 1974, 2.

48 Guofang Daxue dangshi dangjian zheng gong jiaoyanshi 國防大學黨史黨建政工教研室 ed., "*Wenhua dageming*" *yanjiu ziliao* "文化大革命"研究資料, 3 vols., vol. 3 (Beijing: 1988), 90–109, esp.95.

49 Yuehan Xixifusi 約翰西西弗斯 ed., *Mao Zedong de qishou: Jiang Qing yu "Wenge"* 毛澤東的旗手:江青與「文革」,vol. 2 (Taipei: Xixifusi wenhua chuban, 2015), 225.

50 Tong Xiaopeng 童小鵬, "Zhou Enlai zai 'PiLin PiKong' zhong 周恩來在'批林批孔'中," *Lingdao wencui*, no. 12 (1996): 48–52; MacFarquhar and Schönhals, *Mao's Last Revolution*, 371–2; Fan Daren 范達人, "'Liangxiao' jipian," *Yan Huang chunqiu*, no. 3 (2014): 19.

51 For the development of comic books in the PRC, see John A. Lent and Ying Xu, *Comic Art in China* (2017), 79–106. For the spread of comic books and their readership, see Mary Ann Farquhar, *Children's Literature in China: From Lu Xun to Mao Zedong* (Armonk: M.E. Sharpe, 1999), 191–248.

52 For a survey of comic books during the Cultural Revolution, see Barbara Mittler, *A Continuous Revolution: Making Sense of Cultural Revolution Culture* (Cambridge, MA: Harvard University Asia Center, 2012), 331–70; Farquahar, *Children's Literature in China*, 191–244.

53 For a comprehensive publication list of the seventies, see Wang Guanqing 汪觀清 and Li Minghai 李明海 eds., *Xin Zhongguo lianhuanhua: 70 niandai* 新中國連環畫:70年代 (Shanghai: Shanghai huabao, 2003).

54 For the process of creating a comic book in the PRC, see Yang Zhaolin 楊兆麟, "*Sanguo yanyi* lianhuanhua de chuangzuo yu chuban 《三國演義》連環畫的創作與出版," in *Xin Zhongguo lianhuanhua: 50-60 niandai* 新中國連環畫 50-60 年代, ed. Wang Guanqing 汪觀清 and Li Minghai 李明海 (Shanghai: Shanghai Huabao, 2001), 23–4; Hou Benben 侯奔奔, "Yu lianhuanhua *Jiangpan zhaoyang* xiangguan de He Youzhi riji he shougao yanjiu 與連環畫《江畔朝陽》相關的賀友直日記和手稿研究" (Ha'erbin Shifan Daxue, 2021), 33–41; Li Lu 黎魯, "Xin Meishu Chubanshe shimo 新美術出版社始末," *Bianji xuekan*, no. 2 (1993): 71–5; Dai Dunbang 戴敦邦, "Bukan huishou shuo wangshi: 'wenge' shiqi yangban xi lianhuanhua huizhi guocheng 不堪回首說往事——'文革'時期樣板戲連環畫繪製過程," in *Xin Zhongguo lianhuanhua: 70 niandai* 新中國連環畫:70年代, ed. Wang Guanqing 汪觀清 and Li Haiming 李海明 (Shanghai: Shanghai huabao, 2003), 6–8.

55 Yu Huiyong 于會泳, "Rang wenyi wutai yongyuan chengwei xuanchuan Mao Zedong sixiang de zhendi 讓文藝舞台永遠成為宣傳毛澤東思想的陣地," *Wenhui bao* May 23, 1968, 1; Shanghai jingju tuan *Zhiqu Weihushan* juzu 上海京劇團《智取威虎山》劇組, "Nuli suzao wuchan jieji yingxiong renwu de guanghui xingxiang 努力塑造無產階級英雄人物的光輝形象," *Hongqi*, no. 11 (1969): 68–70.

56 Chen Guying, *Zhuangzi*, 775–80.

57 Tang Xiao 湯嘯, "Guanyu Liuxia Zhi de fanKong shiji 關於柳下跖的反孔事跡," *Renmin ribao* February 26, 1974, 3; Tang Xiaowen 唐曉文, "Liuxia Zhi tongma Konglao'er 柳下跖痛罵孔老二,". Both author names are the pennames for the propaganda writing group of the Central Party School of the Chinese Communist Party.

58 At the time, comic titles referring to Confucius include Gan Tanghui 甘棠惠, *Kong lao'er xiaozhuan* 孔老二小傳 (Nanning: Guangxi Renmin, 1973; Xiaogan 蕭甘, Gu Bingxin 顧炳鑫, and He Youzhi 賀友直, *Kong Lao'er zui'e de yisheng* 孔老二罪惡的一生 (Beijing: Renmin, 1974; repr., Zhongguo Dazhong Yishu); Shaanxi Shifan Daxue zhongwen xi gong, bing xueyuan, jiaoshi 陝西師範大學中文系工農兵學員、教師 et al., Kong Lao'er de chou'e mianmu 孔老二的醜惡面目 (Xi'an: Shaanxi Renmin, 1974); Sichuan Shifan Xueyuan 四川師範學院 et al., Fandong jieji de "shengren": Kong Lao'er 反動階級的"聖人"——孔老二 (Chengdu: Sichuan

Renmin, 1974); Shandongsheng "Wu Qi" Yixiao meishudui 山東省"五七"藝校美術隊, Kong Lao'er de zui'e yisheng 孔老二的罪惡一生 (Ji'nan: Shandong Renmin, 1974); Zhang Yiqian 張義潛, *Kong Lao'er lieguo pengbi ji* 孔老二列國碰壁記 (Xi'an: Shaanxi Renmin, 1974); Xiang Liling 項立嶺 and Luo Yijun 羅義俊, *Zhi chi Kong Qiu* 跖斥孔丘 (Kunming: Yunnan Renmin, 1974); Wang Jindong 王今棟 and Qin Yunhai 秦雲海, *Liuxia Zhi tongchi Kong Lao'er* 柳下跖痛斥孔老二 (Zhengzhou: Henan Renmin, 1975); Zhou Shen 周申, *Liuxia Zhi tongma Kong Lao'er* 柳下跖痛罵孔老二 (Ji'nan: Shandong Renmin, 1975); Guangxi Yishu Xueyuan 廣西藝術學院, *Woguo lishi shang laodong renmin de fanKong douzheng* 我國歷史上勞動人民的反孔鬥爭 (Nanning: Guangxi Renmin, 1974); Ren Mei 任梅 and Lu Zhanmei 魯展美, *Lishi shang laodong renmin fanKong douzheng de gushi* 歷史上勞動人民反孔鬥爭的故事 (Beijing: Renmin Meishu, 1975). Also see the series of reports on the topic from *People's Daily*: Tian Kai 田凱, "Lishi shang laodong renmin de fanKong douzheng 歷史上勞動人民的反孔鬥爭," *Renmin ribao* January 9, 1974, 2; Zhong Da 鐘達, "Taiping Tianguo de fanKong douzheng 太平天國的反孔鬥爭," *Renmin ribao* July 18, 1974, 2; Beijing Di'er Jichuangchang gongren lilun xiaozu 北京第二機床廠工人理論小組, "Huangjin qiyi de fanKong douzheng 黃巾起義的反孔鬥爭". October 21, 1974; Beijing Yongding Jixiechang gongren lilunzu 北京永定機械廠工人理論組, "Huang Chao nongmin qiyi de fanKong douzheng 黃巢農民起義的反孔鬥爭," ibid. November 10, 1974; Changkong Jixiechang gongren lilun xiaozu 長空機械廠工人理論小組, "Fang La nongmin qiyi de fanKong douzheng 方臘農民起義的反孔鬥爭." November 24, 1974; Zhengzhou Tielüju Zhuangxie Jixiechang gongren lilun xiaozu 鄭州鐵路局裝卸機械廠工人理論小組 and Beijingshi Shunyixian Tianzhu Gongshe pinxiazhongnong lilun 北京市順義縣天竺公社貧下中農理論, "Woguo lishishang laodongfunü de fanKong douzheng 我國歷史上勞動婦女的反孔鬥爭," ibid. December 29, 1974; Beijing Diyi Jichuangchang gongren lilun xiaozu 北京第一機床廠工人理論小組, "Mingmo nongmin qiyi de fanKong douzheng 明末農民起義的反孔鬥爭" December 31, 1974.

59 There was a back and forth regarding the evaluations of certain historical figures. And being on the wrong side could be consequential. See, for example, the situation for the vice mayor of Beijing, Wu Han 吳晗, in MacFarquhar and Schönhals, *Mao's Last Revolution*, 15–18.

60 Gan Liyue 甘禮樂, "Xinqin de kaituozhe, tansuozhe: Gu Bingxin yu lianhuanhua yishu 辛勤的開拓者、探索者——顧炳鑫與連環畫藝術," *Meishu*, no. 9 (1980): 13–14.

61 Liu Xiuming, "Kongzi zhuan," 83–91. For the history of the journal and its relationship with Jiang Qing and her allies, see the interview by Chen Hanrong 陳菡蓉, "Guanyu *Xuexi yu pipan* de ren he shi 關於《學習與批判》的人和事," *Shilin*, no. 1 (2010): 127–34.

62 Xiaogan, Gu Bingxin, and He Youzhi, *Kong Lao'er*. "Xiaogan" is the penname of Gan Liyue, who worked as a word editor at Shanghai Art Press.

63 See Chapter 1.
64 Xiaogan, Gu Bingxin, and He Youzhi, *Kong Lao'er*, 58. The Classical Chinese word for "dog" (*quan* 犬) does not necessarily have a curse word usage, so the authors are using the Mandarin translation, namely *sangjia gou* 喪家狗 to insert such meaning.
65 Xiaogan, Gu Bingxin, and He Youzhi, *Kong Lao'er*, 28–9.
66 For the textual formation and dating of the *Commentary of Zuo*, see Michael Loewe ed., *Early Chinese Texts: A Bibliographical Guide* (Berkeley: The Society for the Study of Early China and The Institute of East Asian Studies, University of California, 1993), 70. Interestingly, in the original text, Confucius did express his disapproval of the blur of division between the noble and the petty. See Yang Bojun, *Chunqiu Zuozhuan zhu*, 1504.
67 We can see this as early as in *Mozi*, Sun Yirang 孫詒讓 ed., *Mozi jiangu* 墨子閒詁 (Beijing: Zhonghua, 2001), 9:298–99. The more proper way was to use one's style name, or *zi* 字, which would be Zhongni 仲尼 in Confucius' case.
68 One of the earliest examples can be found in Wu Yu, "Chiren yu lijiao."
69 One of the earliest examples of using Kong lao'er can be found in a poem commemorating the May Fourth Movement in 1950: Li Luo 黎落, "Shengli de 'Wusi'" 勝利的'五四'," *Guangming ribao* May 4, 1950, 6.
70 For example, Xiaogan, Gu Bingxin, and He Youzhi, *Kong Lao'er*, 12, 14, 22, 23.
71 Xiaogan, Gu Bingxin, and He Youzhi, *Kong Lao'er*, 3, 7, 33, 45.
72 Xiaogan, Gu Bingxin, and He Youzhi, *Kong Lao'er*, 10, 12, 17, 18, 24, 26.
73 Xiaogan, Gu Bingxin, and He Youzhi, *Kong Lao'er*, 44, 46, 49, 50, 56, 58. Fig. 3 is from *Kong Lao'er*, 7, 30, 71, 79.
74 Xiaogan, Gu Bingxin, and He Youzhi, *Kong Lao'er*, 5, 6, 25, 53.
75 Zhuge Ming 諸葛明, "Fanmian renwu de 'rang, duo, ying, ai, bei' 反面人物的'讓、躲、迎、矮、背'," *Xiju yishu*, no. 4 (1978): 56–7.
76 Xiaogan, Gu Bingxin, and He Youzhi, *Kong Lao'er*, 26; 64.
77 Xiaogan, Gu Bingxin, and He Youzhi, *Kong Lao'er*, 58, 59, 71.
78 Sima Qian, *Shiji*, 47: 1909.
79 Xiaogan, Gu Bingxin, and He Youzhi, *Kong Lao'er*, 62, 76.
80 Ruth Rogaski, *Hygienic Modernity: Meanings of Health and Disease in Treaty-port China* (Berkeley: University of California Press, 2004), 238.
81 Xiaogan, Gu Bingxin, and He Youzhi, *Kong Lao'er*, 9, 10, 12, 14, 75–9.
82 Xiaogan, Gu Bingxin, and He Youzhi, *Kong Lao'er*, 48, 50, 58–60.
83 Xiaogan, Gu Bingxin, and He Youzhi, *Kong Lao'er*, 36, 37, 78.
84 Xiaogan, Gu Bingxin, and He Youzhi, *Kong Lao'er*, 7.
85 Xiaogan, Gu Bingxin, and He Youzhi, *Kong Lao'er*, 30.
86 See He Youzhi 賀友直, *He Youzhi shuohua* 賀友直說畫 (Shanghai: Shanghai Renmin, 2008), 68–75. Spiderwebs are rather common for portraying Confucius. See, for example, Gan Tanghui 甘棠惠, *Kong lao'er xiaozhuan* 孔老二小傳, 21. In the work *Shiwu guan* 十五貫 from 1979, He also used the assembly of flies to

indicate smelliness and bad business. See the author's own reasoning in He Youzhi, *He Youzhi shuohua*, 18–19.

87 Xiaogan, Gu Bingxin, and He Youzhi, *Kong Lao'er*, 7, 8, 18, 22.
88 Xiaogan, Gu Bingxin, and He Youzhi, *Kong Lao'er*, 1, 2, 9, 11, 27.
89 Yu Huiyong 于會泳, "Rang wenyi wutai." Mittler, *A Continuous Revolution*, 340–1.
90 For example, only toward the end is there a symbolic depiction of different reactionaries through history worshipping Confucius. Xiaogan, Gu Bingxin, and He Youzhi, *Kong Lao'er*, 82. This realistic style is especially in contrast with the caricatures of Confucius and Lin Biao on propaganda posters of the time. See *Pi Lin pi Kong manhua xuanchuanhua xuanbian* 批林批孔漫畫宣傳畫選編 (Tianjin: Tianjin Yishu Xueyuan gongyi meishu xi, 1974).
91 MacFarquhar and Schönhals, *Mao's Last Revolution*, 366–78; 454–7.
92 MacFarquhar and Schönhals, *Mao's Last Revolution*, 380–1; 96–400.
93 Li Jinquan, *Xiandai sixiang shijia Yang Rongguo*, 129–32.
94 Mittler, *A Continuous Revolution*, 156, 62–3.

Chapter 6

1 For the traits of cuteness, see the later part of this chapter.
2 The company's full name is registered as Shenzhen Bolin Jituan Youxian Gongsi 深圳博林集團有限公司, or Shenzhen Chuangyi Industry Development Co., Ltd.
3 "Wenhua zaizao zhi Hello Kongzi quanqiu gongyi zhan 文化再造之Hello Kongzi 全球公益展," https://www.szcharity.org/News/Detail/16592.
4 For the development of private education in China since the eighties, see Feng Qiangwei 馮薔薇, "Huisu yu zhanwang: Woguo minban gaodeng jiaoyu fazhan zhi lu 回溯與展望：我國民辦高等教育發展之路," *Daxue* 511, no. 17 (2021): 16–9; Lei Fang 雷芳, "Minban peixun jiaoyu de gongxian, wenti, yu fazhan jianyi 民辦培訓教育的貢獻、問題與發展建議," *Hunansheng Shehuizhuyi Xueyuan xuebao* 19, no. 105 (2018): 84–6; Liu Yan 劉艷 and Lin Hualing 林華玲, "Woguo minban peixun jiaoyu ruhe yu 'lang' gongwu: yi Xindongfang Jiaoyu Keji Jituan weijian 我國民辦培訓教育如何與'狼'共舞——以新東方教育科技集團為鑒," *Renli ziyuan guanli*, no. 7 (2013): 172–3.
5 For the popularity of traditional Chinese learning in twenty-first-century China, or the "Fever for National Learning" (*guoxue re* 國學熱) as the media has referred to it, see the salient documentations by Arif Dirlik, "Guoxue/National Learning in the Age of Global Modernity," *China Perspectives* 85, no. 1 (2011): 4–13; John Makeham, "The Revival of Guoxue: Historical Antecedents and Contemporary Aspirations,": 14–21; Fan Peng 樊鵬, "Jin ershinian lai Dalu 'Guoxue xure' zhi guaixianzhuang 近二十年來大陸'國學虛熱'之怪現狀," *Wenhua zongheng* 文化縱橫, June 12, 2020,

http://culture.ifeng.com/c/7xFVuerUhWF (accessed October 24, 2023). Also see a periodization of the phenomenon by Chen Lai 陳來, "Xinshiji guoxuere de fazhan 新世紀國學熱的發展," *Beijing Daxue xuebao* 48, no. 6 (2011): 43–5.

6 TigerloveHoney, "'qimeng, chuancheng, wenhua zaizao zhi Hello Kongzi quanqiu gongyi xunzhan: Taiwan zhan' zai Gugong「啟蒙 傳承 文化再造之Hello Kongzi 全球公益巡展: 台灣站」在故宮," Pixnet, January 9, 2015, https://tigerlovehoney.pixnet.net/blog/post/254803198 (accessed October 24, 2023).

7 Konrad Lorenz, *Studies in Animal and Human Behavior*, trans. Robert Martin, vol. 2 (Cambridge, MA: Harvard University Press, 1971), 154; *The Foundations of Ethology*, trans. Konrad Lorenz and Robert Warren Kickert (New York and Vienna: Springer Verlag, 1981), 154–64.

8 See the discussion of cute later in the chapter.

9 I thank Sarah Brooker for pointing me in the direction of the iconography of Confucius and its relationship with Hello Kongzi. I have also benefited from her article manuscript "The Many Faces of Confucius: The Textual Foundation and Visual Evolution of Confucius' Image."

10 Stephen Jay Gould, *The Panda's Thumb: More Reflections in Natural History* (New York: Norton, 1980), 95–107; R. A. Hinde and L. A. Barden, "The Evolution of the Teddy Bear," *Animal Behaviour* 33 (1985): 1371–73. For a further discussion on the case of Mickey Mouse also see Simon May, *The Power of Cute* (Princeton: Princeton University Press, 2019), 50–7.

11 Gould, *The Panda's Thumb: More Reflections in Natural History*, 97. Scholars have made abundant theorizations of the commodification of cuteness. See, for example, Lori Merish, "Cuteness and Commodity Aesthetics: Tom Thumb and Shirley Temple," in *Freakery: Cultural Spectacles of the Extraordinary Body*, ed. Rosemarie Thomson-Garland (New York: New York University Press, 1996), 185–203; Christine Reiko Yano, *Pink Globalization: Hello Kitty's Trek across the Pacific* (Durham: Duke University Press, 2013); Gary S. Cross, *Freak Show Legacies: How the Cute, Camp and Creepy Shaped Modern Popular Culture* (New York: Bloomsbury Academic, 2021), 103–40.

12 See, for example, the traditional Chinese portrait of Confucius in compulsory education middle school textbooks: Jiaoyubu, *Yuwen*, 50.

13 TigerloveHoney, "qimeng, chuancheng, wenhua zaizao".

14 TigerloveHoney, "qimeng, chuancheng, wenhua zaizao."

15 *Time*, "10 Questions for Yūko Yamaguchi" *Time*, August 21, 2008, https://web.archive.org/web/20080826115227/http://www.time.com/time/magazine/article/0,9171,1834451,00.html (accessed October 10, 2023).

16 For how Yamaguchi designed Hello Kitty and Sanrio's perspectives, see the interview on Yamaguchi, Aaron Marcus et al., *Cuteness Engineering: Designing Adorable Products and Services* (Cham: Springer, 2017), 119–46. It is noteworthy that the designer actually does not consider Hello Kitty "cute" to her own taste. For a more comprehensive study

on Hello Kitty, her merchandise, and the cultural impacts, see Yano, *Pink Globalization*, esp. 58–68, 79, 87–92; Marcus et al., *Cuteness Engineering*, 119–46.

17 The rare occasions where Hello Kongzi talks include a promotion video of Hello Kong tour in North America, where he raps; and an eight-episode spin-off cartoon, where he teaches Chinese characters. Hello Kongzi, "HelloKongzi—Rap Battle," YouTube, February 13, 2016, https://www.youtube.com/watch?v=gGMNDtcAl-o (accessed October 25, 2023); Broad Link, "Wen yi ruizhi 文以睿智," in *Hellokongzi shuo hanzi Hellokongzi* 說漢字 (Iqiyi, 2018).

18 For the multiple meanings of winking in our contemporary societies, see, for example, Autumn Sprabary, "Why do people wink?," All About Vision, https://www.allaboutvision.com/resources/why-people-wink/ (accessed October 25, 2023). For Hello Kitty's wink and its implication especially in the context of global consumerism, see Yano, *Pink Globalization*, 28; 54–5, 226–9, 64–8.

19 See the explanation from the authors of the manga in Frederik L. Schodt, *Dreamland Japan: Writings on Modern Manga* (Berkeley: Stone Bridge Press, 1996), 218.

20 For a summary and insightful analysis of the character Doraemon and the manga, see Saya S. Shiraishi, "Japan's Soft Power: Doraemon Goes Overseas," in *Network Power: Japan and Asia*, ed. Peter J. Katzenstein and Takashi Shiraishi (Ithaca: Cornell University Press, 1997), 234–72, esp. 38, 60.

21 "'Mengmengda' Kongzi xiang liangxiang Shenzhen wenbohui '萌萌噠'孔子像亮相深圳文博會," Zhongguo xinwen wang, June 12, 2022, http://www.onezh.com/news/news_show.asp?id=10894.

22 Jiaoyubu 教育部, *Yuwen*, 50–3. The selection of the *Analects* and the angle can be traced back to earlier versions of the textbooks in the nineties. For Confucius' appearance in the textbooks after the Cultural Revolution and the changing narratives, see "Jinian Gaige Kaifang 30 zhounian: Jiaokeshu 30 nian bianlian ji 紀念改革開放30週年: 教科書30年變臉記," *Jinghua shibao*, November 10, 2008, https://news.sina.com.cn/c/2008-11-10/155016624496.shtml (accessed October 25, 2023).

23 Jiaoyubu 教育部, *Zhongguo lishi: Qinianji, shangce* 中國歷史: 七年級上冊 (Beijing: Renmin jiaoyu, 2016), 38.

24 For the general principles of evaluating historical figures as well as views on Confucius in Chinese textbooks since the seventies, see one of the main editors of history textbooks Wang Hongzhi's 王宏志 articles: Wang Hongzhi 王宏志, "Luetan zai xinbian zhongxue *Zhongguo lishi* keben zhong xie lishi renwu de jige wenti 略談在新編中學《中國歷史》課本中寫歷史人物的幾個問題," *Lishi jiaoxue*, no. 2 (1978): 28–32, esp. 31; "Shehui jinbu he lishi jiaocai de gaige 社會進步和歷史教材的改革," *Kecheng, jiaocai, jiaofa*, no. 11 (1990): 17; Wang Hongzhi 王宏志, Li Longgeng 李隆庚, and Zang Rong 臧嶸, "Yiwu jiaoyu chuzhong *Zhongguo lishi* 義務教育初中《中國歷史》," *Kecheng, jiaocai, jiaofa*, no. 5 (1992): 4–9; Wang Hongzhi 王宏志, "Lishi renwu he lishi jiaocai 歷史人物和歷史教材," *Kecheng, jiaocai, jiaofa*, no. 11 (1997): 6–10, esp. 8.

25 Lin Ruiyi 林瑞益, "Hello Kongzi quanqiu xunzhan chuancheng xiaodao Hello Kongzi 全球巡展傳承孝道," Zhongshi xinwen wang, December 22, 2014, https://www.chinatimes.com/cn/realtimenews/20141222000790-260514?chdtv (accessed October 25, 2023).
26 Michael Martinez and Jaqueline Hurtado, "Hello Kitty Turns 40, Draws 25,000 Fans to First Hello Kitty Con," CNN, June 14, 2022, https://edition.cnn.com/2014/11/01/us/hello-kitty-convention-40th-year/index.html.
27 Yano, *Pink Globalization*, 199–250, esp. 3–13, 47.
28 Shiraishi, "Japan's Soft Power," 262–72.
29 Justin McCurry, "Japan enlists cartoon cat as ambassador," *The Guardian*, June 14, 2022, https://www.theguardian.com/world/2008/mar/20/japan.
30 Lorenz, *The Foundations of Ethology*, 154, 64; *Studies in Animal and Human Behavior*, 154.
31 Daniel Harris, *Cute, Quaint, Hungry and Romantic: The Aesthetics of Consumerism* (New York: Basic Books, 2000), 3–5, 15–16.
32 Ngai's work on cute was first published as a journal article in 2005: Sianne Ngai, "The Cuteness of the Avant-Garde," *Critical Inquiry* 31, no. 4 (2005): 811–47.
33 Ngai, *Our Aesthetic Categories: Zany, Cute, Interesting* (Cambridge, MA: Harvard University Press, 2012), 53–109, esp. 29, 87, 93.
34 Gary D. Sherman and Jonathan Haidt, "Cuteness and Disgust: The Humanizing and Dehumanizing Effects of Emotion," *Emotion Review* 3, no. 3 (2011): 245–51.
35 Joshua Paul Dale, "The Appeal of the Cute Object: Desire, Domestication, and Agency," in *The Aesthetics and Affects of Cuteness*, ed. Joshua Paul Dale et al. (New York: Routledge, 2017), 35–55, esp. 35, 40, 46, 50.
36 Megan Arkenberg, "Cuteness and Control in *Portal*," ibid., 56–74, esp. 65.
37 Viviana A. Zelizer, *Pricing the Priceless Child: The Changing Social Value of Children* (New York: Basic Books, 1985), 3–21; Gary S. Cross, *The Cute and the Cool: Wondrous Innocence and Modern American Children's Culture* (Oxford; New York: Oxford University Press, 2004), 43–82.
38 Cross, *Kids' Stuff: Toys and the Changing World of American Childhood* (Cambridge, MA: Harvard University Press, 1999), 102–8, 59, 90.
39 Sharon Kinsella, "Cuties in Japan," in *Women, Media and Consumption in Japan*, ed. Lise Skov and Brian Moeran (Honolulu: University of Hawai'i Press, 1995), 221–39. For cuteness in the history of Japan and a reflection on why "cuteness" became such a visible trend in Japanese society, see May, *The Power of Cute*, 59–91.
40 Olympics, "Rio 2016 Closing Ceremony Full HD Replay," YouTube, August 21, 2016, https://www.youtube.com/watch?v=ssc5eLjLoMQ&t=6722s (accessed October 24, 2023).
41 Kinsella, "Cuties in Japan," 250–52.

42 Tom Smith, "How Kumamon Became a National Sensation in Japan," Culture Trip, March 3, 2020, https://theculturetrip.com/asia/japan/articles/how-kumamon-became-a-national-sensation/ (accessed October 24, 2023).
43 Yano, *Pink Globalization*, 60–7; May, *The Power of Cute*, 66–70; 155–7.
44 May, *The Power of Cute*, esp. xii, 6–7, 23–27, 33, 41, 114
45 See Liu Yiqing 劉義慶, Xu Zhen'e 徐震堮 ed., *Shishuo xinyu jiaojian* 世說新語校箋 (Beijing: Zhonghua, 1984), 2:217; 2:43; 3:487.
46 Jia Sixie 賈思勰, *Qimin yaoshu* 齊民要術, 4 vols., vol. 353–6, Sibu congkan (Shanghai: Commercial, 1922), 4:13b; 9:12a; Li Fang 李昉 et al., *Taiping yulan*, 479: 2197.
47 Wu Shan 吳山 and Lu Yuan 陸原 eds., *Zhongguo lidai wanju cidian* 中國歷代玩具辭典 (Fuzhou: Fujian Jiaoyu, 2020), 5, 42, 53, 229.
48 Wei Wei 魏巍, "Shui shi zui ke'ai de ren 誰是最可愛的人," *Renmin ribao* April 11, 1951, 1.
49 Meixuan 美宣, "Douren xiai de meishu pian 逗人喜愛的美術片," *Dianying pingjie*, no. 6 (1985): 41
50 Shao Wenjing 邵文菁, "Milaoshu zai Zhongguo 米老鼠在中國," *Dang'an Chunqiu*, no. 8 (2016): 13–17; Kelisitingna Gangtian 克莉絲汀娜剛田, "[Dalu] Jinian Yangshi *Jiqimao* bochu 30 zhounian de *Duolaeimeng dongman xiao baike* zhongchou shangxian [大陸]紀念央視《機器貓》播出30週年的《哆啦A夢動漫小百科》眾籌上線," Duolaeimeng Zhongwen wang, April 20, 2022, https://chinesedora.com/news/35824.htm (accessed October 24, 2023).
51 "*Pleasant Goat and Big Big Wolf*," Wikipedia, October 23, 2023, https://en.wikipedia.org/wiki/Pleasant_Goat_and_Big_Big_Wolf (accessed October 24, 2023).
52 The number in the report is in Chinese Yuan: 87,085,000,000. See Xinhua She 新華社, "2013 nian woguo dongman chanye zongchanzhi yu 870 yi yuan 2013年我國動漫產業總產值逾870億元," Zhongyang zhengfu menhu wangzhan, June 10, 2014, http://www.gov.cn/xinwen/2014-07/10/content_2715703.htm (accessed October 24, 2023).
53 From 1841 to 1984, the Chinese government gifted the panda bears. But afterwards it only leased them.
54 For Panda Diplomacy, see Kathleen Carmel Buckingham, Jonathan Neil William David, and Paul Jepson, "Diplomats and Refugees: Panda Diplomacy, Soft 'Cuddly' Power, and the New Trajectory in Panda Conservation," *Environmental Practice* 15, no. 3 (2013): 262–70.
55 See the Weibo accounts like Zaozhuang Gong'an 棗莊公安 and Qufu Gong'an 曲阜公安: Zaozhuang Gong'an 棗莊公安, Sina Weibo, June 27, 2022, https://weibo.com/1839681925?refer_flag=1001030103_ (accessed October 24, 2023); Qufu Gong'an 曲阜公安, June 27, 2022, https://weibo.com/u/2018539543 (accessed October 24, 2023). For an example of using cartoon characters as the representative of the police force, see "Xinzhou Gong'an katong jingcha jinri he dajia jianmian la!

忻州公安卡通警察今日和大家見面啦!", Tengxun shipin, April 22, 2022, https://v.qq.com/x/page/ u333103l52d.html (accessed October 24, 2023).

56 We can see this by searching the word 可愛 in the image search of Baidu, a search engine used almost exclusively by users in mainland China: ""Ke'ai 可愛"," Baidu, June 26, 2022, https://image.baidu.com/search/index?tn=baiduimage&ps=1&ct=2013265 92&lm=-1&cl=2&nc=1&ie=utf-8&dyTabStr=MCwzLDUsMSw3LDgsNCw2LDIsO Q%3D%3D&word=%E5%8F%AF%E7%88%B1 (accessed October 25, 2023). For an early use of the expression *Q ban*, see "Q ban 'Weita nai' wenshi Q版'維他奶'問世," *Zhongguo shipin gongye*, no. 12 (1996). For the meaning of *moe* and its relationship with cuteness, see Gabriele de Seta, "'Meng'! It Just Means Cute': A Chinese Online Vernacular Term in Context," *M/C Journal* 17, no. 2 (2014). For an overview of cuteness in contemporary China, see Marcus et al., *Cuteness Engineering*, 63–91.

57 See the news reports and the official posters in Chen Xiaoling 陳小凌, "Hello Kongzi quanqiu gongyi xunzhan Hello Kongzi全球公益巡展," YamNews, December 23, 2014, https://n.yam.com/Article/20141224767330 (accessed October 25, 2023); Lin Ruiyi 林瑞益, "Hello Kongzi quanqiu xunzhan chuancheng xiaodao Hello Kongzi 全球巡展傳承孝道"; "Kongzi ye lai chuanyue shikong? 孔子也來穿越時空?," TVBS, January 2, 2015, https://news.tvbs.com.tw/travel/561142 (accessed October 25, 2023).

58 Lin Ruiyi 林瑞益, "Hello Kongzi."

59 "Kongzi ye lai chuanyue shikong?".

60 The expression in Min dialect is a shortened version of *chhut-lâi kóng*, corresponding to the Chinese characters 出來講. For the history of the expression, see "*Chuaigong* 踹貢," PTT Xiangmin baike, December 18, 2014, https://pttpedia.fandom.com/zh/wiki/%E8%B8%B9%E5%85%B1 (accessed October 25, 2023).

61 Johnny Kong, "Halou, Kongzi 哈嘍, 孔子," YouTube, December 22, 2014, https://www.youtube.com/watch?v=F6ZfS_bJdQc (accessed October 25, 2023).

62 In addition, the quotation from the *Analects* was in fact from his disciple Zengzi instead of himself. *Lunyu*, 4: 104.

63 Kong, "Halou, Kongzi."

64 Kong, "Halou, Kongzi."; Kevin A. Leman II, "Ellen Show," (Warner Bros. Television Distribution, May 8, 2014).

65 Gilbert Rozman, "Comparisons of Modern Confucian Values in China and Japan," in *The East Asian Religion: Confucian Heritage and its Modern Adaptation*, ed. Gilbert Rozman (Princeton: Princeton University Press, 1991), 181–3.

66 Wu Yinhui 吳垠慧, "Kongzi gongzai dao Gugong, rewu xian liuyi 孔子公仔到故宮 熱舞現六藝," Chinatimes December 27, 2014, https://www.chinatimes.com/realtimenews/20141227003848-260405?chdtv (accessed October 24, 2023); Vreranda, "Kongzi Hello Kongzi quanqiu gongyi xunzhan-Taiwan zhan 孔子 Hello Kongzi全球公益巡展 - 臺灣站," Pixnet, January 4, 2015, https://vreranda.pixnet.net/blog/post/192216174 (accessed October 24, 2023); TigerloveHoney, "qimeng, chuancheng, wenhua zaizao".

67 Yu-Ting Feng, Hello Kongzi in New York (feng-yuting.com, 2016).
68 Hello Kongzi, "HelloKongzi—Taxi!," YouTube, March 3, 2016 https://www.youtube.com/watch?v=_WjOE6hk1QE&t=6s (October 24, 2023).
69 Ibid.
70 Hello Kongzi, "Hello Kongzi + Skateboard," YouTube, February 3, 2016, https://www.youtube.com/watch?v=8UwU8kT9SX0 (accessed October 27, 2023); "HelloKongzi + BUNGEE," YouTube, January 22, 2016, https://www.youtube.com/watch?v=_WjOE6hk1QE (accessed October 24, 2023).
71 For the effects of the projection, see the video in Feng, Hello Kongzi in New York.
72 Sha Huang, "HelloKongzi in New York Documentary," feng-yuting.com, July 8, 2022, https://feng-yuting.com/work/hello-kongzi-world-tour-new-york (accessed October 24, 2023).
73 Hello Kongzi, "HelloKongzi in New York—Hiphop Dance," YouTube, March 3, 2016, https://www.youtube.com/watch?v=b9zvrflJJCg (accessed October 24, 2023).
74 "HelloKongzi—Rap Battle"; "HelloKongzi in New York—Hiphop Dance".
75 Cross, *Kids' Stuff*, 105.

Conclusion

1 Alex Lo, "Would Confucius Condone Same-Sex Marriage?," *South China Morning Post* November 17, 2022; Fukuda Kōichi 福田晃市, *Moe yaku Kōshi-chan no Rongo* 萌訳孔子ちゃんの論語 (Tokyo: Sōgō Kagaku Shuppan, 2010); Zhenshuo 朕說, "Zuiqiang jirounan laoshi, zaixian jiaoshou zhexue? 最強肌肉男老師,在線教授哲學?," Zhihu, December 3, 2019, https://zhuanlan.zhihu.com/p/94994674 (accessed October 24, 2023). For more discussions on Confucius and same-sex marriage and the political controversies around it, see Tongdong Bai, "Confucianism and Same-Sex Marriage," *Politics and Religion* 14 (2021): 132–58; Bryan W. Van Norden, "Confucius on Gay Marriage," *The Diplomat* (July 13, 2015).
2 Ann-ping Chin, *The Authentic Confucius: A Life of Thought and Politics* (New York: Scribner, 2007); Gan Lin 甘霖, *Benlai de Kongzi*: Lunyu *xinjie* 本來的孔子——《論語》新解 (Beijing: Zhonghua, 2018). Bai Tongdong has made an eloquent defense of reading the early Confucians philosophically for the contemporary world instead of historically. See his *Against Political Equality: The Confucian Case* (Princeton: Princeton University Press, 2020), 5–19. Also see Joseph Chan, *Confucian Perfectionism: A Political Philosophy For Modern Times* (Princeton: Princeton University Press, 2014).
3 We can already see the advertisement of a younger looking Confucius for children. See, for example, the cover design of Meng Zhuo 孟琢, Yin Meng 尹夢, and Mei Ruyu 梅茹瑜, *Kongzi yue: Gei haizi de guoxue manhua* 孔子曰——給孩子的國學漫畫 (Beijing: Zhongguo qingnian, 2020).

Bibliography

Aarim-Heriot, Najia. *Chinese Immigrants, African Americans, and Racial Anxiety in the United States, 1848-82*. Urbana: University of Illinois Press, 2006.

"Advertisement." *Boston Evening-Post*, September 12, 1743, 2.

"Ah Bak, the Christian. The Chinaman Who Embraced Modern Religion But Clung to His Opium Habit." *Boston Daily Globe*, September 25, 1882, 1.

"Ah Sin–Chin Shin Yin." *Pomeroys Democrat*, August 17, 1878, 6.

Ames, Roger. *The Art of Rulership: A Study of Ancient Chinese Political Thought*. Albany: SUNY, 1994.

Arkenberg, Megan. "Cuteness and Control in *Portal*." In *The Aesthetics and Affects of Cuteness*, edited by Joshua Paul Dale, Joyce Goggin, Julia Leyda, P. Anthony McIntyre and Dinae Negra, 56–74. New York: Routledge, 2017.

Armstrong, Karen. *The Great Transformation: The Beginning of Our Religious Traditions*. New York: Knopf, 2006.

Bai, Tongdong. *Against Political Equality: The Confucian Case*. Princeton: Princeton University Press, 2020.

Bai, Tongdong. "Confucianism and Same-Sex Marriage." *Politics and Religion* 14 (2021): 132–58.

Ban Gu 班固. *Baihu tong shuzheng* 白虎通疏證. Beijing: Zhonghua, 1994.

Ban Gu 班固. *Hanshu* 漢書. Beijing: Zhonghua, 1962.

Banck, Werner. *Das chinesische Tempelorakel*. Taipei: Guting Book Store, 1976.

Bao Pengshan 鮑鵬山. *Kongzi yuanlai: Bei wujie de Kongzi* 孔子原來: 被誤解的孔子. Beijing: Zhongguo qingnian, 2019.

Beijing Daxue Qinghua Daxue da pipanzu 北京大學、清華大學大批判組. "Lin Biao yu Kong Meng zhi dao 林彪與孔孟之道." *Guangming ribao*, February 7, 1974, 1–2.

Beijing Dier Jichuangchang gongren lilun xiaozu 北京第二機床廠工人理論小組. "Huangjin qiyi de fanKong douzheng 黃巾起義的反孔鬥爭." *Renmin ribao*, October 21, 1974, 2.

Beijing Diyi Jichuangchang gongren lilun xiaozu 北京第一機床廠工人理論小組. "Mingmo nongmin qiyi de fanKong douzheng 明末農民起義的反孔鬥爭." *Renmin ribao*, December 31, 1974, 2.

Beijing Yongding Jixiechang gongren lilunzu 北京永定機械廠工人理論組. "Huang Chao nongmin qiyi de fanKong douzheng 黃巢農民起義的反孔鬥爭." *Renmin ribao*, November 10, 1974, 2.

Bielenstein, Hans. "Wang Mang, The Restoration of the Han Dynasty, and Later Han." In *The Cambridge History of China*. Vol. 1, *The Ch'in and Han Empires, 221*

B.C.–A.D. 220, edited by Denis Twitchett and Michael Loewe, 223–90. Cambridge: Cambridge University Press, 1987.

Bindman, David. "Am I Not a Man and a Brother? British Art and Slavery in the Eighteeth Century." *Anthropology and Aesthetics* 26, no. 26 (1994): 68–82.

Blaine, James G. *Life and Work of James G. Blaine*. New York: Western W. Wilson, 1893.

Blake, John. "This World-class Athlete Talks like Aristotle and Acts like Confucius. We Can All Learn from Him." CNN, May 27, 2022. https://edition.cnn.com/2022/05/27/world/rafael-nadal-philosophy-blake-cec/index.html#:~:text=Tennis%20great%20Rafael%20Nadal%20talks,all%20learn%20from%20him%20%7C%20CNN (accessed October 25, 2023).

Boltz, William G. "*Lao tzu Tao te ching* 老子道德經." In *Early Chinese Texts: A Bibliographical Guide*, edited by Michael Loewe, 269–92. Berkeley: University of California Press, 1993.

Bottoms, Michael. *An Aristocracy of Color: Race and Reconstruction in California and the West, 1850–1890*. Norman: University of Oklahoma Press, 2013.

Brashier, K. E. *Public Memory in Early China*. Cambridge, MA: Harvard University Asia Center, 2014.

Broad Link. "Wen yi ruizhi 文以睿智." In *Hellokongzi shuo hanzi Hellokongzi* 說漢字. Beijing: Iqiyi, 2018.

Brockey, Liam Matthew. *Journey to the East: The Jesuit Mission to China, 1579–1724*. Cambridge, MA: The Belknap Press of Harvard University Press, 2007.

Brown, Miranda, and Uffe Bergeton. "'Seeing' like a Sage: Three Takes on Identity and Perception in Early China." *Journal of Chinese Philosophy* 35, no. 4 (2008): 641–62.

Buckingham, Kathleen Carmel, Jonathan Nei William David, and Paul Jepson. "Diplomats and Refugees: Panda Diplomacy, Soft 'Cuddly' Power, and the New Trajectory in Panda Conservation." *Environmental Practice* 15, no. 3 (2013): 262–70.

Campany, Robert. "The Earliest Tales of the Bodhisattva Guanshiyin." In *Religions of China in Practice*, edited by Donald S., Lopez Jr., 82–96. Princeton: Princeton University Press, 1996.

Campany, Robert. "On the Very Idea of Religions (in the Modern West and in Early Medieval China)." *History of Religions* 42 (2003): 287–319.

Campany, Robert. "The Real Presence." *History of Religions* 32 (1993): 233–72.

Campany, Robert. *Signs from the Unseen Realm: Buddhist Miracle Tales from Early Medieval China*. Honolulu: University of Hawai'i Press, 2012.

Campany, Robert. *Strange Writing: Anomaly Accounts in Early Medieval China*. Albany: State University of New York Press, 1996.

"Celestial Chess." *Boston Daily Globe*, August 25, 1889, 18.

Chan, Adrian. *Chinese Marxism*. London: Continuum, 2003.

Chan, Joseph. *Confucian Perfectionism: A Political Philosophy For Modern Times*. Princeton: Princeton University Press, 2014.

Changkong Jixiechang gongren lilun xiaozu 長空機械廠工人理論小組. "Fang La nongmin qiyi de fanKong douzheng 方臘農民起義的反孔鬥爭." *Renmin ribao*, November 24, 1974, 2.

Cheek, Timothy. *The Intellectual in Modern Chinese History*. Cambridge: Cambridge University Press, 2015.
Chen Biao 陳標. "*Mao Zedong sixiang wansui* zai haiwai de liyong 《毛澤東思想萬歲》在海外的利用." *Dangdai Zhongguo shi yanjiu* 16, no. 4 (2009): 114–19.
Chen Guying 陳鼓應, ed. *Zhuangzi jinzhu jinyi* 莊子今注今譯. Beijing: Zhonghua, 1983.
Chen Hanrong 陳菡蓉. "Guanyu *Xuexi yu pipan* de ren he shi 關於《學習與批判》的人和事." *Shilin* no. S1 (2010): 127–34.
Chen Hung-sen 陳鴻森. "*Zixia Yi zhuan* kaobian 子夏易傳考辨." *Zhongyang Yanjiuyuan Lishi Yuyan Yanjiusuo jikan* 56, no. 2 (1985): 359–404.
Chen, Jack. "On the Act and Representation of Reading in Medieval China." *Journal of the American Oriental Society* 129, no. 1 (2009): 57–71.
Chen jin 陳晉. "Mao Zedong yuedu shilüe wu 毛澤東閱讀史略(五)." *Zhonggong dangshi yanjiu* no. 10 (2013): 11–21.
Chen jin 陳晉. *Mao Zedong zhi hun* 毛澤東之魂. Beijing: Zhongyang wenxian, 1997.
Chen Lai 陳來. "Xinshiji guoxuere de fazhan 新世紀國學熱的發展." *Beijing Daxue xuebao* 48, no. 6 (2011): 43–5.
Chen, Ning. "The Etymology of sheng (Sage) and its Confucian Conception in Early China." *Journal of Chinese Philosophy* 27, no. 4 (2000): 409–27.
Chen Pan 陳槃. *Gu Chenwei yantao ji qi shulu jieti* 古讖緯研討及其書錄解題. Shanghai: Guji, 2009.
Chen Qinghao 陳慶浩. "*Gu xian ji jiaozhu* 古賢集校注." *Dunhuang xue* 3 (1976): 63–102.
Chen Shiyun 陳世昀. "Weijin Nanbeichao zhiguai xiaoshuo 'yi' de xushu 魏晉南北朝志怪小說「異」的敘述." *Changgeng renwen shehui xuebao* 12, no. 2 (2019): 235–70.
Chen Xiaoling 陳小凌. "Hello Kongzi quanqiu gongyi xunzhan Hello Kongzi全球公益巡展." YamNews. December 23, 2014. https://n.yam.com/Article/20141224767330 (accessed October 25, 2023).
Chen, Yong. *Chop Suey, USA: The Story of Chinese Food in America*. New York: Columbia University Press, 2014.
Cheng, Shude, Junying Cheng, Jianyuan Jiang, and Confucius. *Lunyu ji shi* 論語集釋. 4 vols. Beijing: Zhonghua, 1990.
Chin, Ann-ping. *The Authentic Confucius: A Life of Thought and Politics*. New York: Scribner, 2007.
"A Chinaman Was Testifying in Richmond." *New York Tribune*, May 17, 1878, 8.
"The Chinese." *Chicago Daily Tribune*, December 26, 1879, 2.
"Chinese Characteristics: Fifth Discourse in Rev. Dr. Newman's Series–'Confucius and Confucianism.'" *New York Herald*, May 27, 1878, 11.
"A Chinese Gambling Hell." *New York Times*, October 2, 1883, 8.
"Chinese in America." *American Missionary*, October 1875, 229.
"The Chinese New Year." *Worcester Daily Spy*, January 28, 1884, 1.
"The Chinese, Shall He Be Welcome?". *Elevator*, March 8, 1873, 3.

"The Chinese: Moon-eyed Knights of the Wash-Tub and Sad-Iron. How They Dress, Eat, Sleep and Earn Their Living. Their Peculiarities, Superstitions and Vices as a People." *Boston Daily Globe*, August 19, 1878, 2.

"*Chuaigong* 踹貢." PTT Xiangmin baike. December 18, 2014. https://pttpedia.fandom.com/zh/wiki/%E8%B8%B9%E5%85%B1 (accessed October 25, 2023).

Chunqiu Gongyang zhuan zhushu 春秋公羊傳注疏. *Shisanjing zhushu* 十三經注疏. Edited by Ruan Yuan 阮元. Beijing: Zhonghua, 1980.

Clinton, Maggie. *Revolutionary Nativism: Fascism and Culture in China, 1925–1937*. Durham: Duke University Press, 2017.

Coe, Andrew. *Chop Suey: A Cultural History of Chinese Food in the United States*. Oxford: Oxford University Press, 2009.

Collins, Randall. *Interaction Ritual Chains*. Princeton: Princeton University Press, 2004.

Collins, Randall. *The Sociology of Philosophy: A Global Theory of Intellectual Change*. Cambridge, MA: Belknap Press of Harvard University Press, 1998.

"Confucius." *Christian Messenger*, March 10, 1819, 4.

"The Continuation of the Morals of Confucius." *New-York Weekly Journal*, February 13, 1737, 1–3.

Cook, Constance A., and Zhao Lu. *Stalk Divination: A Newly Discovered Alternative to the I Ching*. Oxford: Oxford University Press, 2017.

Coolidge, Mary Roberts. *Chinese Immigration*. New York: Henry Holt, 1909.

Crane, Beverly "The Structure of Value in 'The Roommate's Death': A Methodology for Interpretive Analysis of Folk Legends." *Journal of the Folklore Institute* 14 (1977): 133–51.

Creel, Herrlee G. *The Origins of Statecraft in China*. Chicago and London: University of Chicago Press, 1970.

Cross, Gary S. *The Cute and the Cool: Wondrous Innocence and Modern American Children's Culture*. Oxford; New York: Oxford University Press, 2004.

Cross, Gary S. *Freak Show Legacies: How the Cute, Camp and Creepy Shaped Modern Popular Culture*. 2021.

Cross, Gary S. *Kids' Stuff: Toys and the Changing World of American Childhood*. Cambridge, MA: Harvard University Press, 1999.

Dai Dunbang 戴敦邦. "Bukan huishou shuo wangshi: 'wenge' shiqi yangban xi lianhuanhua huizhi guocheng 不堪回首說往事——'文革'時期樣板戲連環畫繪製過程." In *Xin Zhongguo lianhuanhua: 70 niandai* 新中國連環畫: 70年代, edited by Wang Guanqing 汪觀清 and Li Haiming 李海明, 6–8. Shanghai: Shanghai huabao, 2003.

Dai Jun 戴軍. "Tangdai siyuan jiaoyu yu wenxue 唐代寺院教育與文學." Zhongguo Shehui Kexueyuan, 2003.

Dale, Joshua Paul. "The Appeal of the Cute Object: Desire, Domestication, and Agency." In *The Aesthetics and Affects of Cuteness*, edited by Joshua Paul Dale, Joyce Goggin, Julia Leyda, P. Anthony McIntyre and Dinae Negra, 35–55. New York: Routledge, 2017.

de Seta, Gabriele. "'Meng? It Just Means Cute': A Chinese Online Vernacular Term in Context." *M/C Journal* 17, no. 2 (2014). https://doi.org/10.5204/mcj.789. (accessed October 25, 2023).

DeLapp, Kevin Michael, ed. *Portraits of Confucius: The Reception of Confucianism from 1560 to 1960*. London; New York: Bloomsbury Academic, 2022.

"Democratic Logic." *Elevator*, August 30, 1867, 2.

Deng Tuo 鄧拓. "Shui lingdao le Wusi yundong? 誰領導了五四運動." *People's Daily*, April 29, 1950.

Dijkstra, Trude, and Thijs Weststeijn. "Constructing Confucius in the Low Countries." *De Zeventiende Eeuw* 32 (2016): 137–64.

Dirlik, Arif. "Guoxue/National Learning in the Age of Global Modernity." *China Perspectives* 85, no. 1 (2011): 4–13.

Dirlik, Arif. "The Ideological Foundations of the New Life Movement: A Study in Counterrevolution." *The Journal of Asian Studies* 34, no. 4 (1975): 945–80.

Dirlik, Arif. *Marxism in the Chinese Revolution*. Lanham: Rowman & Littlefield Publishers, Inc., 2005.

Dull, Jack L. "A Historical Introduction to the Apocryphal (Ch'an-wei) Texts of the Han Dynasty." Seattle: University of Washington, 1966.

Durand-Dastès, Vincent. "Divination and Fate Manipulation in a Popular Myth of Late Imperial China: *The Wedding of Zhougong and Peach Blossom Girl*." In *International Consortium for Research in the Humanities: Selected Lectures*, edited by International Consortium for Research in the HumanitiesInter, 1–34: International Consortium for Research in the Humanities, November 11, 2010.

Durrant, Stephen W. *The Cloudy Mirror: Tension and Conflict in the Writings of Sima Qian*. Albany: SUNY, 1995.

"Editorial Article." *Boston Daily Globe*, April 17, 1877, 4.

Elman, Benjamin A. *A Cultural History of Civil Examinations in Late Imperial China*. Berkeley: University of California Press, 2000.

Elman, Benjamin A., and Martin Kern, eds. *Statecraft and Classical Learning: The Rituals of Zhou in East Asian History*. Leiden: Brill, 2010.

Elstein, David. "Beyond the Five Relationships: Teachers and Worthies in Early Chinese Thought." *Philosophy East and West* 62, no. 3 (2012): 375–91.

"Enterprise of the Chinese." *The Daily Graphic*, January 31, 1876, 7.

Eoyang, Eugene. "Oral Narration in the *Pien* and *Pien-wen*." *Archiv orientální: Journal of the Czechoslovak Oriental Institute* 46 (1978): 232–52.

Epstein, Brian. "The Diviner and the Scientist: Revisiting the Question of Alternative Standards of Rationality." *Journal of the American Academy of Religion* 78, no. 4 (2010): 1048–86.

Fairbank, John K., and Kwang-Ching Liu, eds. *Late Ch'ing, 1800–1911, Part 2: The Cambridge History of China*. Cambridge: Cambridge University Press, 1980.

Fan Daren 范達人. "'Liangxiao' de chengli yu zhongjie '梁效'的成立與終結." *Yan Huang chunqiu* no. 6 (2014): 17–25.

Fan Daren 范達人. "'Liangxiao' jipian zhongdian wenzhang de xiezuo jingguo '兩效' 幾篇重點文章的寫作經過." *Yan Huang chunqiu* no. 3 (2014): 16–24.

Fan Ge 凡歌. "Yang Rongguo: Yige lishi xuezhe de xuanze ti 楊榮國: 一個歷史學者的選擇題." *Guojia lishi* no. 2 (2010): 35–42.

Fan Peng 樊鵬. "Jin ershinian lai Dalu 'Guoxue xure' zhi guaixianzhuang 近二十年來大陸'國學虛熱'之怪現狀." *Wenhua zongheng* 文化縱橫. June 12, 2020. http://culture.ifeng.com/c/7xFVuerUhWF (accessed October 24, 2023).

Fan Wenlan 范文瀾. *Zhongguo tongshi jianbian* 中國通史簡編. Fan Wenlan quanji 范文瀾全集. Vol. 7-8, Shijiazhuang: Hebei Jiaoyu, 2002.

Fan Ye 范曄. *Houhan shu* 後漢書. Beijing: Zhonghua, 1965.

Farquahar, Mary Ann. *Children's Literature in China: From Lu Xun to Mao Zedong*. Armonk: M.E. Sharpe, 1999.

Feng Qiangwei 馮薔薇. "Huisu yu zhanwang: Woguo minban gaodeng jiaoyu fazhan zhi lu 回溯與展望: 我國民辦高等教育發展之路." *Daxue* 511, no. 17 (2021): 16–19.

Feng Youlan 馮友蘭. "Duiyu Kongzi de pipan he duiyu wo guoqu de zunkong sixiang de ziwo pipan 對於孔子的批判和對於我過去的尊孔思想的自我批判." *Guangming ribao*, December 3, 1973, 3.

Feng Youlan 馮友蘭. "Fugu yu Fanfugu shi liangtiao luxian de douzheng 復古與反復古是兩條路線的鬥爭." *Guangming ribao*, December 4, 1973, 3.

Feng, Yu-Ting. *Hello Kongzi in New York*. feng-yuting.com, 2016.

Flath, James A. *Traces of the Sage: Monument, Materiality, and the First Temple of Confucius*. Honolulu: University of Hawai'i Press, 2016.

"From Our Exchanges." *Zion's Herald*, November 29, 1877, 1.

"From the Morals of Confucius." *New-York Weekly Journal*, January 24, 1737, 1–3.

Fukuda Kōichi 福田晃市. *Moe yaku Kōshi-chan no Rongo* 萌訳孔子ちゃんの論語. Tokyo: Sōgō Kagaku Shuppan, 2010.

Gan Bao 干寶. *Sou shen ji* 搜神記. Beijing: Zhonghua, 1979.

Gan Lin 甘霖. *Benlai de Kongzi*: Lunyu *xinjie* 本來的孔子——《論語》新解 Beijing: Zhonghua, 2018.

Gan Liyue 甘禮樂. "Xinqin de kaituozhe, tansuozhe: Gu Bingxin yu lianhuanhua yishu 辛勤的開拓者、探索者——顧炳鑫與連環畫藝術." *Meishu* no. 9 (1980): 13–16; 33.

Gan Tanghui 甘棠惠. *Kong lao'er xiaozhuan* 孔老二小傳. Nanning: Guangxi Renmin, 1973.

Gao Mingshi 高明士. *Zhongguo zhonggu de jiaoyu yu xueli* 中國中古的教育與學禮. Taipei: Taida, 2005.

Ge Hong 葛洪. *Shenxian zhuan jiaoshi* 神仙傳校釋. Beijing: Zhonghua, 2010.

Genz, Joachim. "Elf Thesen zur Eigenart und Systematik früher chinesischer Chronomantik." *Oriens Extremus* 44 (2003/4): 101–10.

Gjertson, Donald E. "The Early Chinese Buddhist Miracle Tale: A Preliminary Survey." *Journal of the American Oriental Society* 101 (1981): 287–301.

Goldin, Paul R. *Confucianism*. Berkeley: University of California Press, 2011.

Gould, Stephen Jay. *The Panda's Thumb: More Reflections in Natural History*. New York: Norton, 1980.

Grafton, Anthony, and Megan Williams. *Christianity and the Transformation of the Book: Origen, Eusebius, and the Library of Caesarea*. Cambridge, MA: Belknap Press, 2006.

Graham, A. C. "The Origins of the Legend of Lao Tan." In *Lao-tzu and the Tao-te-ching: Studies in Ethics, Law, and the Human Ideal*, edited by Livia Kohn and Michael LaFargue, 23–40. Albany: SUNY, 1998.

Guan Changlong 關長龍, ed. *Dunhuang ben shushu wenxian jijiao* 敦煌本數術文獻輯校. Beijing: Zhonghua, 2019.

Guangxi Yishu Xueyuan 廣西藝術學院. *Woguo lishi shang laodong renmin de fanKong douzheng* 我國歷史上勞動人民的反孔鬥爭. Nanning: Guangxi Renmin, 1974.

Guo Moruo 郭沫若. *Shi pipan shu* 十批判書. Shanghai: Qunyi, 1945.

Guofang Daxue dangshi dangjian zheng gong jiaoyanshi 國防大學黨史黨建政工教研室, ed. *"Wenhua dageming" yanjiu ziliao* "文化大革命"研究資料. 3 vols. Vol. 3. Beijing, 1988.

Guoxue yuan 國學園. "Kongzi weishenme bu yuanyi tanlun guishen 孔子為什麼不願意談論鬼神." Wangyi. March 5, 2020. https://www.163.com/dy/article/F6VO4UN805431K92.html (accessed October 25, 2023).

Gyory, Andrew. *Closing the Gate: Race, Politics, and the Chinese Exclusion Act*. Chapel Hill: The University of North Carolina Press, 1998.

Halloran, Fiona Deans. *Thomas Nast: The Father of Modern Political Cartoons*. Chapel Hill: The University of North Carolina Press, 2012.

Han Yanming 韓延明. "Mao Zedong tan Kongzi 毛澤東談孔子." *Dangshi wenhui* no. 10 (2020): 37–41.

Hansen, Valerie. *The Silk Road: A New History*. Oxford: Oxford University Press, 2012.

Harkness, Ethan R. "Cosmology and the Quotidian: Day Books in Early China." PhD dissertation: University of Chicago, 2011.

Harris, Daniel. *Cute, Quaint, Hungry and Romantic: The Aesthetics of Consumerism*. New York: Basic Books, 2000.

He Youzhi 賀友直. *He Youzhi shuohua* 賀友直說畫. Shanghai: Shanghai Renmin, 2008.

Hello Kongzi. Hello Kongzi YouTube channel. YouTube. https://www.youtube.com/@hellokongzi2504/videos (accessed October 27, 2023).

Heyd, Uriel. *Reading Newspapers: Press and Public in Eighteenth-century Britain and America*. Oxford: Voltaire Foundation, 2012.

Higby, William. *Privileges and Immunities of Citizenship*. Washington: Government Printing Office, 1866.

Hinde, R. A., and L. A. Barden. "The Evolution of the Teddy Bear." *Animal Behaviour* 33 (1985): 1371–3.

Hiroshi Arami 荒見泰史. *Dunhuang bianwen xieben de yanjiu* 敦煌變文寫本的研究 Beijing: Zhonghua, 2010.

Holcombe, Charles. *In the Shadow of the Han: Literati Thought and Society at the Beginning of the Southern Dynasties*. Honolulu: University of Hawai'i Press, 1994.

Hou Benben 侯奔奔. "Yu lianhuanhua *Jiangpan zhaoyang* xiangguan de He Youzhi riji he shougao yanjiu 與連環畫《江畔朝陽》相關的賀友直日記和手稿研究", Ha'erbin Shifan Daxue, 2021.

Hu Shi 胡適. *Zhongguo zhexueshi dagang* 中國哲學史大綱. Vol. 1, Shanghai: Shangwu, 1947.

Hu Weixiong 胡為雄, ed. *Mao Zedong shizhuan* 毛澤東詩傳. Beijing: Zhongyang Dangxiao, 2014.

Huang Chin-shing 黃進興. "Xueshu yu Xinyang: Lun Kong Miao congsi zhi yu Rujia daotong yishi 學術與信仰: 論孔廟從祀制與儒家道統意識". *Xin shixue* 5, no. 2 (1994): 1–82.

Huang, Sha. "HelloKongzi in New York Documentary." feng-yuting.com. https://feng-yuting.com/work/hello-kongzi-world-tour-new-york (accessed October 25, 2023).

Huang Zhengjian 黃正建. *Dunhuang zhanbu wenshu yu Tang Wudai zhanbu yanjiu* 敦煌占卜文書與唐五代占卜研究. Beijing: Xueyuan, 2001.

Hunter, Michael. *Confucius beyond the Analects*. Leiden: Brill, 2017.

Jaspers, Karl. *The Great Philosophers*. Translated by Ralph Manheim. 4 vols. New York: Harcourt, Brace & World, Inc., 1962–1995.

Jensen, Lionel M. *Manufacturing Confucianism: Chinese Traditions & Universal Civilization*. Durham: Duke University Press, 1997.

Jia Sixie 賈思勰. *Qimin yaoshu* 齊民要術. Sibu congkan. 4 vols. Vol. 353–356, Shanghai: Commercial, 1922.

Jiaoyubu 教育部, ed. *Yuwen: Qinian ji, shangce* 語文: 七年級上冊, Yiwu jiaoyu jiaokeshu. Beijing: Renmin jiaoyu, 2016.

Jiaoyubu 教育部. *Zhongguo lishi: Qinianji, shangce* 中國歷史: 七年級上冊. Beijing: Renmin jiaoyu, 2016.

"Jinian Gaige Kaifang 30 zhounian: Jiaokeshu 30 nian bianlian ji 紀念改革開放: 30週年: 教科書30年變臉記." *Jinghua shibao*. November 10, 2008. https://news.sina.com.cn/c/2008-11-10/155016624496.shtml (accessed October 25, 2023).

Johnsen, Leigh Dana. "Equal Rights and the 'Heathen Chinee': Black Activism in San Francisco, 1865–1875." *Western Historical Quarterly* 11, no. 1 (1980): 57–68.

Johnson, David. "The Wu Tzu-hsü Pien-wen and Its Sources: Part I." *Harvard Journal of Asiatic Studies* 40, no. 1 (1980): 93–156.

Johnson, David. "The Wu Tzu-hsü Pien-wen and Its Sources: Part II." *Harvard Journal of Asiatic Studies* 40, no. 2 (1980): 465–505.

Johnson, Sylvester A. *The Myth of Ham in Nineteenth-Century American Christianity: Race, Heathens, and the People of God*. New York: Palgrave Macmillan, 2004.

Jones, Michael Owen. "What's Disgusting, Why, and What Does it Matter?" *Journal of Folklore Research* 37, no. 1 (2000): 53–71.

Kalinowski, Marc. *Divination et société dans la Chine médiévale: Étude des manuscrits de Dunhuang de la Bibliothèque nationale de France et de la British Library*. Paris: Bibliothèque Nationale de France, 2003.

Kalinowski, Marc. "Dunhuang shuzhan xiaokao 敦煌數占小考." *Faguo Hanxue* 5 (2000): 187–214.

Kalinowski, Marc. "Typology and Classification of the Mantic Arts in China." In *Handbook of Divination and Prognostication in China*, edited by Michael Lackner and Zhao Lu. Handbook of Oriental Studies. Section 4 China, 171–251. Leiden: Brill, 2022.

Kang Li 康立. "Kongzi he Lin Biao doushi zhengzhi pianzi 孔子和林彪都是政治騙子." *Renmin ribao*, March 11, 1974, 2.

Kang Youwei 康有為. *Kongzi gaizhi kao* 孔子改制考. Kang Youwei quanji 康有為全集. Edited by Jiang Yihua 姜義華 and Zhang Ronghua 張榮華. Vol. 3, Beijing: Zhongguo Renmin Daxue, 2007.

"'Ke'ai 可愛.'" Baidu. June 26, 2022. https://image.baidu.com/search/index?tn=baiduimage&ps=1&ct=201326592&lm=-1&cl=2&nc=1&ie=utf-8&dyTabStr=MCwzLDUsMSw3LDgsNCw2LDIsOQ%3D%3D&word=%E5%8F%AF%E7%88%B1 (accessed October 25, 2023).

Kelisitingna Gangtian 克莉絲汀娜剛田. "[Dalu] Jinian Yangshi *Jiqimao* bochu 30 zhounian de *Duolaeimeng dongman xiao baike* zhongchou shangxian [大陸]紀念央視《機器貓》播出30週年的《哆啦A夢動漫小百科》眾籌上線." Duolaeimeng Zhongwen wang. April 20, 2022. https://chinesedora.com/news/35824.htm (accessed October 25, 2023).

Kinsella, Sharon. "Cuties in Japan." In *Women, Media and Consumption in Japan*, edited by Lise Skov and Brian Moeran, 220–54. Honolulu: University of Hawai'i Press, 1995.

Kluver, Randy. "Chinese Culture in a Global Context: The Confucius Institute as a Geo-Cultural Force." In *China's Global Enagagement: Cooperation, Competition, and Influence in the 21st Century*, edited by Jacques Delisle and Avery Goldstein, 389–416. Washington: Brookings Institution Press, 2017.

Knapp, Keith. *Selfless Offspring: Filial Children and Social Order in Medieval China*. Honolulu: University of Hawai'i Press, 2005.

Kohn, Livia. "The Lao-tzu Myth." In *Lao-tzu and the Tao-te-ching: Studies in Ethics, Law, and the Human Ideal* edited by Livia Kohn and Michael LaFargue, 41–62. Albany: SUNY, 1998.

Kong, Johnny. "Halou, Kongzi 哈嘍, 孔子." YouTube. December 22, 2014. https://www.youtube.com/watch?v=F6ZfS_bJdQc (accessed October 25, 2023).

"Kongzi duidai guishen de taidu shi zenyang de 孔子對待鬼神的態度是怎樣的." Douban. https://www.zhihu.com/question/25408139.

"Kongzi ye lai chuanyue shikong? 孔子也來穿越時空?." TVBS. January 2, 2015. https://news.tvbs.com.tw/travel/561142 (accessed October 25, 2023).

Kudō Motoo 工藤元男. *Suikochi Shinkan yori mita Shindai no kokka to shakai* 睡虎地秦簡よりみた秦代の國家と社會 Tokyo: Sōbunsha, 1998.

Kwok, D. W. Y. *Scientism in Chinese Thought, 1900–1950* New Haven: Yale University Press, 1965.

Lam, Joseph S. C. "Musical Confucianism: The Case of 'Jikong yuewu.'" In *On Sacred Grounds: Culture, Society, Politics, and the Formation of the Cult of Confucius*, edited by Thomas A. Wilson, 134–74. Cambridge, MA: Harvard University Asia Center, 2002.

Legge, James. *The Chinese Classics with a Translation, Critical and Exegetical Notes Prolegomena, and Copious Indexes. Vol. 1: Confucian Analects, The Great Learning, and the Doctrine of the Mean.* London: Trübner, 1961.

Lei Fang 雷芳. "Minban peixun jiaoyu de gongxian, wenti, yu fazhan jianyi 民辦培訓教育的貢獻、問題與發展建議." *Hunansheng Shehuizhuyi Xueyuan xuebao* 19, no. 105 (2018): 84–6.

Leman II, Kevin A. "Ellen Show." Edited by Warner Bros. Television Distribution, May 8, 2014.

Lent, John A., and Xu Ying. *Comics Art in China.* Jackson: University of Mississippi Press, 2017.

Lew-Williams, Beth. *The Chinese Must Go: Violence, Exclusion, and the Making of the Alien in America.* Cambridge, MA: Harvard University Press, 2018.

Lewis, Mark Edward. *China Between Empires: The Northern and Southern Dynasties.* Cambridge, MA: Belknap Press of Harvard University Press, 2009.

Li Fang 李昉 et al., ed. *Taiping yulan* 太平御覽. Beijing: Zhonghua, 1960.

Li Feng. "'Feudalism' and Western Zhou China: A Criticism." *Harvard Journal of Asiatic Studies* 63, no. 1 (2003): 115–44.

Li Guangbi 李光璧. "Guanyu gao chuzhong benguoshi gudai bufen jiaocai jiaofa de yixie wenti 關於高初中本國史古代部分教材教法的一些問題." *Lishi jiaoxue* no. 2 (1952): 18–23.

Li Jianfeng 李劍鋒. "Wei Jin Nanchao zhiguai xiaoshuo zhong de Kongzi xingxiang 魏晉南朝志怪小說中的孔子形象." *Kongzi yanjiu* no. 1 (2008): 102–8.

Li Jianguo 李建國. *Tang qian zhiguai xiaoshuo shi* 唐前志怪小說史. Tianjin: Jiaoyu, 2005.

Li Jinquan 李錦全. *Xiandai sixiang shijia Yang Rongguo* 現代思想史家楊榮國. Guangzhou: Zhongshan Daxue press, 2009.

Li Junling 李俊領. "Kangzhan shiqi Guomindang yu Nanjing Guomin Zhengfu dui Kongzi de jisi dianli 抗戰時期國民黨與南京國民政府對孔子的祭祀典禮." *Shehui kexue pinglun* no. 4 (2008): 45–62.

Li Ling 李零. *Sangjia gou: Wo du Lunyu* 喪家狗：我讀《論語》. Taiyuan: Shanxi renmin, 2007.

Li Lu 黎魯. "Xin Meishu Chubanshe shimo 新美術出版社始末." *Bianji xuekan* no. 2 (1993): 71–5.

Li Luo 黎落. "Shengli de 'Wusi' 勝利的'五四'." *Guangming ribao,* May 4, 1950.

Li Tao 李燾. *Xu Zizhi tongjian changbian* 續資治通鑑長編. Beijing: Zhonghua, 1979.

Li Xiaorong 李小榮. *Dunhuang bianwen* 敦煌變文 Lanzhou: Gansu jiaoyu, 2013.

Li You 李攸, ed. *Songchao shi shi* 宋朝事實 Vol. 11, Songdai Biji Xiaoshuo 宋代筆記小說. Shijiazhuang: Hebei jiaoyu, 1995.

Li Yu 李雨. "Jianguo chuqi (1949–1953) zhongxue lishi jiaokeshu jiazhi quxiang yanjiu 建國初期(1949–1953) 中學歷史教科書價值取向研究." Henan Shifan Daxue, 2016.

Li Zehou 李澤厚. *Lunyu jindu* 論語今讀. Hefei: Anhui wenyi, 1998.

Li Zhengyu 李正宇. "Dunhuang xuelang tiji jizhu 敦煌學郎題記輯注." *Dunhuang xue jikan* no. 1 (1987): 27–40.

Li Zhizhong 李志忠. "Gushu xuanfeng zhuang kao bian 古書旋風裝考辨." *Wenwu* no. 2 (1981): 75–8.

Liao, Hsien-huei. "Critique and Recognition: Mantic Arts and Their Practitioners in the Writings of Song Literati." In *Handbook of Divination and Prognostication in China*, edited by Michael Lackner and Zhao Lu. Handbook of Oriental Studies. Section 4 China, 305–44. Leiden: Brill, 2022.

Liji zhengyi 禮記正義. *Shisanjing zhushu* 十三經注疏. Edited by Ruan Yuan 阮元. Beijing: Zhonghua, 1980.

Lin Ruiyi 林瑞益. "Hello Kongzi quanqiu xunzhan chuancheng xiaodao Hello Kongzi 全球巡展傳承孝道." Zhongshi xinwen wang. December 22, 2014. https://www.chinatimes.com/cn/realtimenews/20141222000790-260514?chdtv (accessed October 25, 2023).

Lin, Shen-yu. "The Tibetan Image of Confucius." *Revue d'Etudes Tibétaines* 12 (2007): 105–29.

Lin Sujuan 林素娟. "Handai gansheng shenhua suo chuanda de yuzhouguan jiqi zai zhengjiao shang de yiyi 漢代感生神話所傳達的宇宙觀及其在政教上的意義." *Cheng Da zhongwen xuebao* 4, no. 28 (2010): 35–82.

Ling Yuxuan 凌玉萱. "Jian'gou shenshengzhe chuanqi: Cong *Shishi Yuanliu* dao *Shengji tu* de chuanqi yunsheng tuxiang fazhan guocheng 建構神聖者傳奇——從《釋氏源流》到《聖蹟圖》的傳奇孕生圖像發展過程." *Yishu fenzi* no. 8 (2007): 15–42.

Lingqi benzhang zheng jing 靈棋本章正經. Zhengtong daozang 正統道藏. Vol. 23, Shanghai: Shudian, Guji, 1988.

Liu, Alan P. L. "Mass Communication and Media in China's Cultural Revolution." *Journalism Quarterly* 42, no. 2 (1969): 314–19.

Liu An 劉安. *Huainanzi jishi* 淮南子集釋. Beijing: Zhonghua, 1998.

Liu Jinbao 劉進寶. "20 shiji Dunhuang cangjing dong fengbi shijian ji qi yuanyin yanjiu de huigu 20世紀敦煌藏經洞封閉時間及其原因研究的回顧." *Dunhuang yanjiu* no. 2 (2000): 29–35.

Liu Lexian 劉樂賢. *Shuihudi Qin jian rishu yanjiu* 睡虎地秦簡日書研究. Taipei: Wenjin, 1994.

Liu Xiang 劉向. *Shuiyuan jiaozheng* 說苑校證. Beijing: Zhonghua, 1987.

Liu Xiuming 劉修明. "Kongzi zhuan 孔子傳." *Xuexi yu pipan* no. 2 (1973): 83–91.

Liu Yan 劉艷, and Lin Hualing 林華玲. "Woguo minban peixun jiaoyu ruhe yu 'lang' gongwu: yi Xindongfang Jiaoyu Keji Jituan weijian 我國民辦培訓教育如何與'狼'共舞——以新東方教育科技集團為鑒." *Renli ziyuan guanli* no. 7 (2013): 172–3.

Liu Yiqing 劉義慶. *Shishuo xinyu jiaojian* 世說新語校箋. Beijing: Zhonghua, 1984.

Liu Yuanru 劉苑如. "Xingxian yu mingbao: Liuchao zhiguai xushu de fengyu—yi ge 'daoyi wei chang' moshi de kaocha 形見與冥報: 六朝志怪敘述的諷喻——一個'導異為常'模式的考察." *Zhongyang yanjiuyuan zhongguo wenzhe yanjiu jikan* 29 (2006): 1–45.

Liu Zhen 劉珍, Li You 李尤, Liu Taotu 劉騊騟, and Liu Yi 劉毅. *Dongguan Han ji* 東觀漢記. Beijing: Zhonghua, 2008.

Lo, Alex. "Would Confucius Condone Same-Sex Marriage?" *South China Morning Post*, November 17, 2022.

Loewe, Michael. *Crisis and Conflict in Han China, 104 BC to AD 9*. London: George Allen & Unwin, 1974.

Loewe, Michael. *Divination, Mythology and Monarchy in Han China*. Cambridge, UK: Cambridge University Press, 1995.

Loewe, Michael. *Early Chinese Texts: A Bibliographical Guide*. Berkeley: The Society for the Study of Early China and The Institute of East Asian Studies, University of California, 1993.

Loewe, Michael. "The Former Han Dynasty." In *The Cambridge History of China. Vol. 1, The Ch'in and Han Empires, 221 B.C.-A.D. 220*, edited by Denis Twitchett and Michael Loewe, 103–222. Cambridge: Cambridge University Press, 1985.

Loewe, Michael. *The Men Who Governed Han China: Companion to* A Biographical Dictionary of Qin, Former Han, and Xin Periods. Leiden: Brill, 2011.

Loomis, A. W. *Confucius and the Chinese Classics; or Readings in Chinese Literature*. San Francisco: A. Roman & Company, 1867.

Lorenz, Konrad. *The Foundations of Ethology*. Translated by Konrad Lorenz and Robert Warren Kickert. New York and Vienna: Springer Verlag, 1981.

Lorenz, Konrad. *Studies in Animal and Human Behavior*. Translated by Robert Martin. Vol. 2, Cambridge, MA: Harvard University Press, 1971.

Lü Buwei 呂不韋. *Lüshi chunqiu zhushu* 呂氏春秋注疏. Chengdu: Bashu, 2002.

Lu Deming 陸德明. *Jingdian shiwen* 經典釋文 Beijing: Zhonghua, 1983.

Lu Jia 陸賈. *Xinyu jiaozhu* 新語校注 Beijing: Zhonghua, 1986.

Lu Xun 魯迅, ed. *Gu xiaoshuo gouchen* 古小說鉤沈. Beijing: Renmin wenxue, 1973.

Lu Jia 陸賈. *Zhongguo xiaoshuo shilue* 中國小說史略 Beijing: Renmin wenxue 1973.

Lum, Kathryn Gin. *Heathen: Religion and Race in American History*. Cambridge, MA: Harvard University Press, 2022.

Lunyu jizhu 論語集注. *Sishu zhangju jizhu* 四書章句集注. Beijing: Zhonghua, 1983.

Luo Xinhui 羅新慧. "Zhoudai tianming guannian de fazhan yu shanbian 周代天命觀念的發展與嬗變." *Lishi yanjiu* no. 5 (2002): 4–18.

MacFarquhar, Roderick. *The Origins of the Cultural Revolution: Volume 1. Contradictions Among the People, 1956–1957*. London: Oxford University Press, 1974.

MacFarquhar, Roderick. *The Origins of the Cultural Revolution: Volume 2. The Great Leap Forward, 1958–1960*. New York: Columbia University Press, 1983.

MacFarquhar, Roderick. *The Origins of the Cultural Revolution: Volume 3. The Coming of the Cataclysm, 1961–1966*. Oxford and New York: Oxford University Press and Columbia University Press, 1997.

MacFarquhar, Roderick, and Michael Schönhals. *Mao's Last Revolution*. Cambridge, MA: Harvard University Press, 2006.

Mair, Victor H. "Lay Students and the Making of Written Vernacular Narrative: an Inventory of Tun-huang Manuscripts." *Journal of Chinese Oral and Performing Literature* 10, no. 1 (1981): 5–96.

Mair, Victor H. *T'ang Transformation Texts: A Study of the Buddhist Contribution to the Rise of Vernacular Fiction and Drama in China* Cambridge, MA: Harvard University Press, 1989.

Makeham, John. "The Revival of Guoxue: Historical Antecedents and Contemporary Aspirations." *China Perspectives* 85, no. 1 (2011): 14–21.

Mao Zedong 毛澤東. "*Mao Zedong sixiang wansui* 1958-1960 毛澤東思想萬歲 1958–1960." Edited Gang'er si Wuhan Daxue zongbu 鋼二司武漢大學總部, 1969.

Maoshi zhengyi 毛詩正義. *Shisanjing zhushu* 十三經注疏. Edited by Ruan Yuan 阮元. Beijing: Zhonghua, 1980.

Marcus, Aaron, Massaki Kurosu, Xiaojuan Ma, and Ayako Hashizume. *Cuteness Engineering: Designing Adorable Products and Services*. Cham: Springer, 2017.

Martinez, Michael, and Jaqueline Hurtado. "Hello Kitty Turns 40, Draws 25,000 Fans to First Hello Kitty Con." CNN. June 14, 2022. https://edition.cnn.com/2014/11/01/us/hello-kitty-convention-40th-year/index.html.

May, Jennifer. "Sources of Authority: Quotational Practice in Chinese Communist Propaganda". PhD dissertation, University of Heidelberg, 2008.

May, Simon. *The Power of Cute*. Princeton: Princeton University Press, 2019.

McCurry, Justin. "Japan enlists cartoon cat as ambassador." The Guardian. June 14, 2022. https://www.theguardian.com/world/2008/mar/20/japan.

Meisner, Maurice. *Li Ta-Chao and the Origins of Chinese Marxism*. Cambridge, MA: Harvard University Press, 1967.

Meixuan 美宣. "Douren xiai de meishu pian 逗人喜愛的美術片." *Dianying pingjie* no. 6 (1985).

Meng Zhuo 孟琢, Yin Meng 尹夢, and Mei Ruyu 梅茹瑜. *Kongzi yue: Gei haizi de guoxue manhua* 孔子曰——給孩子的國學漫畫. Beijing: Zhongguo qingnian, 2020.

"'Mengmengda' Kongzi xiang liangxiang Shenzhen wenbohui '萌萌噠'孔子像亮相深圳文博會." Zhongguo xinwen wang. June 12, 2022. http://www.onezh.com/news/news_show.asp?id=10894.

Mengzi jizhu 孟子集注. *Sishu zhangju jizhu* 四書章句集注. Beijing: Zhonghua, 1983.

Merish, Lori. "Cuteness and Commodity Aesthetics: Tom Thumb and Shirley Temple." In *Freakery: Cultural Spectacles of the Extraordinary Body*, edited by Rosemarie Thomson-Garland, 185–203. New York: New York University Press, 1996.

Meynard, Thierry. *The Jesuit Reading of Confucius: The First Complete Translation of the Lunyu (1687) Published in the West*. Leiden: Brill, 2015.

Mitter, Rana. *A Bitter Revolution: China's Struggle with the Modern World*. Oxford: Oxford University Press, 2004.

Mittler, Barbara. *A Continuous Revolution: Making Sense of Cultural Revolution Culture*. Cambridge, MA: Harvard University Asia Center, 2012.

"A Modern Chinese Moralist." *Philadelphia Enquirer*, February 14, 1884, 3.

Mungello, D. E. *Curious Land: Jesuit Accommodation and the Origins of Sinology*. Honolulu: University of Hawai'i Press, 1985.

Murray, Julia K. "Confucian Iconography." In *Modern Chinese Religion I: Song-Liao-Jin-Yuan (960–1368 AD)*, edited by Pierre Marsone and John Lagerway. Handbook of Oriental Studies. Section 4 China, 801–43. Leiden: Brill, 2015.

Murray, Julia K. "Illustrations of the Life of Confucius: Their Evolution, Functions, and Significance in Late Ming China." *Artibus Asiae* 57, no. 1/2 (1997): 73–134.

Murray, Julia K. "Miraculous Portraits of Confucius: Images and Auspicious Presences." *Ars Orientalis* 50 (2021): 78–105.

Murray, Julia K. "Visual Representations of Confucius." In *A Concise Companion to Confucius*, edited by Paul R. Goldin. Blackwell Companions to Philosophy, 92–129. Hoboken, NJ Wiley, 2017.

Naha Toshisada 那波利貞. "Tōshōhon zatsushō kō: Tōdai shomin kyōiku kenkyū no ichi shiryō 唐鈔本雜抄考——唐代庶民教育研究の一資料." *Shinagaku kenkyū* 10 (1942): 1–91.

Nast, Thomas. "Civilization of Blaine." *Harper's Weekly* XXIII (March 8, 1879): cover page.

Nast, Thomas. "A Matter of Taste." *Harper's Weekly* XXIV (March 15, 1879): 118.

Ngai, Mae M. *The Chinese Question: The Gold Rushes and Global Politics*. New York: W. W. Norton & Company, Inc., 2021.

Ngai, Sianne. "The Cuteness of the Avant-Garde." *Critical Inquiry* 31, no. 4 (2005): 811–47.

Ngai, Sianne. *Our Aesthetic Categories: Zany, Cute, Interesting*. Cambridge, MA: Harvard University Press, 2012.

Nickerson, Peter S. "Taoism, Death, and Bureaucracy in Early Medieval China." PhD. dissertation, University of California, 1996.

Nielsen, Bent. *A Companion to Yi Jing Numerology and Cosmology: Chinese Studies of Images and Numbers from Han 漢 (202 BCE–220 CE) to Song 宋 (960–1279 CE)*. London: RoutledgeCurzon, 2003.

Norris, Pippa, and Ronald Inglehart. *Sacred and Secular: Religion and Politics Worldwide*. Cambridge: Cambridge University Press, 2011.

Nylan, Michael, and Thomas Wilson. *Lives of Confucius: Civilization's Greatest Sage Through the Ages*. New York: Doubleday, 2010.

Olympics. "Rio 2016 Closing Ceremony Full HD Replay." YouTube, August 21, 2016. https://www.youtube.com/watch?v=ssc5eLjLoMQ&t=6722s (accessed October 24, 2023).

Ou, Hsin-yun. "Mark Twain's Racial Ideologies and His Portrayal of the Chinese." *Concentric: Literary and Cultural Studies* 36, no. 2 (2010): 33–59.

Ouyang Xun 歐陽詢. *Songben yiwen leiju* 宋本藝文類聚. Shanghai: Guji, 2013.

Paddison, Joshua. *American Heathens: Religion, Race, and Reconstruction in California*. Berkeley: University of California Press, 2012.

Paine, Thomas. *The Age of Reason*. Toronto: W.B. Cooke & W.M. Scott, 1887.

People v. Hall, 4 California (1854).

Pi Lin pi Kong manhua xuanchuanhua xuanbian 批林批孔漫畫宣傳畫選編. Tianjin: Tianjin Yishu Xueyuan gongyi meishu xi, 1974.

"*Pleasant Goat and Big Big Wolf.*" Wikipedia. October 23, 2023. https://en.wikipedia.org/wiki/Pleasant_Goat_and_Big_Big_Wolf (accessed October 24, 2023).

Powers, Stephen. "Aborigines of California: An Indo-Chinese Study." *The Atlantic* 33 (1874), 313–23.

Pregadio, Fabrizio, ed. *The Encyclopedia of Taoism*. London; New York: Routledge, 2004.

Prieto, Andrés I. "The Perils of Accommodation: Jesuit Missionary Strategies in the Early Modern World." *Journal of Jesuit Studies* 4 (2017): 395–414.

Puett, Michael J. "Following the Commands of Heaven: The Notion of Ming in Early China." In *The Magnitude of Ming: Command, Allotment, and Fate in Chinese Culture*, edited by Christopher Lupke, 49–69. Honolulu: University of Hawai'i Press, 2005.

Puett, Michael J. "Sages, Creation, and the End of History in the *Huainanzi*." In *The Huainanzi and Textual Production in Early China*, edited by Sarah A. Queen and Michael J. Puett, 267–90. Leiden: Brill, 2014.

"Q ban 'Weita nai' wenshi Q版'維他奶'問世." *Zhongguo shipin gongye* no. 12 (1996): 12.

Qian, Nancy, and Pierre Yared. "The Institutional Causes of China's Great Famine, 1959–1961." *Review of Economic Studies* no. 82 (2015): 1568–611.

Qiu Guangming 丘光明, Qiu Long 邱隆, and Yang Ping 楊平. *Zhongguo kexue jishu shi: Du liang heng juan* 中國科學技術史: 度量衡卷 Beijing: Kexue, 2001.

Qu Zhimin 屈直敏. *Dunhuang wenxian yu zhonggu jiaoyu* 敦煌文獻與中古教育. Lanzhou: Gansu jiaoyu, 2011.

Qufu Gong'an 曲阜公安. June 27, 2022. https://weibo.com/u/2018539543 (accessed October 24, 2023).

Raphals, Lisa. *Divination and Prediction in Early China and Ancient Greece*. Cambridge: Cambridge University Press, 2013.

Ren Mei 任梅, and Lu Zhanmei 魯展美. *Lishi shang laodong renmin fanKong douzheng de gushi* 歷史上勞動人民反孔鬥爭的故事. Beijing: Renmin Meishu, 1975.

"Republican State Convention." *Sacramento Daily Record*, June 29, 1871, 3.

Rogaski, Ruth. *Hygienic Modernity: Meanings of Health and Disease in Treaty-port China*. Berkeley: University of California Press, 2004.

Rong Xinjiang 榮新江. *Eighteen Lectures on Dunhuang*. Translated by Imre Galambos. Leiden: Brill, 2013.

Rong Xinjiang 榮新江. *Guiyijun shi yanjiu: Tang Song shidai Dunhuang lishi kaosuo* 歸義軍史研究: 唐宋時代敦煌歷史考索. Shanghai: Guji, 1996.

Rong Xinjiang. "Khotanese Felt and Sogdian Silver: Foreign Gifts to Buddhist Monasteries in Ninth- and Tenth-Century Dunhuang." *Asia Major* 17, no. 1 (2004): 15–34.

Rong Xinjiang. "The Nature of the Dunhuang Library Cave and the Reasons for its Sealing." *Cahiers d'Extrême-Asie* 11 (1999): 247–75.

Rong Xinjiang. "The Relationship of Dunhuang with the Uighur Kingdom in Turfan in the Tenth Century." In *De Dunhuang à Istanbul: Hommage à James Russell Hamilton*, edited by Louis Bazin and Peter Zieme, 275–98. Turnhout: Brepols, 2001.

Rozman, Gilbert. "*Comparisons of Modern Confucian Values in China and Japan.*" In *The East Asian Religion: Confucian Heritage and Its Modern Adaptation*, edited by Gilbert Rozman, 157–203. Princeton: Princeton University Press, 1991.

Russell-Smith, Lilla. *Uygur Patronage in Dunhuang: Regional Art Centres on the Northern Silk Road in the Tenth and Eleventh Centuries.* Leiden: Brill, 2005.

Saxton, Alexander. *The Indispensable Enemy: Labor and the Anti-Chinese Movement in California.* Berkeley: University of California Press, 1971.

Schipper, Kristofer. "*Laozi zhongjing* chutan 《老子中经》初探." *Daojia wenhua yanjiu* 16 (1999): 204–16.

Schipper, Kristofer, and Franciscus Verellen, eds. *The Taoist Canon: A Historical Companion to the Daozang* Vol. 3. Chicago: University of Chicago Press, 2004.

Schodt, Frederik L. *Dreamland Japan: Writings on Modern Manga.* Berkeley: Stone Bridge Press, 1996.

Shaanxi Shifan Daxue zhongwen xi gong, nong, bing xueyuan, jiaoshi 陝西師範大學中文系工農兵學員、教師 et al. Kong Lao'er de chou'e mianmu 孔老二的醜惡面目. Xi'an: Shaanxi Renmin, 1974.

Shandongsheng "Wu Qi" Yixiao meishudui 山東省"五七"藝校美術隊. Kong Lao'er de zui'e yisheng 孔老二的罪惡一生. Ji'nan: Shandong Renmin, 1974.

Shanghai jingju tuan *Zhiqu Weihushan* juzu 上海京劇團《智取威虎山》劇組. "Nuli suzao wuchan jieji yingxiong renwu de guanghui xingxiang 努力塑造無產階級英雄人物的光輝形象." *Hongqi* no. 11 (1969): 62–78.

Shangshu 尚書. Shisan jing zhushu 十三經注疏. Edited by Ruan Yuan 阮元. Beijing: Zhonghua, 1980.

Shao Wenjing 邵文菁. "Milaoshu zai Zhongguo 米老鼠在中國." *Dang'an Chunqiu* no. 8 (2016): 13–17.

Sherman, Gary D., and Jonathan Haidt. "Cuteness and Disgust: The Humanizing and Dehumanizing Effects of Emotion." *Emotion Review* 3, no. 3 (2011): 245–51.

Shi Yan 史燕. "Liuchao xiaoshuo zhong de Kongzi xingxiang 六朝小說中的孔子形象" Master Thesis, Zhengzhou Daxue, 2012.

Shiraishi, Saya S. "Japan's Soft Power: Doraemon Goes Overseas." In *Network Power: Japan and Asia*, edited by Peter J. Katzenstein and Takashi Shiraishi, 234–72. Ithaca: Cornell University Press, 1997.

Sichuan Shifan Xueyuan 四川師範學院, Qionglaixian Wenhuaguan 邛崍縣文化館, Sichuan Renmin Chubanshe 四川人民出版社, and Sichuan Huabaoshe 四川畫報社. Fandong jieji de "shengren": Kong Lao'er 反動階級的"聖人"——孔老二. Chengdu: Sichuan Renmin, 1974.

Sima Qian 司馬遷. *Shiji* 史記. Beijing: Zhonghua, 1963.

Smith, Tom. "How Kumamon Became a National Sensation in Japan." Culture Trip. March 3, 2020. https://theculturetrip.com/asia/japan/articles/how-kumamon-became-a-national-sensation/ (accessed October 24, 2023).

Snow, Jennifer C. *Protestant Missionaries, Asian Immigrants, and Ideologies of Race in America, 1850–1924.* New York: Routledge, 2007.

"Some Remarkable Giants." *San Francisco Bulletin*, May 18, 1889, 6.

Sou, Daniel. "In the government's service: A study of the role and practice of early China's officials based on excavated manuscripts." PhD dissertation, University of Pennsylvania, 2013.

Sprabary, Autumn "Why do people wink?" All About Vision. https://www.allaboutvision.com/resources/why-people-wink/ (accessed October 25, 2023).

"Street Scenes in Papeete, Tahiti." *Chicago Daily Tribune*, May 27, 1876, 2.

Strickmann, Michel. *Chinese Poetry and Prophecy: The Written Oracle in East Asia*. Stanford: Stanford University Press, 2005.

Sugawara Shinkan 菅原信海. "Senzei sho 占筮書." In *Tonkō Kanbun bunken* 敦煌漢文文獻, edited by Ikeda On 池田溫, 439–62. Tokyo: Daitō Shuppansha, 1992.

Sukhu, Gopal. *The Shaman and the Heresiarch: A New Interpretation of the* Li sao Albany: SUNY, 2012.

Sun Xiaochun and Jacob Kistemaker. *The Chinese Sky During the Han: Constellating Stars and Society*. Leiden: E.J. Brill, 1997.

Sun Yirang 孫詒讓, ed. *Mozi jiangu* 墨子間詁. Beijing: Zhonghua, 2001.

Supper, J. C. "From the Rev. J. C. Supper, Secretary of the Java Auxiliary Bible Society, May 18, 1815." *Christian Messenger*, January 22, 1817, 1.

Svarverud, Rune. "Body and Character: Physiognomic Descriptions in Han Dynasty Literature." In *Minds and Mentalities in Traditional Chinese Literature*, edited by Halvor Eifring, 120–46. Beijing: Culture and Art Publishing House, 1999.

"Table Gossip." *Boston Daily Globe*, September 15, 1877, 4.

Takaki, Ronald. *Strangers from a Different Shore: A History of Asian Americans*. Boston, Toronto, and London: Little, Brown and Company, 1989.

Takata Tokio 高田時雄. "Multilingualism in Tun-huang." *Acta Asiatica* 78 (2000): 49–70.

Tanaka Masami 田中麻紗巳. *Ryōkan shisō no kenkyū* 両漢思想の研究. Tokyo: Kenbun Shuppan, 1986.

Tang Xiao 湯嘯. "Guanyu Liuxia Zhi de fanKong shiji 關於柳下跖的反孔事跡." *Renmin ribao*, February 26, 1974.

Tang Xiaowen 唐曉文. "Liuxia Zhi tongma Konglao'er 柳下跖痛罵孔老二." *Renmin ribao*, February 26, 1974.

Tang Yijie 湯一介. "Wo yu 'Liangxiao' 我與'梁效'." *Shiji* no. 1 (2016): 25–8.

Tangherlini, Timothy R. "'It Happened Not Too Far from Here …': A Survey of Legend Theory and Characterization." *Western Folklore* 49 (1990): 371–90.

Tchen, John Kuo Wei. *New York before Chinatown: Orientalism and the Shaping of American Culture 1776–1882*. Baltimore: The Johns Hopkins University Press, 1999.

Thomas, F. W. *Ancient Folk-Literature from North-Eastern Tibet* Berlin: Akademie Verlag, 1957.

Tian Kai 田凱. "Lishi shang laodong renmin de fanKong douzheng 歷史上勞動人民的反孔鬥爭." *Renmin ribao*, January 9, 1974, 2.

TigerloveHoney. "'qimeng, chuancheng, wenhua zaizao zhi Hello Kongzi quanqiu gongyi xunzhan: Taiwan zhan' zai Gugong「啟蒙.傳承 文化再造之Hello Kongzi

全球公益巡展: 台灣站」在故宮." Pixnet. January 9, 2015. https://tigerlovehoney. pixnet.net/blog/post/254803198 (October 24, 2023).

Time. "10 Questions for Yūko Yamaguchi" *Time*. August 21, 2008. https://content.time.com/time/subscriber/article/0,33009,1834451,00.html (accessed October 10, 2023).

Tjan, Tjoe Som. *Po Hu T'ung: The Comprehensive Discussions in the White Tiger Hall*. Leiden: Brill, 1949–52.

Tong Xiaopeng 童小鵬. "Zhou Enlai zai 'PiLin PiKong'" zhong 周恩來在'批林批孔'中." *Lingdao wencui* no. 12 (1996): 48–52.

Twain, Mark. "John Chinaman in New York." In *Mark Twain's Sketches, New and Old*, edited by Mark Twain, 231–2. Hartford: American Publishing, 1875.

Van de Ven, Hans J. *From Friend to Comrade: The Founding of the Chinese Communist Party, 1920–1927*. Berkeley: University of California Press, 1991.

van Ess, Hans. "The Apocryphal Texts of the Han Dynasty and the Old Text/New Text Controversy." *T'oung Pao* 85, no. 1 (1999): 29–64.

Van Norden, Bryan W. "Confucius on Gay Marriage." *The Diplomat* (July 13, 2015).

Van Norden, Bryan W. *Taking back Philosophy: A Multicultural Manifesto*. New York: Columbia University Press, 2017.

Vreranda. "Kongzi Hello Kongzi quanqiu gongyi xunzhan-Taiwan zhan 孔子 Hello Kongzi全球公益巡展 - 臺灣站." Pixnet. January 4, 2015. https://vreranda.pixnet.net/blog/post/192216174 (accessed October 25, 2023).

Walfred, Michele. "Chinese Americans." https://thomasnastcartoons.com/the-chinese-cartoons/ (accessed October 25, 2023).

Walfred, Michele. "'Civilization of Blaine' 1879." April 8, 2014. https://thomasnastcartoons.com/2014/04/08/civilization-of-blaine-8-march-1879/ (accessed October 25, 2023).

Walfred, Michele. "'A Matter of Taste' 15 March 1879." April 1, 2014. https://thomasnastcartoons.com/2014/04/01/a-matter-of-taste-15-march-1879/ (accessed October 25, 2023).

Walters, Kerry S. *The American Deists: Voices of Reason and Dissent in the Early Republic*. Lawrence: University Press of Kansas, 1992.

Wang Aihe. *Cosmology and Political Culture in Early China*. Cambridge: Cambridge University Press, 2000.

Wang Aihe 王愛和. "Dunhuang zhanbu wenshu yanjiu 敦煌占卜文書研究." PhD dissertation, Lanzhou University, 2003.

Wang Chong 王充. *Lunheng jiaoshi* 論衡校釋. Beijing: Zhonghua, 1990.

Wang Chongmin 王重民, Wang Qingshu 王慶菽, Xiang Da 向達, Zhou Yiliang 周一良, and Qi Gong 啟功, eds. *Dunhuang bianwen ji* 敦煌變文集. Beijing: Renmin, 1957.

Wang Chuanlong 王傳龍. "'Xuanfeng zhuang' banben huikao '旋風裝'版本匯考.'" *Daxue tushuguan xuebao* no. 3 (2009).

Wang Dongxing 汪東興. *Wang Dongxing huiyi: Mao Zedong yu Lin Biao fangeming jituan de douzheng* 汪東興回憶: 毛澤東與林彪反革命集團的鬥爭. Beijing: Dangdai Zhongguo, 1997.

Wang guanqing 汪觀清, and Li Minghai 李明海, eds. *Xin Zhongguo lianhuanhua: 70 niandai* 新中國連環畫: 70年代. Shanghai: Shanghai huabao, 2003.

Wang Guoliang 王國良. *Wei Jin Nanbeichao zhiguai xiaoshuo yanjiu* 魏晉南北朝志怪小說研究. Taipei: Wenshizhe, 1984.

Wang Hongzhi 王宏志. "Lishi renwu he lishi jiaocai 歷史人物和歷史教材." *Kecheng, jiaocai, jiaofa* no. 11 (1997): 6–10.

Wang Hongzhi 王宏志. "Luetan zai xinbian zhongxue *Zhongguo lishi* keben zhong xie lishi renwu de jige wenti 略談在新編中學《中國歷史》課本中寫歷史人物的幾個問題." *Lishi jiaoxue* no. 2 (1978): 28–32.

Wang hongzhi 王宏志. "Shehui jinbu he lishi jiaocai de gaige 社會進步和歷史教材的改革." *Kecheng, jiaocai, jiaofa* no. 11 (1990): 16–18; 42.

Wang Hongzhi 王宏志, Li Longgeng 李隆庚, and Zang Rong 臧嶸. "Yiwu jiaoyu chuzhong *Zhongguo lishi* 義務教育初中《中國歷史》." *Kecheng, jiaocai, jiaofa* no. 5 (1992): 4–9.

Wang Jia 王嘉. *Shiyi ji* 拾遺記. Changchun: Jilin Daxue, 1992.

Wang Jindong 王今棟, and Qin Yunhai 秦雲海. *Liuxia Zhi tongchi Kong Lao'er* 柳下跖痛斥孔老二. Zhengzhou: Henan Renmin, 1975.

Wang Jingbo 王晶波. *Dunhuang zhanbu wenxian yu shehui shenghuo* 敦煌占卜文獻與社會生活. Lanzhou: Gansu jiaoyu, 2011.

Wang Jiyun 王際雲. "Kongzi yao ''fuli', Lin Biao yao fubi 孔子要"復禮", 林彪要復辟." *Renmin ribao*, January 28, 1974, 2.

Wang Ka 王卡. *Dunhuang Daojiao wenxian yanjiu: Zongshu, Mulu, Suoyin* 敦煌道教文獻研究——綜述·目錄·索引. Beijing: Shehui kexue, 2004.

Wang Tianhai 王天海, ed. *Xunzi jiaoshi* 荀子校釋. Shanghai: Shanghai guji, 2005.

Wang Weiqin 王偉琴. ""Li Ling bianwen" zuoshi zuozhe kaolun 《李陵變文》作時作者考論." *Yuwen zhishi* no. 2 (2012): 6–8.

Wang Zhenzhong 王振忠. "Cong 'Hongguan changren' dao 'Zhongguo juren': Wanqing Wuyuan Zhan Shichai shengping shiji kaozheng 從'虹關長人'到'中國巨人': 晚晴婺源詹世釵生平事跡考證." *Anhui Shifan Daxue xuebao* 45 (2017): 529–42.

Wang Zijin 王子今. "Mao Zedong lunxi Qin Shihuang 毛澤東論析秦始皇." *Bainian chao* no. 10 (2003): 38–43.

Wei Bin 魏斌. *Shanzhong de Liuchao shi* 山中的六朝史. Beijing: Zhonghua, 2019.

Wei Shou 魏收. *Wei shu* 魏書. Beijing: Zhonghua, 1974.

Wei Wei 魏巍. "Shui shi zui ke'ai de ren 誰是最可愛的人." *Renmin ribao*, April 11, 1951.

Wei Zheng 魏徵, and Linghu Defen 令狐德棻. *Suishu* 隋書. Beijing: Zhonghua, 1973.

"Wenhua zaizao zhi Hello Kongzi quanqiu gongyi zhan 文化再造之Hello Kongzi全球公益展." Shenzhen Charity Federation. May 18, 2015. https://www.szcharity.org/News/Detail/16592 (accessed October 25, 2023).

Williams, Samuel Wells. *Middle Kingdom; A survey of the Geography, Government, Education, Social Life, Arts, Religion, &c., of the Chinese Empire and Its Inhabitants.* New York and London: Wiley & Putnam, 1849.

Wilson, Thomas A. "Ritualizing Confucius/Kongzi: The Family and State Cults of the Sage of Culture in Imperial China." In *On Sacred Grounds: Culture, Society, Politics, and the Formation of the Cult of Confucius*, edited by Thomas A. Wilson, 43–94. Cambridge, MA: Harvard University Asia Center, 2002.

Wilson, Thomas A. "Culture, Society, Politics, and the Cult of Confucius." In *On Sacred Grounds: Culture, Society, Politics, and the Formation of the Cult of Confucius*, edited by A. Thomas Wilson, 1–42. Cambridge, MA: Harvard University Asia Center, 2002.

Wu Qiyu 吳其昱. "Tonkō Kanbun shahon Gaikan 敦煌漢文写本概観." Translated by Itō Mieko 伊藤美重子. In *Tonkō Kanbun bunken* 敦煌漢文文獻, edited by Ikeda On 池田溫, 29–43. Tokyo: Daitō Shuppansha, 1992.

Wu Shan 吳山, and Lu Yuan 陸原, eds. *Zhongguo lidai wanju cidian* 中國歷代玩具辭典. Fuzhou: Fujian Jiaoyu, 2020.

Wu Yinhui 吳垠慧. "Kongzi gongzai dao Gugong, rewu xian liuyi 孔子公仔到故宮 熱舞現六藝." Chinatimes. December 27, 2014. https://www.chinatimes.com/realtimenews/20141227003848-260405?chdtv (accessed October 24, 2023).

Wu Yu 吳虞. "Chiren yu lijiao 吃人與禮教." *Xin qingnian* 6, no. 6 (1919).

Xiang Liling 項立嶺, and Luo Yijun 羅義俊. *Zhi chi Kong Qiu* 跖斥孔丘. Kunming: Yunnan Renmin, 1974.

Xiao Ji 蕭吉. *Wuxing dayi* 五行大義. Tokyo: Kyūko shoin, 1984.

Xiao Yi 蕭繹. *Jinlouzi jiaojian* 金樓子校箋. Beijing: Zhonghua, 2011.

Xiaogan 蕭甘, Gu Bingxin 顧炳鑫, and He Youzhi 賀友直. *Kong Lao'er zui'e de yisheng* 孔老二罪惡的一生. Beijing: Renmin, 1974. Zhongguo Dazhong Yishu.

Xin Deyong 辛德勇. *Zhizao Hanwudi* 制造漢武帝. Beijing Sanlian, 2015.

Xing Yitian 邢義田. *Huawai zhi yi: Handai Kongzi jian Laozi huaxiang yanjiu* 畫外之義: 漢代孔子見老子畫像研究. Beijing: Sanlian, 2020.

Xinhua She 新華社. "2013 nian woguo dongman chanye zongchanzhi yu 870 yi yuan 2013年我國動漫產業總產值逾870億元." Zhongyang zhengfu menhu wangzhan. July 10, 2014. http://www.gov.cn/xinwen/2014-07/10/content_2715703.htm (accessed October 24, 2023).

"Xinzhou Gong'an katong jingcha jinri he dajia jianmian la! 忻州公安卡通警察今日和大家見面啦!". Tengxun shipin. Apirl 22, 2022. https://v.qq.com/x/page/u333103l52d.html (accessed October 24, 2023).

Yan Gengwang 嚴耕望. "Tangren dushu shanlin siyuan zhi fengshang: Jianlun shuyuan zhidu zhi qiyuan 唐人讀書山林寺院之風尚——兼論書院制度之起源." *Zhangyang Yanjiuyuan Lishi Yuyan Yanjiusuo jikan* 30 (1959): 689–728.

Yan Jiayan 嚴家炎. "Ping 'Wusi,' 'Wenge,' yu chuantong wenhua de lunzheng 評'五四'、'文革'與傳統文化的論爭." *Zhongwai wenhua yu wenlun* (1999): 58–73.

Yan Wenru 閻文儒. "Mogao ku de chuangjian yu Cangjing dong de kaizao jiqi fengbi 莫高窟的創建與藏經洞的開鑿及其封閉." *Wenwu* no. 6 (1980): 59–62.

Yan Zhitui 顏之推. *Yanshi jiaxun jijie* 顏氏家訓集解. Shanghai: Shanghai Guji, 1980.

Yan Zhitui 顏之推. *Liezi jishi* 列子集釋. Beijing: Zhonghua, 1985.

Yang Bojun 楊伯峻, ed. *Chunqiu Zuozhuan zhu* 春秋左傳注. Beijing: Zhonghua, 1990.

Yang Mingzhang 楊明璋. "Dunhuang ben 'Qian Han Liu jia taizi zhuan' kaolun 敦煌本《前漢劉家太子傳》考論." *Dunhuang xue* 28 (2010): 91–110.

Yang Rongguo 楊榮國. *Kong Mo de sixiang* 孔墨的思想. Hong Kong: Shenghuo shudian, 1943.

Yang Rongguo 楊榮國. "Kongzi: Wangu di weihu nulizhi de sixiangjia 孔子——頑固地維護奴隸制的思想家." *Renmin ribao*, August 7, 1973, 2.

Yang Xiong 揚雄. *Fayan yishu* 法言義疏. Beijing: Zhonghua, 1987.

Yang Zhaolin 楊兆麟. "*Sanguo yanyi* lianhuanhua de chuangzuo yu chuban 《三國演義》連環畫的創作與出版." In *Xin Zhongguo lianhuanhua: 50-60 niandai* 新中國連環畫 50-60年代, edited by Wang Guanqing 汪觀清 and Li Minghai 李明海, 23–4. Shanghai: Shanghai Huabao, 2001.

Yano, Christine Reiko. *Pink Globalization: Hello Kitty's Trek across the Pacific*. Durham: Duke University Press, 2013.

Yasui Kōzan 安居香山. "Kanseitei setsu no tenkai to Isho shisō 感生帝說の展開と緯書思想." *Nihon Chūgoku Gakkai hō*, 20 (1968): 63–78.

Yasui Kōzan 安居香山, and Nakamura Shōhachi, 中村璋八, eds. *Weishu jicheng* 緯書集成. Shijiazhuang: Hebei renmin, 1994.

Yasui Kōzan 安居香山, and Nakamura Shōhachi 中村璋八. *Isho no kisoteki kenkyū* 緯書の基礎的研究. Tokyo: Kokusho Kankōkai, 1976.

Yi Baisha 易白沙. "Kongzi pingyi shang 孔子平議（上）." *Xin qingnian* 1, no. 6 (1916): 1–6.

Yi Baisha 易白沙. "Kongzi pingyi xia 孔子平議（下）." *Xin qingnian* 2, no. 1 (1916): 1–6.

Ying Shao 應劭. *Fengsu tongyi* 風俗通義. Beijing: Zhonghua, 2010.

Yu Huiyong 于會泳. "Rang wenyi wutai yongyuan chengwei xuanchuan Mao Zedong sixiang de zhendi 讓文藝舞台永遠成為宣傳毛澤東思想的陣地." *Wenhui bao*, May 23, 1968, 1.

Yu Jiaxi 余嘉錫. *Siku tiyao bianzheng* 四庫提要辨正. Beijing: Zhonghua, 1980.

Yu Shinan 虞世南, ed. *Beitang shuchao* 北堂書鈔. Beijing: Zhongguo Shudian, 1989.

Yu Taolai 俞陶來. "'Li Ling bianwen' chu tan 《李陵變文》初探." *Dunhuang yanjiu* no. 4 (1988): 72–7.

Yuan Ke 袁珂, ed. *Shan hai jing jiaozhu* 山海經校注 Chengdu: Bashu, 1996.

Yuehan Xixifusi 約翰西西弗斯, eds. *Mao Zedong de qishou: Jiang Qing yu "Wenge"* 毛澤東的旗手:江青與「文革」.Edited by Yuehan Xixifusi 約翰西西弗斯 and Li Jia 李佳. 2 vols. Vol. 2. Taipei: Xixifusi wenhua chuban, 2015.

Zagury, Guillaume, and Laurie Underwood. "How Pandemic Proves China's 'Digital Confucianism' is Superior to the West." *South China Morning Post*, September 16, 2021.

Zaozhuang Gong'an 棗莊公安. Sina Weibo, June 27, 2022. https://weibo.com/1839681925?refer_flag=1001030103_ (accessed October 24, 2023).

Zelizer, Viviana A. *Pricing the Priceless Child: The Changing Social Value of Children*. New York: Basic Books, 1985.

Zhang Peiyuan 張培元. "Kongzi shi sangjia gou, ni shi shenme 孔子是喪家狗, 你是什麼." May 18, 2007. Henan shangbao. https://news.sina.com.cn/c/pl/2007-05-18/050113015692.shtml (accessed October 24, 2023).

Zhang Tao 張濤. *Kongzi zai Meiguo: 1849 nian yilai Kongzi zai Meiguo baozhi shang de xingxiang bianqian* 孔子在美國: 1849年以來孔子在美國報紙上的形象變遷. Beijing: Beijng Daxue, 2011.

Zhang, Wenxian. "Standing up against Racial Discrimination: Progressive Americans and the Chinese Exclusion Act in the Late Nineteenth Century." *Phylon* 56, no. 1 (2019): 8–32.

Zhang Yiqian 張義潛. *Kong Lao'er lieguo pengbi ji* 孔老二列國碰壁記. Xi'an: Shaanxi Renmin, 1974.

Zhang Yongjun 張永軍. "Xueshi guiqiu jingren ju, xuewen shenzuo jingren yu: Li Ling jiaoshou *Sangjia gou: Wo du* Lunyu duhou 學詩貴求驚人句,學問慎作驚人語——李零教授《喪家狗:我讀<論語>》讀後." *Shehui kexue luntan* no. 8 (2008): 131–2.

Zhang, Zhenjun. *Buddhism and Tales of the Supernatural in Early Medieval China: A Study of Liu Yiqing's (403–444)* Youming lu. Leiden: Brill, 2014.

Zhang Zhiqing 張志清, and Lin Shitian 林世田. "S.6015 Yi sanbei zhuihe yu jiaolu: Dunhuang ben Yi sanbei yanjiu zhi yi S.6015 <易三備>綴合與校錄——敦煌本 <易三備>研究之一." *Dunhuang Tulufan yanjiu* 9 (2006): 389–401.

Zhang Zhiqing 張志清, and Lin Shitian 林世田 "S.6349 yu P.4924 Yi sanbei xiejuan zhuihe zhengli yanjiu S.6349與P.4924易三備寫卷綴合整理研究." *Wenxian* no. 1 (2006): 47–54.

Zhao Libin 趙立彬. "Wanqing zhi Minguo shiqi xihua sixiang de fasheng yu fazhan shulun 晚清至民國時期西化思想的發生與發展述論." *Zhongshan Daxue xuebao luncong* no. 3 (2000): 139–49.

Zhao Lu. *In Pursuit of the Great Peace: Han Dynasty Classicism and the Making of Early Medieval Literati Culture*. Albany: SUNY, 2019.

Zhao Lu. "Introduction to Thought and Mantic Arts." In *Handbook of Divination and Prognostication in China*, edited by Michael Lackner and Zhao Lu, 35–60. Leiden: Brill, 2022.

Zhao Lu. "To Become Confucius: Political Legitimacy and Han Apocryphal Texts in the Case of Emperor Ming (r. A.D. 58–75)." *Asia Major* 28, no. 1 (2015): 115–44.

Zhen Luan 甄鸞. *Laughing at the Tao: Debates among Buddhists and Taoists in Medieval China*. Translated by Livia Kohn. Princeton: Princeton University Press, 1995.

Zheng A'cai 鄭阿財. "Dunhuang xieben 'Kongzi beiwen shu' chutan 敦煌寫本《孔子備問書》初探." *Dunhuang xue* 17 (1991): 101–15.

Zhengzhou Tieluju Zhuangxie Jixiechang gongren lilun xiaozu 鄭州鐵路局裝卸機械廠工人理論小組, and Beijingshi Shunyixian Tianzhu Gongshe pinxiazhongnong lilun 北京市順義縣天竺公社貧下中農理論. "Woguo lishishang laodongfunü de fanKong douzheng 我國歷史上勞動婦女的反孔鬥爭." *Renmin ribao*, December 29, 1974, 2.

Zhenshuo 朕說. "Zuiqiang jirounan laoshi, zaixian jiaoshou zhexue? 最強肌肉男老師, 在線教授哲學?" December 3, 2019. Zhihu. https://zhuanlan.zhihu.com/p/94994674 (accessed October 24, 2023).

Zhong Da 鐘達. "Taiping Tianguo de Fankong douzheng 太平天國的反孔鬥爭." *Renmin ribao*, July 18, 1974, 2.

Zhonggong zhongyang wenxian yanjiushi 中共中央文獻研究室. *Mao Zedong nianpu: 1949–76* 毛澤東年譜: 1949–1976. 6 vols. Vol. 5, Beijing: Zhonguang wenxian, 2013.

Zhonggong zhongyang wenxian yanjiushi 中共中央文獻研究室.. *Mao Zedong nianpu 1949–1976* 毛澤東年譜: 1949–1976. 6 vols. Vol. 6,Beijing: Zhongyang wenxian, 2013.

Zhou Ciji 周次吉. *Liuchao zhiguai xiaoshuo yanjiu* 六朝志怪小說研究. Taipei: Wenjin, 1990.

Zhou Shen 周申. Liuxia Zhi tongma Kong Lao'er 柳下跖痛罵孔老二. Ji'nan: Shandong Renmin, 1975.

Zhu Hong 朱洪. "Cong chongji Kongjia dian dao faqi wenxue geming: Chen Duxiu 1916 nian zhubian *Xin qingnian* di'er juan sixiang pingxi 從衝擊孔家店到發起文學革命——陳獨秀1916年主編《新青年》第二卷思想評析." *Wenhua xuekan* no. 1 (2018): 109–15.

Zhu Lei 朱雷. "'Li Ling bianwen,' 'Zhang Yichao bianwen,' 'Pomo bian' zhupian bianyi 《李陵變文》、《張義潮變文》、《破魔變》諸篇辨疑." *Wei Jin Nanbeichao Sui Tang shi ziliao* 13 (1994): 48–55.

Zhu Yanbing 朱雁冰. "*Zhongguo zheren Kongzi* zhong de Kongzi xingxiang 《中國哲人孔子》中的孔子形象." *Fudan xuebao* (1990): 12–17.

Zhuge Ming 諸葛明. "Fanmian renwu de 'rang, duo, ying, ai, bei' 反面人物的'讓、躲、迎、矮、背'." *Xiju yishu* no. 4 (1978): 56–7.

Zhu Xi 朱熹, ed. *Sishu zhangju jizhu* 四書章句集注. Beijing: Zhonghua, 1983.

Zürcher, Erik. "Buddhism and Education in T'ang Times." In *Neo-Confucian Education: The Formative Stage*, edited by W. Theodore de Bary and John W. Chaffee, 19–56. Berkeley: University of California Press, 1989.

Index

Please note that page references to Tables will be in **bold**

Adams, Hannah, *Dictionary of All Religions and Religious Denominations* 82
atheism 83
African Americans 83
Ah Bak 87
American Missionary Association 89–90
Analects 2, 3–8, 31, 34, 39, 40, 42–3, 55, 69, 110, 157n5, 180n44, 186n22, 189n62
   and *Book of Changes* 55, 74
   as a compilation of sayings by Confucius 3–4
   Confucius's teaching of individual differences in 97
   creditability of 24
   ethics, teaching of 42–3
   first sentence 131
   image of Confucius in 8, 13, 37
   interpretation of title 79
   and the Jesuits 77, 79
   moral philosophy of Confucius in 7, 79
   most reliable source of life/thought of Confucius 4
   rote memorization 100
   sayings in 4, 34, 79, 112
   study of 100, 150
   title, interpretation of 79
   translation 77, 147, 172n3, 172n4
   wooden mallet reference 20
   Yan Yuan featured in 42, 59
Angell Treaty (1880) 84
anime, manga and video games (ACG) 138
anime characters 131, 135, 136
Annals (biographies of kings and emperors) 5
   see also Annals of Spring and Autumn (Confucious)
Annals of Spring and Autumn (Confucious) 13
authorship
   in apocrypha 16–18, 22–5, 38
   disputes as to 16–18
   and Duan Gate mandate 38
   in Han dynasty 37–8
   chronicle of State of Lu 16, 37
   declining social order as stimulation for 17
   heavenly nature 25, 34
   "obtaining the *qilin*" 22–3
   as a prophecy 34
Antebellum America, image of Confucius as universal philosopher in 78, 80–4
anti-Confucius sentiment 101, 115
   movement 99
apocrypha (corpus of texts) 13, 30–1
   appearance of Confucius in 29
   banning of public access to 15
   chenwei metaphor 14
   Confucius as a prophet 13–31
   Confucius's authorship of the *Annals* in 22–5
   Five Phases theory 19–22
   history 14–16, 20, 27–8, 30
   image of Confucius in 19
   and literati 13
   political messages 15
   reconstruction of texts 15–16
   vs. strange stories records 38
   themes 14
appearance of Confucius
   see also portraits of Confucius
   face
      beard 1, 121, 127, 129, 148
      depicted in portraits 127–8
      eyebrows 127
      features 26, 28
      forehead 1, 26, 28, 29, 127, 128
      mustache 127
   finger nails 121

head 127
heavenly 28, 30
height 1, 29, 120, 127, 156n70
physiognomic reading 29
in *Records of the Grand Historian* 5, 29, 120
unusual 28–9
Aristotle 8
Arkenberg, Megan 134
Arthur, Chester 84
attributes of Confucius *see* images/attributes of Confucius

bianwen texts 171n104
binding of text
  Book of Changes 55
  landscape binding 113–14
  methods 167n69
  scrolls 62
  "whirlwind binding" 62
biographies, categorization of 5
  see also Records of the Grand Historian (Sima Qian)
"Biography of Confucius" (Gu Bingxin and He Youzhi) 116, 117
"Biography of the Liu Family Heir of the Former Han" 70
birth of Confucius 19, 21, 27–8, 35, 69
  see also under Confucius; miraculous birth of Confucius; miraculous births; miraculous conception narrative
  historical Confucius, in Zou (later Gufu) 4
  in a hollow mulberry tree 13, 26, 27
Black Cat Detective (animation) 137
Blaine, James 88–9, 93–4
Bolshevik Revolution, Russia 101, 102
Book Excerpts from the Northern Hall 61
Book of Changes 5, 158n22
  see also Five Classics
  binding of text 55
  Confucius as a transmitter 63
  divination in 9, 38–9, 51, 55, 63, 68, 69, 167n75
    see also hexagrams
  "Explanation of the Trigrams" chapter 67
  genealogy 58
  mentioned in *Analects* 55, 74

  mentioned in *Records of the Grand Historian* 39, 55, 58, 74
  preface 57, 58
  symbols in 167n75
  text 58–9, 163n28
  yin and *yang* 62
Book of Documents 5, 169n90
  see also Five Classics
The Book of Han 71
Book of Lord Shang (*Shangjun shu*, *Han Feizi*, and *Xunzi* 107
Book of Poetry 5, 60, 166n57
  see also Five Classics
  Han tradition 45
Boston Daily Globe 86–7, 88
  Feast of Confucius 86
Broad Link Cultural & Creative 126
Broad Link Group 126–7, 128–30, 140, 141, 145
Buddhism 33, 34, 43, 53–5, 91, 157n3
  chanting 46, 48
  communities 54
  and Confucianism 159n37
  and Daoism 49, 159n37
  Fo Guang Mountain, Kaohsiung 139
  Great Anti-Buddhist Persecution (845 CE) 53
  grottoes 53
  Khotan, Buddhist kingdom of 54
  monks 44
  promoting 175n53
  sutras 48
  temples 53
  texts 55, 159n37, 162n19

Caishu 67
Cang Jie (sage king) 30
Categorized Collection of Literary Texts 61
CCP *see* Chinese Communist Party (CCP)
Central Cultural Revolution Group 111
Central Pacific Railroad (CPRR) 80
Chae Chan Ping v. United States 85
chanting
  of the classics 46–8
  and concentration 44
  curses, protection from 44–5
  power of 43–6
  supernatural power behind 44
Chart of the Duke of Zhou Traveling through Eight Days 67

Chen, State of 40
Chen Lanbin 96
Cheng of Zhou, King 67
Chicago Daily Tribune 85–6
children
   and cuteness 134
   television channels 137
Chin Shin Yin 96
China
   see also Chinese Communist Party (CCP); Cultural Revolution (1966–76); Dunhuang, Northwest China;Great Leap Forward movement (1958–60); Imperial China (221 BCE–1911 CE); People's Republic of China (PRC)
   civil war 15
   comic books in 113–15
   Communist 75
   contemporary, Confucius in 34
   cuteness tradition 136–8
   early medieval (220–581 CE) 9, 33, 35, 44, 49
   feudal society 31, 103, 104, 105, 109
   image of Confucius as a Chinese philosopher 76, 78–80
   Literary Chinese 51
   modern textbooks 7–8
   Opium War (1842) 100
   panda policy 137–8
   PRC, founding of 7
   Pre-Qin China 131
   racial stereotyping of Chinese 2, 3
   Republican Era (1912–49) 99, 100, 101, 102, 113
   revolutions in 100–106
   streaming websites 137
   turning heathen 82–4
   twentieth-century 7
   word for "loveable" 136–7
China Central Television (CCTV) 137
Chinese Communist Party (CCP) 99, 112, 116
   "Biography of Confucius" 112
   and the May Fourth Movement 102–103
   "Right Leaning Opportunism and Confucian Thought" 112
   "smashing down the Confucian shop" 102–104

Chinese Exclusion Act (1882) 75–6, 84, 96
Chinese exclusion debate 80–1
Chinese immigrants, in the United States 76, 83, 84–5
Chinese New Year 85
Chinese philosopher, image of Confucius as 76, 78–80
Chinese Wisdom 77
Christian Messenger 81, 82
Christianity 53, 54, 81, 92
   Biblical teaching 92
   evangelism 90
   missionaries 82, 83
Chronicle of Master Lü 27
Civil Examination 77
Classic of Filial Piety, chanting 34, 47
"classical" Confucius 8, 43
codex 62, 167n68
Collected Commentaries on the Chapters and Sentences of the Four Books 77
comic books 10, 99, 113–16, 119, 122
   American 113
   artists 116
   in China 113–14
      Chinese-history-themed 120
      Cultural Revolution 181n52
   in the PRC 180n51
   Great Changes of the Mountainous Village 116
   images of 114
   Li Shuangshuang 116
   Red Crag 116
   The Red Guards on Honghu Lake 116
   Wedding of Xiao'erhei 116
   working-class people 121
Communist International (Comintern) 102
Communist Party of the Soviet Union, 20th Congress 106
conception of Confucius, miraculous see miraculous conception narrative
Confucianism 7, 33, 34, 44
   see also Confucius
   and Buddhism 159n37
   Confucius the founder of 3, 131
   and COVID policies in mainland China 97
   defining 150n9
   in Imperial China 1, 3, 104

and Legalism 108
linked to dynastic cycles 104
Mao on 108
Neo-Confucianism 79
villainizing 103
Confucius
   appearance *see* appearance of Confucius
   benevolence 1, 42
   birth *see* birth of Confucius
   compared with Christ 92
   death of (479 BCE) 4, 36–7
   disparaging of 106–113
   filial piety 1
   hatred in CCP media 112
   images of *see* images/attributes of Confucius
   Jesuit depictions, impacts 76–80
   miraculous conception narrative *see* miraculous conception narrative
   moral teaching 82
   posthumously titled King of Transmitting Culture 6
   relationship with Heaven 5, 22, 23–5
   sacrificing to 7, 30, 78, 100, 177n12
   as stereotype 75–97
   strangeness of 33–49
   travel by *see* travel by Confucius
   ubiquity of 88
   as "uncrowned king" 18, 21
   in the United States 81–4
   why not a powerful political figure 5, 16, 20–1
   works of
      Annals of Spring and Autumn 13, 16–18, 22–5
      Five Classics *see* Five Classics
   worship of 100
Confucius and the Chinese Classics (Loomis) 85
Confucius Did Not Say (Yuan Mei) 34
Confucius Institutes 8
Confucius temples 6, 59, 125
consumerism 10, 132
cool Confucius 142–6
Couplet, Philippe
   Confucius, the Philosopher of China, or the Knowledge of China Translated into Latin 77–8, 79, 91
   retitled *The Morals of Confucius, a Chinese Philosopher* 81, 85
critical textual studies 15–16
"Criticism on Confucius and Self-Criticism on my Confucian Worship in the Past" 112
Criticizing Lin and Confucius movement 112, 115, 122–3, 124
'Cultural rebuild' campaign 126
Cultural Revolution (1966–76) 10, 99, 106, 110, 116, 121, 124
   comic books 181n52
cuteness 125–46
   in China 136–8
   combining with coolness 142–3
   of Confucius
      making Confucius cute 126–32
      managing the cute Confucius 139–46
   expansion of in private and public sectors 138
   many meanings of cute 132–9
   traits associated with 125, 134
   uncertainty created by 136
cuteness of Confucius 10

Da Costa, Inàcio 77
Dale, Joshua Paul 133, 134
Daoism 33, 34, 43, 44, 48, 53
   and Buddhism 49, 159n37
   Inner Scripture of Laozi 57–8
   Laozi 169n95
Daoist Canon of the Zhengtong Reign 60–1
dark emperor, Confucius seen as son of 26, 28, 31, 35
   see also Shuliang He (alleged father of Confucius)
"day books" 66
demon hunter, Confucius seen as 33–49
   see also strangeness of Confucius
   Confucius and disciples as "ghostbusters" 39–43
   ghost stories 39, 42, 43, 49, 59
Deng Xiaoping 106, 123
Di Ku 30
Diagrams Elaborating Confucius (apocryphal text) 23
Dictionary of All Religions and Religious Denominations 82
Dijkstra, Trude 172n3

disciples of Confucius
see also Yan Yuan (disciple of Confucius); Zigong (disciple); Zilu (disciple); Zixia (disciple of Confucius)
   adventures with 34–43
   as apostles 82
   audiences as 138
   disagreements 158n21
   as "ghostbusters" 39–43
divination
   in *Book of Changes* 9, 38, 39, 51, 55, 58, 62, 63, 68, 69, 167n75
   Confucius as diviner 9, 51–74
   Confucius as interpreter 55–9
   divinatory manuals 9, 47, 51–2, 55, 56, 59, 62–4, 66, 67
      see also *Three Completions of the Changes*
   in Dunhuang, Northwest China 2, 9, 55–69
      texts 69–75
   method of Confucius 62–4
      and Duke of Zhou 64–7
   texts 163n24
   "Twelve Coins Divination" 67–9
   Yan Yuan, commentaries of 59–62
Divinatory Method [using]' the Sublime Tokens 59, 61, 63
Divinatory Method of Confucius [Leaning toward] the Horse Head 62, 64
Divinatory Method of the Duke of Zhou and Confucius 64, 66
diviner, Confucius as 51–74
"Doctrine of the Mean" 77, 79
Doraemon (Japanese manga character) 129–32, 135
dreams 67, 70
   see also miraculous conception narrative
   of Confucius 37
   of Emperor Ming 91, 175n53
   Five Phases theory 28
   and miraculous conception
      of Confucius 21, 26, 27, 35
      of Liu Bang 27
   occurring at the "water margin" 26, 27
   spirits in 27
   and transmission from Heaven 28
Duan Gate incident 24–5, 38

The Duke of Zhou Interpreting Dreams 67
Dunhuang, Northwest China 73
   development as a metropolitan city 52, 53
   divination 2, 9, 55–69
      in texts, perceptions of sages 69–75
   documents 51
   geographical location and history 52–4
   literati immigrants 53
   texts 54, 170n100, 171n110

Earth, Five Phases theory 20, 28
Eastern Han (25–220 CE) 30, 45, 69
education 6, 52–4, 131
   Broad Link Group as program 126
   and Buddhism 162n20
   Civil Examination 77
   compulsory 185n12
   cross-cultural 146
   current system 140
   evangelist 90
   investment of 126
   national 126
   official learning 77
   popularity of traditional Chinese learning 184n5
   private 126, 184n4
   public 126
   traditional Chinese learning 126–7
Eight-Legged Essay, Civil Examination 77
Eisner, Michael 137
evangelism 90
"Explanation of the Trigrams" 67
External Tradition of Han's Book of Poetry 39

Fan Ye 45
Feng Youlan 112
Fire, Five Phases theory 20, 22, 28
Five Classics 13–15, 19, 33, 39, 43, 150n9, 157n3
   commentaries 31
   compiling by Confucius 15
   editing by Confucius 5, 15, 51
   elaboration of 14
   transmission of ancient sage kings through 6
Five Phases theory 19–22, 40, 51, 153n31
   colors
      black (Water) 28

green-brown (Wood) 21, 28
red (Fire) 22, 28
white (Metal) 28
yellow (Earth) 28
Earth 20, 28
Fire 20, 28
five emperors 28
Metal 20, 28
virtues 20–1
Water 20, 21
Wood 20, 21, 28
Fo Guang Mountain, Kaohsiung 139
Foreign Miners' Tax Act (1850) 80
Four Books (*Analects*, *Mencius*, "Great Learning" and "Doctrine of the Mean") 77
Fuxi (sage) 58

gambling 87
Gan Bao, *Records of Searching the Wondrous* 39, 40, 42, 46, 48
Gang of Four 123
Gansu, Dunhuang 52
Gao Yao 29
Garden of Persuasion (Liu Xiang) 18, 41
generation **20**, 164n31
    see also hexagrams
    fifth-generation hexagram 164n31
    first-generation hexagram 164n31
    generation line 56, 57, 164n32, 164n33
    second-generation hexagram 164n31
ghost stories 39, 42, 43, 49, 59
    see also demon hunter, Confucius seen as
Gold Rush, California (1849) 80
Golden Rule 90
Goldin, Paul R. 150n9
Gong Gong 21
Gongyang tradition 22
Gould, Stephen Jay, *The Panda's Thumb* 185n10, 185n11
Great Leap Forward movement (1958–60) 105, 106, 178n26
"Great Learning" 77, 79
Great Peace (ideal society) 67
grottoes 53, 161n14, 161n15, 162n16
Gu Bingxin 116, 117–19, 121–3
Guangdong, Jesuits in 76
Guanshu 67
Guiyi Circuit 53–4

Guo Moruo, *Ten Critiques* 108
Guomindang (GMD) 102, 121, 177n12

Haidt, Jonathan 133, 134
Hamlin, Hannibal 89
Han dynasty (206 BCE–220 AD) 34, 37
    see also Western Han period (207 BC–25 AD)
    Book of Poetry (Confucius) 45
    bureaucratic practices 14
    Confucius's prediction of rise of 9
    Eastern Han (25–220 CE) 30, 45, 69
    fall of 30, 52–3
    First Emperor 100
    image of Confucius at end of Western Han 16–19
    Liu Bang as founder 15, 27
    restoring 13
    rise of 38
    role of Confucius in helping 21, 22
    ruling house 13
Harper's Weekly 93
Harries, Daniel 132–3
He Youzhi 116–19, 121–3
heathenism 76, 81, 82–4
    and atheism 83
    deficiencies 83
    and denial of US citizenship 89
    heathen image of Confucius 9, 84–96
    and Judaism 83
    linked to non-Christian religious beliefs 83–4
    unequal treatment of non-white groups 83
    in the United States 82
Heaven
    Mandate of 14–15, 20, 78, 104, 153n28
    relationship with Confucius 5–6, 22, 23–5
    seen as an arbitrary agent 19
    will of 19
heavenly sage, image of Confucius as
    see sage (heavenly), image of Confucius as
Hello Kitty (Japanese fictional character) 129–32, 143
Hello Kongzi (merchandized character) 10, 126–30, 132–4, 137, 143
    application to Confucius 139
    based on the historical Confucius 145

campaign for 146
Hello Kongzi World Tour (2014) 139–42, 144
and "Hiphop Dance" video 145
hemerological tradition 66
Hen Peng 70
hexagrams 39, 56–8, 63
  see also divination; trigrams
  Eight Palace Hexagrams 164n31
  fifth-generation 164n31
  first-generation 164n31
  hexagram Tripod 38
  Jing Fang, based on 56
  master 164n31
  second-generation 164n31
Hexi Corridor 52
"historical" Confucius 8
History of the Later Han 91
Holt, Leslie, *Hello Dali* 131
"homeless dog," Confucius compared with 2, 4, 29, 117
Hongbian (Monk-supervisor) 54
Hou Ji 28
Huainanzi 17–18, 47
Hunter, Michael 2

iconoclastic attitudes towards Confucius 10, 99
images/attributes of Confucius 139
  in the *Analects* 8, 13
  in apocrypha *see* apocrypha (corpus of texts)
  as Black dragon 22
  as Chinese philosopher 76, 78–80
  choice of 10
  as cool 142–6
  as cute 10, 125–46
  as demon hunter 9, 39–43
  deviating from mainstream attributes 8
  diversity of/multiple 1–2, 8
  as diviner/divination interpreter 9, 51–74
  as heathen 9, 84–96
  as heavenly sage 5, 6, 16, 18–19, 24, 25–30, 154n45
  as "homeless dog" 2, 4, 29, 117
  mainstream *see* mainstream images of Confucius
  Maoist 109–111
  negative, in the media 76, 112
  perceptions historically made 2
  as prophet 13–31
    half-human and half-heavenly 9, 27
    in *Records of the Grand Historian see Records of the Grand Historian* (Sima Qian)
    rejected 2
  as universal philosopher in Antebellum America 78, 80–4
  as villain 99–124
  "weird," defining 8, 9
Imperial China (221 BCE–1911 CE) 1, 3, 6, 100, 104
Imperial Reader of the Taiping Reign 61
Imperii Gymnasium 79
Inner Scripture of Laozi 57–8, 165n44
Intellectual History of Ancient China 110

Japan
  culture of cuteness (*kawaii*) 135–6
  Hello Kitty (fictional character) 129–32, 143
  Kumamoto Prefecture 136
  manga characters 113, 129–32
Jensen, Lionel 2
Jesuits 7, 76, 90
  Confucius, the Philosopher of China, or the Knowledge of China Translated into Latin 77–8, 79, 91
    retitled *The Morals of Confucius, a Chinese Philosopher* 81, 85
  depictions of Confucius, impacts 78–80
  hermeneutic strategies 79
  legacy 7, 80
  and mainstream images of Confucius 6–7
  missionaries 2, 6
  on philosophizing 78
  translation of the *Analects* 77
Jesus Christ 90, 91
  compared with Confucius 92
Ji Huanzi 24
jian chu divination system 66
Jiang Qing 107, 111, 113, 114, 116, 122–3
Jiang Yuan 28
Jin dynasty (265–420) 61
Jing Fang 56
"John Confucius" cartoon character 93, 96
Judaism 83

Kara-Khanid Khanate dynasty (Islamic) 54
Khotan, Buddhist kingdom of 54
Khrushchev, Nikita 105, 106
Kingly Way, reluctance of Confucius to practice 18
Kong Qiu 8
Kongzi *see* Confucius
Korean War (1950–53) 137

Laozi (teacher) 68, 69
Laozi (text) 58, 68
Legalism 107, 108
Li Desheng 113
Li Ling 71, 72, 73
Li Zhizhong 167n67
Liang dynasties (301–421 CE) 53
Liangxiao group (1973) 111–12, 113, 123
Lin Biao 106, 107, 111, 112, 115
Lin Biao and the Way of Confucius and Mencius 112
Lin Shitian 57, 164n29
Lin Xiaogong 64
Lin Youwu 131, 140
Ling Sing 83
Lingfu (green emperor), Five Phases theory 28
"Listed Biographies" 5
literati 6, 36
   and apocrypha 13
   and chanting 46
   culture 4, 69, 73
   and divination 55
   in Dunhuang, Northwest China 53
   early medieval 31, 44, 49, 61, 69
   Five Classics, chanting 43
   and Heaven's will 19
   of imperial China 15, 16, 59
   individual concerns of 31
   Qing dynasty (1644–1912) 78, 79
   representations of Confucius among 51
   and "strangeness" 159n35
   in Western Han dynasty 16, 37
Little Fox (animation) 137
Liu Bang (Han dynasty founder) 15
   birth story 27
Liu imperial family 14, 15, 22
Liu Shaoqi 106
Liu Song dynasty (420–479 CE) 61
Liu Xiang 19
   The Garden of Persuasion 18, 41

Liu Xiu 15, 19
Liu Zongyuan 108
Liuxia Zhi 115, 116
Loomis, A.W., *Confucius and the Chinese Classics* 85
Lorenz, Konrad 127, 132, 133
Louis XIV, King 77
Lu, State of 4, 22, 26, 103, 117
   Annals as chronicle of 16, 37
Lu Deming, *Textual Explanations of Classics and Canons* 58
Lu Xun 101

Ma Guohan, *Jade Sack Mountain House's Collection of Lost Books* 15–16
Ma Yuan 128
mainstream images of Confucius 2, 3, 6–7, 8, 141
   see also images/attributes of Confucius
   deviation from the mainstream 3, 10, 115, 125
   place of 10
manga, Japanese 113
   see also Doraemon (Japanese manga character)
Manicheism 53, 54
Mao Zedong 99, 102, 106, 111, 112, 122, 123
   criticism of Confucius 116
   will of 107–108
Marx, Karl, *Das Kapital* 101
Marxism 7, 101
Master Kong (reference to Confucius) 118
Master of the Golden Mansion (Xiao Yi) 36
Matthews, Thomas Stanley 89
May, Simon 136
May Fourth Movement 101, 104
   and the CCP 102–103
Mencius (advocate of Confucius) 16, 17, 19, 44, 153n28
Mencius (text) 6, 77, 100
   on Confucius's authorship of the *Annals* 17
Metal, Five Phases theory 20, 28
Methodist Episcopal Church 86
methods of numbers 55
Mexican Americans 83
Mickey Mouse (cartoon character) 128, 132, 135, 137, 143, 145, 185n10
The Middle Kingdom 81, 85

Min dialect 140
Ming, Emperor 30
Ming dynasty (1368–1644) 76, 77, 79
mining, Antebellum America 80
Minor Sayings 37
miraculous births
    of Confucius 19, 21, 26, 27–8, 35, 69
    in a hollow mulberry tree 13, 26, 27
    of Liu Bang 27
    of Xie 28
    of Yi Yin 27
miraculous conception narrative 26–8, 31, 35–6
    see also dark emperor, Confucius seen as son of; dreams; Shuliang He (alleged father of Confucius); Zhengzai (mother of Confucius)
    in *Records of the Grand Historian* 26, 28
    taking place in a dream 21, 26, 27, 35
Mogao, Buddhist grottoes in 53
moral philosophy of Confucius 3
    in *Analects* 7, 79
The Morals of Confucius, a Chinese Philosopher 81, 85

Nadal, Rafael 8
Nakamura Shōhachi 15
Nast, Thomas 176n58
    "The Civilization of Blaine" 93, 95
Native Americans 83
Neo-Confucianism 79
New Life Movement 102
The New York Herald 91
Newman, John, "Confucius and Confucianism" 90, 91
Ngai, Sianne, *Our Aesthetic Categories: Zany, Cute, Interesting* 133
Nobita, Nobi 130
nobles 4, 69, 104, 109, 118
    "Hereditary Houses" (biographies) 5
    progressive 117
    slave-owning 110
North of Heavenly Court (constellation) 30
Nylan, Michael 2

opium smoking 86

paganism 82, 83
Paine, Thomas 81

Peng Zheng 106
People's Daily 102, 107, 109, 110, 111, 115, 123
People's Fine Arts Publishing House 137
People's Liberation Army (PLA) 137
People's Republic of China (PRC) 9, 104
    comic books 180n51
    communes 105
    founding of (1949) 7, 102, 105
    leadership 105
    Ministry of Education 8
    official records 105–106
    policies 105
Philadelphia Inquirer 91–2
Ping of Chu, King 72
Plato 78
Pleasant Goat and Big Big Wolf (animation program) 137
pop culture characters, for children 128
Portal/Portal 2 (videogames) 134
portraits of Confucius
    see also appearance of Confucius
    Hello Kongzi image 127, 128
    traditional 127–8
Pre-Qin China 131
prophecies 14, 15, 22, 23, 33, 34
    of Confucius, in his tomb 36–8, 154n48
prophet, Confucius as 13–31
    and messenger of Heaven 13
    narratives 13–14

Qi, State of 4
Qin dynasty (221–207 BC) 14, 21, 23, 36–8, 168n83
    fall of 38
    First Emperor 37
    Pre-Qin China 131
Qing dynasty (1644–1912) 76–7, 79, 84, 93, 96, 100
    anti-Christian persecution 77
    Burlingame Treaty (1868) 80
    literati 78, 79
Qingdao 101
Quakers 81

Records of Searching the Wondrous (Gan Bao) 39, 40, 42, 46, 48
Records of the Grand Historian (Sima Qian) 3, 16, 24, 39, 40, 41, 103, 169n90

on appearance of Confucius 5, 29, 120
biography of Confucius 3, 5–6, 55
    lifting to the "lineage" 16
and *Book of Changes* 39, 55, 58, 74
categorization of biographies 5
on conception of Confucius 26, 28
depicting Confucius as a human child 26
"homeless dog" categorization of Confucius 117
images of Confucius in 8, 117
most reliable source of life/thought of Confucius 4
scope of 117
on social class of Confucius 103
vision of demise of Confucius in 37
on world knowledge of Confucius 34–5
Records of the Left-out (Wang Jia) 35–6
"Records of the Strange" 9, 33, 38, 44
    chanting the classics in 46–8
religion *see* Buddhism; Christianity; Daoism; Judaism; Manicheism; Zoroastrianism
"Restoration of the Past and Anti-Restoration of the Past Is the Struggles of Two Path" 112
revolutions in China 99–124
    gone too far 105–106
"Rhapsody of Han Peng" 70
Ricci, Matteo 77
Riot Grrrl (punk movement) 131
Rites 5
    see also Five Classics
Rites of Zhou 67
Romance of the Three Kingdom and *Journey to the West* 114
Rong Xinjiang 161n1, 161n11, 162n16
Ruggieri, Michele 77

sacrifice 6, 37, 137
    sacrificing to Confucius 7, 30, 78, 100, 177n12
sage (heavenly), image of Confucius as 5, 6, 16, 18–19, 24, 25–30, 154n45
    "dark sage" 21
    including with other sage kings 28, 29–30
Santley, Catherine 91
Scott Act (1888) 84–5

Scripture of Divine Incantations of the Abyssal Caverns 43
Scripture of Laozi Converting the Barbarians 68
Scripture of the Names and Images of Laozi in Ten Direction 169n94
"Seven Epitomes" (bibliographical work) 58
Shang dynasty (1600–1046 BC) 5, 27, 103, 109, 154n45
Shanghai Animation Film Studio 137
Shaozheng Mao 110, 117, 118, 120
    Confucius's execution of 109
Shendou (yellow emperor), Five Phases theory 28, 30
Shenzhen Charity Foundation 126
Sherman, Gary 133, 134
Shuliang He (alleged father of Confucius) 26
Shun (sage king) 44
Silk Road 52
Sima Qian 4, 5, 7, 9
    Records of the Grand Historian see Records of the Grand Historian (Sima Qian)
    reference to Confucius as ultimate sage 16
Sinful Life of Kong the Second 99, 113, 118, 123
social status 5
Society of Jesus 76
Socrates 76, 78
Song, King of 70
Song, State of 4
Song dynasty (960–1279) 31, 156n79
    Northern Song dynasty (960–1127 CE) 157
South China Morning Post 97
Spring and Autumn Annals of Master Lü 44
Spring and Autumn (Confucius) 5
    see also Five Classics
Stalin, Joseph 106
State of Lu *see* Lu, State of
State of Qi *see* Qi, State of
State of Song *see* Song, State of
statues of Confucius 125
stereotype, Confucius as 75–97
    in American newspapers during Chinese Exclusion Act (1882) 75–6, 84–6, 174n30

heathenism *see* heathenism
Jesuit depictions, impacts 76–80
universal philosopher in Antebellum America 80–4
Stoics 8
strangeness 33–49
  as an anxiety of the literati 159n35
  of Confucius
    and adventures with disciples 34–43
    Confucius and disciples as "ghostbusters" 9, 39–43
    death of Confucius as strange 36–7
    miraculous conception narrative *see* miraculous conception narrative
    supernatural powers 33
    perceiving the future 37–9
  "Records of the Strange" 9, 33
  strange creatures 49
  of trees in Confucius's cemetery 36
Sublime Tokens see Divinatory Method [using]' the Sublime Tokens
Sui dynasty (581–618) 15, 53, 64, 167n70
Supper, Reverend J. C. 81

Taiwei (constellation) 28, 30
Taklamakan Desert 52
talents of Confucius 17–18
Tang dynasty (618–907) 53, 54, 59, 62, 67, 157n9, 158n25, 164n29, 170n97
Tang Yijie 111
Tao Zhu 106
Textual Explanations of Classics and Canons (Lu Deming) 58
Thévenot, Melchisédech 77
The Thought of Confucius and Mozi 110
Three Completions of the Changes 56–9, 61, 63, 68
Three Realms Monastery 54
Tibet
  and divination method 68
  language 51, 161n9
  occupation of Dunhuang 53, 54
  Tibetan Empire (618–842 CE) 69
Tokyo Olympics (2021) 135
transcontinental railroad, United States 83–4
"Transformation Text of Li Ling" 71
"Transformation Text of Wu Zixu" 72

travel by Confucius 4, 16, 30, 62, 119
  in state of Chen 40
Treaty of Guadalupe Hidalgo (1848) 83
Treaty of Versailles (1919) 101
trigrams 56, 58, 67, 164n31, 164n33
  see also divination; hexagrams
Triplet (constellation) 30
Twain, Mark, "John Chinaman in New York" 92, 93
"Twelve Coins Divination" 67–9
The Twelve Coins Divination Method of the Book of Changes 68

United States
  see also Antebellum America, Confucius seen as universal philosopher in
  American Missionary Association 89–90
  Burlingame Treaty (1868) 80
  Chinese immigrants in 76, 83, 84–5
  Confucius in 81–4
  Constitution of the State of California (1879) 84
  Democrats and Republicans 83, 84
  Fifteenth Amendment 83
  heathenism in 82
  independence 81
  newspapers 75–6, 84–6, 174n30
  Protestant Church 89
  transcontinental railroad 83–4
Unity of Three 114
universal philosopher, image of Confucius as 80–4
  defending the universal philosopher 89–96

video games 134, 135
villain, image of Confucius as 99–124
  how to visualize Confucius as a villain 118–22
  telling a bad story of Confucius 117–18
  villain as the hero 115–16
virtues, Five Phases theory 20–1

Wang Anshi 107
Wang Chong 74
Wang Jia, *Records of the Left-out* 35–6
Wang Mang 15, 70
Wang Yangming 79

Wang Yun 47
Warring States period (476–221 BCE) 3, 107, 168n83
Water, Five Phases theory 20, 21
Wei Wei 137
weird attributes of Confucius
see also under Confucious; strangeness of Confucius
defining 8
Wen (sage king) 30
Wen, Emperor 64
Wenzu (red emperor), Five Phases theory 28
Western Han period (207 BC– 25 AD)
see also Han dynasty (206 BCE–220 AD)
Confucius identifying odd objects in 24
image of Confucius at end of 16–19
literati in dynasty 16, 37
Western Xia empire 54
Weststeijn, Thijs 172n3
"whirlwind binding" 62
Williams, Samuel Wells 83
The Middle Kingdom 82, 85
Wood, Five Phases theory 20, 21, 28
Wu, Emperor (265–317 CE) 15, 45
Wu, Emperor (r. 140–87 BCE) 14, 71
Wu Qiyu 163n25
Wu Yu 101
Wu Zixu 72, 73
Xavier, Francis 76
Xia dynasty (2070–1600 BC) 27, 54, 103
xian ("worthies") 70, 170n100

Xiang Xu 47–8
Xianji (white emperor), Five Phases theory 28
Xiao Yi, *Master of the Golden Mansion* 36
Xin dynasty (9–23 CE) 15
Xiongnu cavalry 71
Xuanju (black emperor), Five Phases theory 28
Xunzi 44, 118

Yamaguchi Yūko 129
Yan Youming 61
Yan Yuan (disciple) 38, 39, 42, 43, 56, 158n21, 165n51, 167n64
commentaries of 59–62, 166n63
death of (481 BCE) 4, 5, 23

Yang, Emperor 15
Yang Rongguo 110, 111, 112, 122
Yang Xiong 18–19
Yao (sage king) 30, 44
Yao Wenyuan 107
Yasui Kōzan 16
Yi Yin 27
Yuan dynasty (1279–1368) 170n97
Yuan Mei 34

Zhan Shichai 85, 91–2
Zhang, Emperor 30
Zhang Chunqiao 116
Zhang Daqing 163n26
Zhang Juzheng 79
Zhang Yichao 53–4
Zhang Zhiqing 57, 164n29
Zhanzong (Song dynasty emperor) 31
Zhao, King of Chu 41
Zhao Jiao 47–8
Zheng people 29
Zhengzai (mother of Confucius) 21, 26, 35, 158n10
Zhi Boyi 46
Zhi Ruozhang 46
Zhou, Duke of 67, 68, 69, 73, 168n86
Zhou dynasty (1046–256 BC) 21, 35, 104
bronze inscriptions 154n45
establishment 67
fall of 23, 25, 38
labeled as "feudal" 178n16
nobles 104, 109
rituals 117
slave ownership 108, 117
Western Zhou dynasty (1047–722 BCE) 103
Zhou Enlai 113, 123
Zhou Yiliang 111
Zhu Xi 77, 79
Zhuangzi 18, 21, 115
Zhuge Ming 119
Zigong (disciple) 38, 39, 40, 42, 61
Zilu (disciple) 23, 40, 42, 44, 158n15
Zixia (disciple) 22, 23, 56–9, 72
Ziyong 72
Zong Zhongshu 45
Zoroastrianism 53, 54, 76
Zou (later Qufu), birth of Confucius in 4
Zuo Commentary on the Spring and Autumn Annals 118

www.ingramcontent.com/pod-product-compliance
Lightning Source LLC
Chambersburg PA
CBHW071832300426
44116CB00009B/1520